I JUST WANT
PEACE

Testimonials for
The Power of Clearing Process
and Sandy Levey-Lunden

"Sandy is like a force of nature complete with her own inter-dimensional wormhole. When traveling the galaxy coming across a shortcut can be of great help and this is how it is when you enter Sandy's orbit. She is connected with the resources and will hook you up with whatever or whomever you have been seeking. If you are seeking the highest truth of yourself, she can help you with that too! She's incredible."

—**Shyralee Mitchell,**
Inter-dimensional Explorer, Singer/Songwriter, Radio Show Host, Professional Hand Analyst & Soul Strategist—Montana, USA

"Sandy taught me that nothing is unforgivable. I can release any upset by clearing my mind. There is only LOVE. The rest is a story I made up. This way of living has transformed my relationship with everyone important to me."

—**Miriam Evers,**
Power of Clearing Coach, Joyous Renegade—British Columbia, Canada

"Hearing Sandy's unmistakable voice reminded me of who I was in my Higher Self. She helped me navigate years of stormy emotional waters with a lot at stake. I remember feelings of utter calm in knowing Divine Strength within me."

—**Iona Leishman,**
Certified Power of Clearing Coach, Visual Artist—Inverness, Scotland

"When I met Sandy in 1999, I was a 46-year-old bachelor who was not a good candidate for a healthy marriage. I had pretty much resigned myself to being alone for life. The relationship principles and communication tools I learned in Sandy's trainings transformed me from being a serial relationship disaster to an excellent and reliable partner. Sandy's unique Clearing Process is the cleanest, most effective tool I've encountered in my many years of personal and spiritual development. It works because it forces both parties to acknowledge and own their issues while at the same time generating compassion and support from the other party. For example, if I'm angry about something, I first own it and report it to my partner, who hears it objectively, knowing it is all about me and has nothing to do with them. It is simply brilliant and has been instrumental in my ability to create 22 years of a happy marriage and family."

—**Andrew Barber-Starkey,**
executive coach, founder, and lead trainer of ProCoach International, and Master Certified Coach—North Vancouver, BC, Canada

"You will discover an abundance of benefits from The Power of Clearing process. You will feel lighter, freer, and more peaceful from uncovering and releasing unproductive patterns of thought that have kept you stuck. You will remember that you are perfect exactly as you are now—complete, whole, and lacking nothing. You will be able to use this practical and straightforward process on your own, and you will discover within all the resources and inherent gifts to lead an abundant, rewarding, and joyful life."

—**Oriana Howes,**
Certified Power of Clearing Coach—London, England

"Convinced that I was unlovable and unworthy of prospects at the end of my marriage, I had no idea how profoundly the Clearing and Holy Relationship work with Sandy and her coaches would pave the way to happiness for me and for those dearest to me. I let go of all guilt, fears, and feelings of unworthiness with The Power of Clearing process. I had many private sessions with the coaches and completed the trainings. There were moments I felt I could die from the emotions until I tapped the truth of my own self, that I was good enough to be wanted and chosen and worthy of love and compassion. From this point forward, I was able to begin my new life. It has been a miraculous healing clearing what was in the way of our family, all joining fully in the family dynamic, accepting each other."

—**David Spooner,**
Certified Power of Clearing Coach—Scotland and England tour guide

"For the more than 20 years that I have known Sandy Levey-Lunden, I have had the privilege to witness and receive countless healing benefits from her work. She is a gifted teacher, healer, and facilitator completely dedicated to easing unnecessary suffering caused by our entrenched belief systems. Of her many gifts, or if you will, superpowers, one that particularly stands out is her way of inspiring people to be courageous, stand out, and be all they truly are. She has been and continues to be a truly beneficial presence to so many, and for that, I am most grateful."

—**Dr. Dennis W. Gaither, MD, Psychiatrist**
Mount Vernon, Washington State
Ordained Ministerial Counselor through Pathways of Light (OMC)
Long-time student, teacher, group and workshop facilitator of
A Course in Miracles (ACIM) Hakomi Therapist, Teacher,
Senior Trainer with Seattle Hakomi Education Network

"Sandy has the gravitational pull of a planet. Her trust is boundless, and her vibrant, empowering energy creates a whole new space for me to exist. Before meeting Sandy, I believed I was just a body, a broken body with symptoms of debilitating pain. The explanation of Big T Truths was my introduction to the idea that I am a spirit inhabiting a body and that I can heal my mind and free my body. In the limitless realm of possibilities, I am learning to expand instead of contract, choose joy instead of punishment, and engage in acceptance instead of struggle. Applying the profound Clearing Process to assist me in giving up blame, shame, and shutting down, I am being ushered back into the light of Love, innocence, and peace. As a mentor, Sandy always makes time for me, offering a safe space, free of judgment, to express myself fully, and guiding me to take responsibility for my feelings. Forgiving myself, I am breaking patterns, finding clarity, and blessing all areas of my life as I hear the truth of my essence spoken to me often. Now, traveling through my heart vortex, I choose to open, connect, and stay true to my Spiritualization path."

—**Kristi Birnie,**
Certified Power of Clearing Coach and student—Vancouver Island, Canada

I JUST WANT PEACE

A GUIDE TO LASTING PEACE IN
YOUR LIFE AND IN THE WORLD

SANDY LEVEY-LUNDEN

Goodyear, AZ

Copyright 2022 by Sandy Levey-Lunden
I Just Want Peace

First Edition – revised in September 2022

All rights reserved. Printed in the United States of America. No part of this book may be used or reproduced in any written form or by electronic or mechanical means, including information storage and retrieval systems, without written permission from the author, except for the use of brief quotations in a book review.

First published in the USA in 2022 by Sandy Levey-Lunden

Paperback ISBN: 978-1-958405-08-6
Hardcover ISBN: 978-1-958405-14-7
eBook ISBN: 978-1-958405-09-3
Library of Congress Control Number: 9781958405086

Publishing House: Spotlight Publishing House™ in Goodyear, AZ
Editor: Lynn Thompson, Living on Purpose Communications
Contributing Editors: Len Satov, Ian Patrick, Christina Ireland, Morgan Hawthorn, Kristi Birnie, Anna Margareta Sundberg Reed
Original scribes: Angela Hahn and Gillian Hibbs
Book Cover: Artida (stock.adobe.com)
Interior Design: Amit Dey
Photographs: Morgan Hawthorn
Illustrations: Joan Trinh Pham
Sketch: Margaret Anne West (Matt Collamer photo, unsplash.com)

Quotes are from *A Course in Miracles*, copyright ©1992, 1999, 2007 Second Edition and Third Edition by the Foundation for Inner Peace, 448 Ignacio Blvd., #306, Novato, CA 94949, USA. www.acim.org and info@acim.org, according to the ACIM Annotation System, used with permission.

For information, contact:
www.sandylevey.com
Phone: +1 (360) 527-2796 (Pacific)
Email: onpurpose@sandylevey.com
Postal: Sandy Levey-Lunden
336 36th Street PMB # 196
Bellingham, WA 98225
United States of America

DISCLAIMER

The author does not intend the material in this book to be a substitute for trained medical or psychological advice. Therefore, please consult with a professional to treat mental and physical illness. The publisher, author, and the author's team assume no liability for injury caused to the reader that may result from the content contained herein.

DEDICATION

To all my clients, friends, and family.

You have openly and transparently shared yourselves
with me since 1980 in your personal process of evolving
and awakening to your true nature.

Our relationship has kept me engaged in my process
of awakening to my authentic Self.

My full attention and intention have always been on
inner peace—my most important goal.

Again, my gratitude to you for what I am learning from our relationship.

By your sharing with me at these deep levels,
you have helped me to live *The Power of Clearing* process.

The many pages of Acknowledgments to you speak for themselves.

TABLE OF CONTENTS

Dedication	ix
Acknowledgments	xvii
Foreword – Ian Patrick	xxix
What is *A Course in Miracles?* (ACIM) – Ian Patrick	xxxi
Preface	xxxiii
The Meaning of Life	xxxiii
"Stuck-ness"	xxxiii
Sandy's Life Mission	xxxv
Introduction	xxxvii
Why did I want to write this book?	xxxvii
And why do you want to read it?	xxxviii
PRELUDE	xli
How and why I became a student of *A Course in Miracles*	xliii
ACIM and *The Power of Clearing*	xliv
Reflections on *The Power of Clearing*	xlix
What is a Sandyism?	lx
PART I – FOUNDATION	3
CHAPTER 1 – I Am Who You Are	5
What is Love?	5
Peace and Joy	6

You Are Light	8
Big T Truth	10
Big T Truths Defined – The Truth of Who I AM	11
Innocence	12
The Mind Cannot Hold Gratitude and Fear Together	17
"I'm So Grateful" song by Karen Drucker	17

CHAPTER 2 – My Definition of Ego — 19

Fear, Guilt, and Separation	19
"What am I hiding?"	22
Making the decision to bring your Ego into the Light	25
little t truth	26
The Complete Way Out of "Stuck-ness"	28

CHAPTER 3 – The World of Illusions — 29

The War is Within	29
Attack and Defense	30
The Goal of Therapy	34
The Projection Factor	37
I Choose to Wake Up NOW!	41

CHAPTER 4 – Ego Games — 45

The Ego Plays to Win	45
Ego Games: Money, Time, Sex, Power, and Control	45
The Money Game	46
The Time Game	48
The Sex Game	54
The Power and Control Game	64
Why Do We Keep Playing Ego Games?	67
"Our Deepest Fear" by Marianne Williamson	69

CHAPTER 5 – Relationships — 71

Reveal Patterns	71
The Movie Called *Your Life*	72
Holy Relationship and Special Relationship	73

The Special Relationship	75
The Holy Relationship	76
Making the Holy Relationship Real: Living in a Healing Partnership	80
How to Create a Holy Relationship	81
Family	84
Getting Divorced?	85
There is No Divorce!	88
Betrayal and Abandonment	89
What Happens Next in Relationship?	92
Association with the Body	94
Revisiting little t truth to Remember	97
The Light You Are	98
"You are the Diamond" song by Carole Isis	99

PART II – CLEARING — 101

CHAPTER 6 – *The Clearing Process* — 103

What is *The Power of Clearing?*	103
How *The Power of Clearing* came about	104
Receiving the Answer	107
Review of little t truth thoughts	111
What is *The Clearing Process?*	112
The Advanced Clearing	126
The Clearing Process with a Friend	128
Disclaimer	129
My Personal Example of *The Clearing Process*	130
"It's What You Are" song by Charley Thweatt from *Wave after Wave*	136

CHAPTER 7 – Important Clearings — 137

God Clearing and Family Clearing	137
Alanna, client, workshop participant, with her Advanced *Clearing Process*	139
Alanna's account after completion of the clearing, days later	148
Some new thoughts from Alanna in 2022	148
"The Guest House" by Rumi, translation by Shahram Shiva	150

PART III – DIVING DEEPER 151

CHAPTER 8 – Healing Accomplished 153

Surrender 153

How Is Healing Accomplished? 154

Further inquiry 157

Questions Answered about the Condition 157

No Order of Difficulty in Miracles 161

If the Sickness Has No Purpose Now, It Can Leave 166

"Love, Serve and Remember" song by John Astin from *Remembrance* 168

CHAPTER 9 – *True Woman's Power* 169

Women's Core Beliefs 169

The Comparison Game 171

My Body Judgment 173

Two Men Having Breakthroughs 174

Women Saying "No" to Men 177

True Woman's Power Testimonials 181

– Embracing the Truth of Who I Truly Am 181

– Three into One—Healing the Triangle 184

"Prayer Dance" by Katya Kudrov 198

PART IV – TESTIMONIALS 199

Chapter 10 – Changing Lives through *The Power of Clearing* 201

The *Fri Sikt* Project 201

Testimonials about *The Power of Clearing* process 211

Case Studies – POCCCP *(Power of Clearing Coaching Certification Program)* 221

Chapter 11 – Moving Forward in Peace 229

Postscript by Sandy 229

Special clarifying points from Sandy in 2022 230

Reflections on the Path of the Past 233

Comments on Relationship as a Path to Enlightenment 234

PART V – ADDITIONAL MATERIAL   239

Appendices   241

   Appendix A   Defining Moments in People's Lives and What They Learned   243

   Appendix B   Articles on Releasing Sexual Guilt and the Physical Body   251

   Appendix C   Understanding and Living in a Holy Relationship   263

   Appendix D   Deeper Meanings of the Trainings   275

   Appendix E   How Is Healing Accomplished? ACIM Manual for Teachers, Pages 17-18   277

Resources   281

   1) List of the *On Purpose* Courses   281

   2) List of Coaches and Therapists   283

   3) Code of Ethics for *Power of Clearing* Coaches   290

   4) Frequently Asked Questions about *The Clearing Process*   292

   5) Books, CDs, and Film   296

   6) The Watcher – Len Satov   298

   7) Daring to Risk – Sandy Levey-Lunden   300

   8) How Healing is Accomplished – Sandy Levey-Lunden   305

Glossary of Terms   309

More About the Author   315

LIST OF ILLUSTRATIONS

1. Sandyism: I Am Awake (Morgan Hawthorn, photo)   xix
2. Man with sign (Margaret Anne West, sketch)   xxxviii
3. Sandyism: In Our True Nature, (Morgan Hawthorn, photo)   xlvi
4. Sandyism: Communicate From Your Heart (Morgan Hawthorn, photo)   lix
5. You are Born Perfect (Joan Trinh Pham, graphic)   9
6. Big T Truths (Joan Trinh Pham, graphic)   16
7. Sandyism: You Don't Have a Secret (Morgan Hawthorn, photo)   23
8. Sandyism: I Choose to Wake Up Now (Morgan Hawthorn, photo)   42
9. Sandyism: You Must Wake Up (Morgan Hawthorn, photo)   68
10. Poop-covered Diamond (Joan Trinh Pham, graphic)   100
11. *I Want the Peace of God* (Morgan Hawthorn, photo)   111
12. Big T and little t chart   124
13. *The Clearing Process* Summary (Joan Trinh Pham, graphic)   125
14. Sandyism: No Amount of Evidence (Morgan Hawthorn, photo)   197
15. Prayer Dance: Katya Kudrov, poem (Morgan Hawthorn, photo)   198
16. Sandyism: Until You Honestly Tell (Morgan Hawthorn, photo)   228
17. Big T-pot (Joan Trinh Pham, graphic)   238

ACKNOWLEDGMENTS

Special acknowledgment to God for all the gifts and talents You gave me. I recognized them from the age of seven when I began using these gifts and they have enabled me to live my life purpose.

Special acknowledgment to my grandmother, Gussie, a healer, who showed me many special healing rituals.

Special acknowledgment to my mother, Dorothy Goodburg, with whom I practiced my telepathic and psychic gifts.

Thank you, Mom and Dad, for always encouraging me that I could be, do, and have anything. You demonstrated to me and taught me my capacity to be limitless, and by acknowledging me, you strengthened my desire to keep going and help people everywhere. Thank you, Dad and Mom, for funding the projects of all the children with special needs and children in the ghetto, whose talents and unique gifts I helped advance, to help them grow and expand.

Special appreciation and acknowledgment to Charisma, my daughter, a massage therapist and healer, for always reminding me of everything I taught you when I forget. Thank you for my four amazing grandchildren, who also remind me if I forget my teaching. You are all living examples of my philosophy and work that will live on through you long after I am gone.

Through these years, I have taught countless trainings with a team of coaches who assisted individuals in every training to go deeply into their ego-mind, release themselves from emotional conflict, and come to peace. The depth that I taught and the knowledge that people have received from these courses would never have been possible without this expertly trained, transformed, and dedicated team of coaches. Each of you embodies the principles, philosophy, and theory of *The Power of Clearing* process, authentically living your life from it and through it. I acknowledge each of you who has selflessly given of yourself so that each person participating in these courses ultimately released themselves to their maximum capacity in that moment. As *Power of Clearing* coaches, each of you was essential to the ultimate success of each person's peace of mind and heart.

I have listed some of the trained coaches who are active and available for clearing sessions in the Resource section of this book.

Special acknowledgment to Richard Unger, the founder of IHA (the Institute of Hand Analysis), who credits me as the midwife of his program and taught me soul psychology. You found, in my fingerprints, my life purpose to which I had always been living: public impact in the healing arts. Richard, you have been like a brother to me for 55 years since we met as teenagers. Later, we reconnected when you were about forty and had developed the IHA system and were writing your first book on hand analysis called *Life Prints*.

Special acknowledgment to my brother, Paul J. Goodberg, and for *What Wants to be Known;* your book poignantly describes our childhood beginning in NYC and about our grandmother, Gussie, who demonstrated to both of us the love of helping people heal.

Thank you to all the children I taught with my Master's in Special Education, who believed in me and opened up a special space in their hearts to allow me to influence their lives with such a high impact.

Special gratitude to Laura Boxer from Oakland, California. Thank you for recognizing my gifts and talents in 1979 and asking me to be the marketing director for the first Women's Success Teams on the West Coast of the USA. I was able to use my special ability in these trainings to find someone's purpose, goal, and vision. I had the chance to discover this talent with hundreds of women in the Women's Success Teams training.

Special gratitude to Justin Sterling of the Sterling Institute. Thank you for believing in me as the first staff member at the Institute and trusting that I could organize and create the first *Women, Sex and Power* and the *Men, Sex and Power* training (*The Guerrilla Training*). Together, we held these trainings to benefit men and women in relationships everywhere. Later, after I left the organization, the training was renamed *The Women's Weekend* and *The Men's Weekend*.

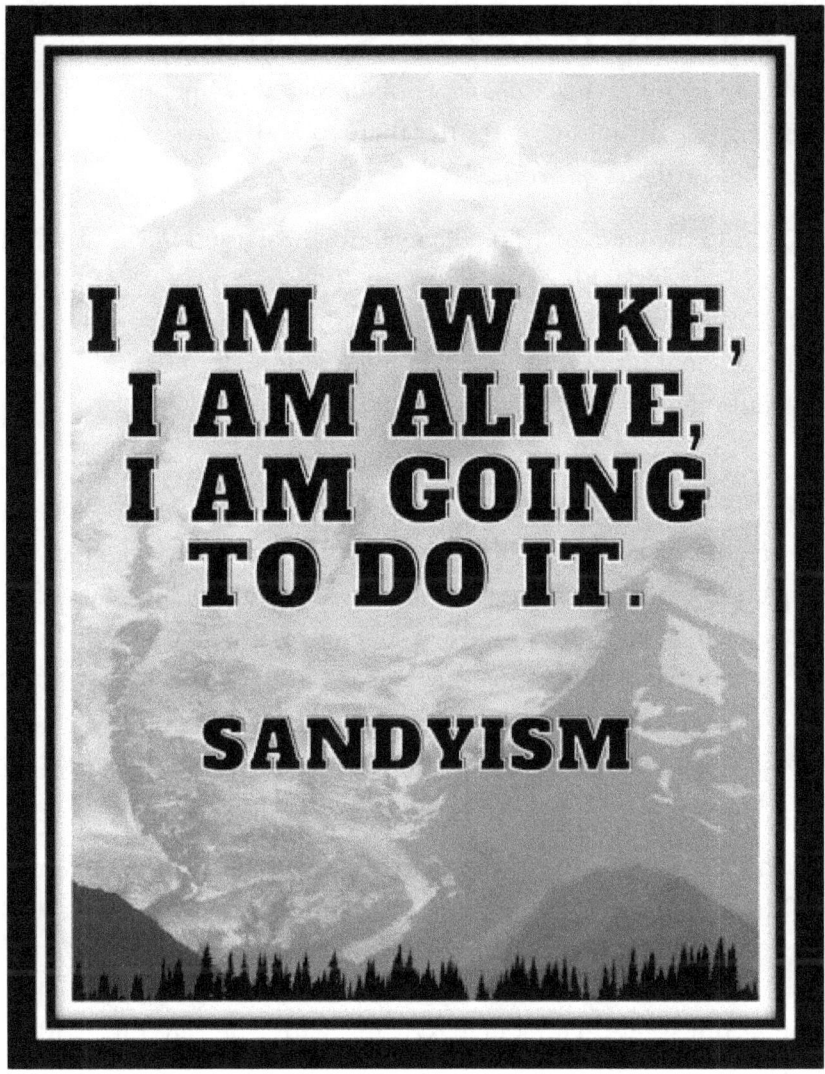

Special gratitude to client Stanley Russell for asking me to create a training on how to make money from your life purpose and for teaching the training with me. I discovered that I had skills as a trainer because of Stanley telling me that he had never been able to make money from his purpose, mission, and vision. At the time, I was a life coach in San Francisco, California, with a fully booked schedule of 12 hours a day. Originally, I thought it was a ridiculous idea for Stanley to teach something he didn't know, but by us teaching together in a course, he realized his goal by learning how to make money from his purpose and market himself.

Special gratitude to Red Payne who was logistically precise and on time in organizing and running the team for a total of 72 hours over a two-weekend training of *The Art of Personal Marketing*. I often had 50-75 people and a coaching team of at least 14. For many years after that, 10,000 people took the training. It was quite a logistical feat.

Special thanks to the team of trained coaches who assisted me in California and Canada from 1984 to 1990 before *The Power of Clearing* process came into vision. Your dedication inspired me to cultivate an efficient coaching team that would deepen the personal process for every individual to help them find the answers they were exploring.

Special acknowledgments to the students I trained who became teachers in their own right over the years and developed their skills and talents—Dr. Dennis Gaither from Mt. Vernon, Washington, USA. In Canada, Diederik Wolsak of Choose Again in Victoria, Christie Dakin of Vancouver, Elaine Clark of Langley, Miriam Evers, Joy Coach, and Howard Staples of Langley, Duane O'Kane of Langley, Teertha Mistleburger of Vancouver, and Len Satov of Vancouver. And in Europe, Paul Goudsmit and Jane Tipping in Holland, Ian Barhydt of Waxthusett, Stockholm, Sweden, Carlos Mosqueda from Spain and Sweden, and Inger Holmqvist from Spain and Stockholm, Sweden.

Special acknowledgment to psychologist Lena Kristina Tuulse from Väddö, Sweden (Stockholm Archipelago) for bringing me to Sweden in 1987 and asking me to teach her everything I knew about *The Art of Personal Marketing* and transformational therapy. Her invitation was a defining moment of my life. I spent three full weeks with Lena Kristina with one day off, working with Volvo, SAS (Scandinavian Airlines), Berol Chemie, and a transformational organization called Humanistic Forum. Thanks to Lena Kristina for inviting me to Sweden that I realize was part of my destiny. A whole Swedish network was born from that meeting when I moved there two years later. For eleven years, I worked with a team of extraordinarily dedicated and skilled Swedish therapists and coaches. I am honored that we accomplished such great success together for the *Fri Sikt* youth project made possible by a private benefactor. Tremendous growth came through my time in Sweden resulting in much of the materials we have gathered for this book. Lena Kristina is one of the most caring, open-minded, adventurous, creative, innovative, forward-thinking, and therapeutically knowledgeable women I have met in my lifetime. She is the 1992 founder of Life University, a model city of healing, on the hundred acres of her property stretching out to the Baltic Sea—where the *Fri Sikt* youth project happened in 1996. Thousands of these students and friends came from Sweden and other European countries and I am still active in many of those relationships today.

I gratefully acknowledge the Swedish team from 1989 to 2001. The depth of the trainings in Sweden were possible because of the great coaching team that helped each participant personally access their emotional traumas and create the possibility for a breakthrough. Alexandra Sjögren, Anna Margareta Sundberg Reed, Katarina Pilotti, Maria Sloth, Anita Mastling, Ingrid Wigh, Martin Dahlborg, Steven Gauvin, Carlos Mosqueda, Inger Holmqvist, Gabriella Saad, Thomas Tuulse, Goran Ziethen, Ragnheld Ziethen, Goran Danrad, Ian Barhydt, Michael Person, Patrik Von Corswant, and Inger Von Corswant: thank you for your one hundred percent support.

Thank you, Anna Margareta Sundberg Reed, for contributing to the writing of this book with your special talents and abilities in journalism. I am grateful you were one of the first promoters of *The Art of Personal Marketing* program in Sweden and one of the ten live translators of my trainings from English to Swedish for many years. You have been a close friend, valued supporter, and an ally of this process for over 30 years.

Thank you, Alexandra Sjögren, for your great interest in metaphysical healing. I value your brilliant ideas. Your kind support enabled many people to heal, and your generosity has made a significant positive difference in many lives.

Special acknowledgment to Mats Stjernqvist and Lottie Stjernqvist of Sandared, Sweden; you have been my dearest friends and colleagues since the early 1990s when we lived together in Skräddaröd, Sweden.

Mats was present with me after *The Art of Surrender* training as I received *The Power of Clearing* materials that would later become *The Holy Relationship* training and *The Power of Clearing* process. Without you, Mats, I feel I would never have received *The Power of Clearing* process initially. Your consistent dedication to Truth and releasing all barriers to total Knowing has been invaluable for me in receiving and sharing *The Power of Clearing* process. Soon after that significant shift in my life, I had a whole community in Sweden to move these trainings and processes forward in transformational thinking.

Then Lottie came into our lives and married Mats. Since then, we have had a triad holy relationship that has lasted over thirty years, with our ongoing purpose of knowing and living Peace and Truth. Lottie, thank you for our thirty-year friendship. You are a living demonstration of *A Course in Miracles* through your knowledge, dedication, and study with full commitment to *The Clearing Process*. Thank you for your support and the five days you spent with me in 1990 in the battle with my ego through my greatest fear of separation to end it in my mind completely. We made it through together. You have always been and will always be a great friend, ally, and supporter.

Special appreciation to the two couples I married in the holy relationship ceremony and ritual. I wrote individual ceremonies for both of these weddings that lasted about an hour and a half. The first in Spain, between Inger Holmqvist and Carlos Mosqueda, and then in Sweden the following year, their friends, Anna-Eva Lohe and Ian Barhydt of Stockholm. Thank you all for the many years you worked together in your relationships as couples in clearing anything that was in the way of you coming to Love, Peace, and Joy together in total joining. Your relationships inspire everyone as dedicated students of your transformation process. Your weddings were highlights in the cornucopia of my life.

Special acknowledgment to Carlos Mosqueda of Stockholm, Sweden; you were the first organizer and leader of the *Fri Sikt* youth project in Stockholm, who organized all the courses and supported weekly team meetings and training for these 120 youths in one and a half years. Your contribution, combining skill, dedication, and commitment to this youth project, was priceless. Thank you for the ten years you worked with me, organizing and promoting all the *On Purpose* trainings in Sweden. Your skill and high-mindedness still inspire me over 25 years later.

Special gratitude to Carlos Mosqueda, the *Fri Sikt* youth project leader in Stockholm, and Martin Dahlburg and Steven Gauvin, project leaders of the Malmo *Fri Sikt* project; thank you all.

Special acknowledgment to Peter Mayer, the award-winning, now-deceased movie maker of the *Fri Sikt* project called *The Difference* in 1998, which won the second-best documentary in Sweden according to the Jul Klippan award. Four million people watched this movie on television, and journalists in 11 newspaper articles wrote about the film documenting the project transforming the lives of 120 youths.

Warm appreciation for Z. Light Miller, my dear friend and sister for over 25 years. I loved supporting you in learning Panchakarma and becoming an Ayurvedic doctor so you could help people cleanse and heal with this ancient Indian tradition. You learned *The Power of Clearing* method and accompanied me with your husband, Brian Miller, to courses all over the world. We created many breakthroughs with much joy and learning; those years were some of the favorites of my life. We were like catalytic combustion together. One of the only reasons I want to be dead one day is to find out why you died since you were one of the healthiest people I knew, following conscious healing practices every day of your life. I'm mystified that the condition you succumbed to when you were 74 years young was one that you and I helped many people heal from with my emotional clearing method and your physical holistic cleansing practices. I will always miss you.

Thanks to my personal assistant, Jennifer Simms, 35 years ago when you were in your 20s and lived near me in Mill Valley, California. We created many fantastic courses and events together in the 1980s. Thank God we reconnected 20 years later when I came to help a client in San Diego, and we rekindled our catalytic relationship. I trust one day we will dance and scream with excitement at the opening of your first movie.

Special gratitude to Ian Patrick in England, founder and manager of the Miracle Network in London for 22 years: Thank you for all your support during the many years we worked together in the *On Purpose* trainings. I appreciate you writing the Foreword and the "What is *A Course in Miracles?*" section of this book, being on the editing team, and creating the glossary of terms with your brilliant knowledge of *A Course in Miracles*. You are a dear friend, fellow teacher, and *Power of Clearing* coach.

Thank you to John and Sue Reynard of Stowmarket, England, the organizers, marketers, and certified *Power of Clearing* coaches holding the England network of participants for many years. I appreciate your dedication to being great friends and supporters of my work and commitment to my *On Purpose* mission of transformation. I will be forever grateful to you.

Special gratitude to the entire organizing team in the UK, Ian Patrick, Sue Reynard, John Reynard, Gillian Hibbs, Angela Hahn, Sally Peace, Roy Gough, Oriana Howes, Susan Culverwell, and Kevin Sandhu; you are valued colleagues and friends.

Special gratitude to the Scotland team of Iona Leishman, Dr. Veronica McBurnie, Lorraine Devlin, and David Spooner; thanks for our deep connections.

In North America, special acknowledgment to the team of coaches and healers, Melanie Aceves, Dr. Dennis Gaither, Len Satov, Jenny Spencer, Michael McDonald, Miriam Evers, Howard Staples, Lorne Rubinoff, Kristi Birnie, Sharon Richlark, Laura Gibson, Christina Ireland, Sue Wilde, Richard Locke, Nisha Helmig, Shelora Fitzgerald, Valerie Shahan, Diane Brewer, Mary Lynn Hart, Krista Voigt, and Gizella Nagy; you continue to make a positive difference of great value in so many people's lives.

Special acknowledgment to Len Satov from Vancouver, Canada, who has been working with me for more than 20 years, traveling to many places in the world and conducting trainings and private sessions for many people. Thank you for all your skill, brilliance, dedication, support, and friendship. I greatly appreciate you. Thank you also for being on my book's editorial team and contributing your article, "The Watcher" (in Resources). The Watcher has become a part of *The Power of Clearing* technology, and many people have found it beneficial in their healing process. In addition, you have contributed other valuable explanations helping people better understand themselves and how their minds work.

Thank you to Christina Ireland of Vancouver, Canada, for your brilliant writings and editorial work for my book and more than 25 years of acknowledgment, support, and additional insights you have given me. Without you and Sue Wilde's intuitive and constant requests for me to create, write, and produce the *True Woman's Power* course, it never would have happened. That course has transformed thousands of women's lives since its inception in 1996.

Acknowledging Miriam Evers of Vancouver, Canada, Joy Coach, whose favorite motto is "Joy First. Then anything else you have time for." Thank you for all the years you worked with me, creating and accounting, recording, and believing in me, and for your friendship, support, and skill.

Acknowledging Howard Staples, life coach; you were the first project leader of the *Youth on Purpose* Project in Vancouver, Canada. For three years, you were leading a group of young adults through transformation and working with me so impeccably, creating our mentors and generating funds. Your commitment, dedication, and skill as a re-birther were unparalleled.

With appreciation for Kathy Middleton, now deceased, one of the organizers of the *On Purpose* trainings; you were such an organized, thorough, meticulous inspiration to all of us on the team with your beautiful support of the network. Those of us who knew you will always miss you.

Special acknowledgment to Kylene Ross, a good friend, certified *Power of Clearing* coach, and soon-to-be lawyer in Nashville, Tennessee; this book would never have been possible without your total loyalty, support, skill, and acknowledgment. The world awaits you for the many brilliant years to come when you serve as a lawyer helping everyone demonstrate their true integrity. Also, I am forever grateful for your help in discovering that someone very close to me, who I trusted implicitly, had stolen hundreds of thousands of dollars from me. This experience of someone betraying me in such a life-altering way provided an opportunity to clearly demonstrate that I do walk the talk I teach by forgiving myself for attracting this betrayal in my life and forgiving that person rather than taking legal action.

To Sharon Browning of Arizona, Kylene Ross' mother, and Diana Calderone of Texas, her best friend, who were some of the original supporters and organizers of the *On Purpose* trainings: Your drive and foresight have been invaluable in the development of this process and 35 years of friendship.

Thank you, Jenny Spencer, one of the outstanding members of the North American support team, a massage therapist, healer, cook, and humanitarian who gave impeccable service and skill to *The Power of Clearing* trainings for over 20 years. Thank you for your friendship and dedication. Thank you for taking time off to support me in Bellingham during the hours of one of the greatest shocks I have experienced in the last 50 years.

Thank you, Joan Trinh Pham, for creating five illustrations of highlights of *The Power of Clearing* learnings—that you drew while participating in the ten-day *Power of Clearing Coaching Certification Program* (**POCCCP**)—we are delighted to feature them in this book.

To Margaret Anne West, thank you for your timely appearance and flexibility for drawing the sketch of a homeless man in the likeness of the person I describe who impacted my life by inspiring the title of this book.

Special acknowledgment to Morgan Hawthorn; you serendipitously came into my life at the exact time when we were preparing my book for promotion and publication. Your ideas, skill, talent, photographs, and graphics, combined with your wholehearted commitment and dedication to my process, have been invaluable. I am so grateful to have received you into my life.

I am grateful for Lynn Thompson, my professional editor; I value your writing and editing skills, flexibility in moving the book forward on all levels, and patience in helping me stay focused. Your acceptance of our team is invaluable for our collaboration. You are meticulous and a pleasure to work with, and I am delighted by your quick wit, organization, and insight. Mutual connections brought us together again twelve years after you organized and attended my trainings in Canada. Your knowledge of *The Power of Clearing* process was so helpful in editing my book.

Kristi Birnie, thank you for showing up at the right moment in divine timing on the final stretch of preparing my book for publication. It's fantastic how your expertise in *The Clearing Process* and brilliant editorial skills combined with your valued and insightful collaboration with Lynn Thompson and the team.

I warmly appreciate Becky Norwood of Spotlight Publishing for your skills, prompt follow-up, follow-through, and fantastic work with my team and me. You are caring, thoughtful, knowledgeable, and filled with new insights and perspectives.

Robert Hand of Bellingham, Washington. Thank you for our exciting new inspirational friendship. I have so enjoyed teaching you *The Power of Clearing* process and *The Holy Relationship* program. Thank you for your interest, dedication, and commitment to learning and awakening to your truest self. It is an inspiration to share with you all that I know. I look forward to teaching new courses at Wise Awakening, your inspirational center for transformation and wellness in Bellingham, Washington.

To Alanna Zackrison of Knoxville, Tennessee, a student committed to your transformation, clearing anything in the way of peace in your life. Thank you for all your inspiration, dedication, one hundred percent friendship, loyalty, and support of my *Power of Clearing* process and for your commitment to using the process to come to one hundred percent Peace, Love, and Joy in your life.

A special thank you to Gizella Nagy for your enthusiastic encouragement to help me gather coaches and materials to increase the impact of *The Clearing Process* in the world today. I am inspired by your passion and willingness to bring together the technology of videos, social media, and website-building to expand my reach and capacity to work with people in *The Clearing Process*.

My heartfelt gratitude to my two angels in England, Angela Hahn, the first scribe and contributor to this book, and Gillian Hibbs, who wrote the second version with me. You two extraordinary ladies are brilliant certified *Power of Clearing* coaches, filled with insight, vision, and open-mindedness. For more than a year, you contributed your remarkable qualities, helping me develop this book. Thank you both for your dedication and commitment that launched and motivated me to write my legacy book.

Finally, I'd like to acknowledge myself for becoming a self-created life coach, among the first in the world, with ideas and methods coming directly from my connection to Spirit. Thank you, God, for my Special Function (ACIM term), and I thank myself for recognizing and utilizing it constantly.

Sandy Levey-Lunden

I Just Want Peace

FOREWORD

I feel truly honored by Sandy Levey-Lunden's invitation to write this foreword and thereby, to contribute to her healing work.

Sandy and I met in 2005, when she was sitting behind a bookstall at an *A Course in Miracles* conference in Salt Lake City, USA. I knew her by reputation as a pioneer. She was revered as a strong woman who could be a little intimidating and would never take no for an answer. When I introduced myself to her that day, instead of the Sandy of reputation, I found her and have since found her to be one of the kindest and most loving people I have ever known. She is enthusiastic, passionate, and simply eager to get her message of healing into the world.

The word "pioneer" is sometimes over-used; however, Sandy is a pioneer in the true sense. In this book, she tells her story, gives her take on the human condition in the world she has observed from an early age and describes how she was "given" *The Clearing Process* material during a time of crisis in her life. From the bottom of her heart, Sandy asked for a way out of her pain and suffering. She received this powerful system of thought transformation, and she used it to heal her situation thoroughly. She continues her clearing practice today on herself because healing is an ongoing journey. Sandy has devoted her life to providing *The Power of Clearing* as a gift to the world, in hundreds of training events globally. In doing so, she has helped thousands of people to find Inner Peace and their True Selves. Sandy's work has since been emulated by many spiritual teachers, psychologists, therapists, and students.

The Clearing Process, described here and pioneered by Sandy, is a dynamic process. By verbalizing, giving voice (out loud) to fears, judgments, doubts, and attack thoughts, in a safe, controlled, and structured way, one can be transformed and released, revealing the True Thoughts, the Thoughts of God, and the Real

Self that were there all along, hidden beneath those raucous ego shrieks. Sandy describes the emergence of *The Clearing Process,* shares the spiritual psychology behind it, and how we can use it to achieve powerful results in our lives. In addition, she includes insights from *A Course in Miracles* (Foundation for Inner Peace, www.acim.org), the book that parallels her work.

While promoting a dozen or more of Sandy's workshops in the UK—under the auspices of the Miracle Network—I attended them all and assisted at many. I've seen people who arrived quiet, withdrawn, scared, angry, in denial, or acting out, transformed into happy, enthusiastic, positive, peaceful, loving, empowered people. Watching their faces, at that moment—when they dropped their mistaken negative beliefs, armor, and anger and suddenly realized that they were, in truth, Whole and Innocent—was truly inspiring and gratifying.

While this book will impart all you need to know about *The Clearing Process*, there is no substitute for actually doing it for yourself and experiencing the profound awareness and healing transformation it provides. I highly recommend this book, and *The Power of Clearing*.

Ian Patrick
Founder, Miracle Network, London UK—www.miracles.org.uk

What is *A Course in Miracles*?

By Ian Patrick

Do you want to let go of fear and anger, and find peace of mind? Do you sometimes reflect on the age-old questions: "What is real?" or "Why do I not feel fulfilled but empty inside?"

Ancient thinkers also asked, pondered, and posed these questions, and many philosophies, spiritual traditions, and religions aim to answer them. The *A Course in Miracles* (ACIM) method, in many ways, overturns the partial or even erroneous answers to these questions.

A Course in Miracles is a self-study book of psychological and spiritual transformation, which aims at replacing our current thought system of fear with one based on love.

Through the study and practice, ACIM will answer many of these questions in a radical and unexpected way.

The Course emphasizes the practical application of its principles, which focus on the key concept of forgiveness and the transformational potential of the mind.

The book comprises 1,250 pages in three volumes, combining profound spiritual teachings with far-reaching and practical psychological insights. The Course is a spiritual teaching rather than a religion. It does not claim any superiority over other paths. In fact, it says that it is one of the thousands of paths that lead to God. It does claim, though, to be able to save us time on that journey.

The three volumes of *A Course in Miracles* consist of:

a) The Text, which provides the theoretical framework
b) The Workbook, which contains 365 daily lessons
c) The Manual for Teachers, which answers many common questions and includes an appendix called the Clarification of Terms.

Have you ever had one of those moments when you just "get it"? Sometimes, we call that an insight, and it can feel like a profound mystical experience—one that shifts our perception completely. We all hunger for those moments, especially in the midst of apparent adversity. *A Course in Miracles* is about those moments, which it calls "miracles."

Much has been written about the Course, with its revolutionary views and understanding of the inner psyche. At a basic level, the Course aims to help us remove the blocks to the awareness of love's presence, which is our natural inheritance, and to start us listening to our inner teacher: the Holy Spirit or "the Voice for God." It is a powerful, complex book that goes beyond what most professionals have encountered in mapping the dynamics of the human mind.

A Course in Miracles says there is no separation between God and ourselves or, therefore, between each of us. God is love, eternal and infinite, and all there is. We are God's one creation. God only creates like Himself, so we remain as He created us, innocent and whole. Only what God created is real. God did not create pain, death, guilt, or fear, so although they exist in our experience, releasing them creates a vehicle to recognizing that they are not real. Rather than trying to change external circumstances, the Course teaches us to change our perceptions about the world.

Forgiveness, a central concept of the Course, provides the means by which we can use our relationships to let go of the past, along with its burden of guilt and grievances. In ACIM, forgiveness does not pardon sins and make them real but sees that there was no sin and recognizes all behavior as either an extension of love or a call for love.

Since *A Course in Miracles* was first published in 1975, more than one million copies have been sold around the world, and it has profoundly changed the lives of many thousands of people. In addition, the Course has been translated into a dozen languages, with many translations in progress. With more than 700 books published by authors inspired by the Course (including those by Marianne Williamson and Jerry Jampolsky), there are now as many as 2,000 ACIM study groups worldwide.

PREFACE

The Meaning of Life

When I was seven years old, I began to think about the meaning of life. All the big questions: *Who am I really? Why am I here? Why did God send me to Earth? What am I supposed to do with my life? What is everybody else supposed to do with theirs?*

In my exploration and clarification of this question, I asked my mother why she was here and what her purpose was on Earth. She told me she didn't know but would think about it and get back to me. After several weeks, she delivered her answer. My mother told me she believed she was here to be my mother. I thought about her response and felt that if that was the truth, that living her purpose as my mother truly fulfilled her here on Earth, then she should have been happy most of the time. However, in my eyes, my mother never appeared to be truly happy at the deepest level of her core being. I believed that if my mother truly understood why she was here on Earth and living her purpose, she would have been completely at peace and experiencing total joy.

"Stuck-ness"

I was born in the Bronx, New York, in 1945. It was a tough neighborhood and a space where everyone seemed to be on high alert. It certainly made the senses come alive, although not always in a peaceful way!

As I observed the people around me, I noticed that it felt as if something was missing when they talked to each other and spoke about their lives. There seemed to be a lack of purpose to their existence. They repeatedly told the same stories about who did what, all in a way that caused them to maintain their victimhood while, at the same time, finding blame. It was as if they had something they couldn't release or move on from, so their patterns would repeat, and their lives would continue going around and around like a record stuck in the same groove. I later called this "stuck-ness" guilt. In every repetitive version of the story, I would also observe my neighbors attempting to defend themselves from this guilt. They perceived themselves as being victimized by those around them.

People have often asked me why some people have more challenging lives while others have seemingly easier or better circumstances. My point of view about how this all came to be is that when we chose to come to Earth, we each chose a specific contract to fulfill. We chose our mother and father, siblings (or not), teachers, children (or not), and the lessons we would learn and grow through in this lifetime. We chose the body we would be in, what would be well and healthy in it and what would be difficult or challenging. We also chose our life partners, husbands, wives, and all the people we are destined to meet and have relationships to share life lessons. We chose the financial situation, where we would live, how, when, for how long, and the amount of ease, struggle, joy, and pain we would go through according to what we contracted. We can choose surrender and release struggle, prioritizing love over fear, so these contracted lessons can become easier. Conscious choices made along the way can change the course of the original contract. Of the thousands of people I have met in my courses, counseling, and workshops, there is no one I have spoken with deeply who has not gone through something difficult on their path to becoming who they are today. I've had several close friends who are heiresses, and many people would say they had it easy; however, they went through so much pain in their lives even with these economic privileges. The ego thinks "the grass is always greener on the other side," however, to me, the amount of struggle experienced would be equal on either side of the fence. No one has it more or better than you do; it's a made-up story on your part if you think they do. What we have is what we choose. To move on, accept what you've got now; it's what you created and attracted. Then choose again what you desire to create and attract in the next now.

My intention in writing this book is for people of all walks of life to understand how to release guilt so that their stories of victimhood are never spoken of again. The energy involved in speaking and expressing is more powerful than you will ever realize. When the negative energy and pain of a stuck pattern in a "story" is released, there will be no need to repeat it because it will be released, let go of, and gone. And you will most likely forget the story you made up.

Sandy's Life Mission

There is always a purpose in how people find their way to my counseling, life coaching, or training room. I trust we are meant to connect and work together. Once we become engaged in this healing process, I am dedicated to their personal breakthrough based on their initial intentions and goals set in the sessions. I am committed to them healing their mind and breaking through to another level according to their vision of their best life. My attention to them can go on for several years after completing our association in the formal sessions. People I work with are never far from my heart. So, when I think of something that will help them, I recommend additional courses, processes, or therapies, which I know from personal experience, or that of close clients or friends.

Sandy Levey-Lunden
Bellingham, Washington, USA

INTRODUCTION

Why did I want to write this book?

This legacy book introduces the world to *The Power of Clearing*, a psycho-spiritual method to release negative belief patterns and limiting mindsets and is intended to summarize decades of using this incredible tool to release trauma, pain, and suffering.

I am also writing this book as a reference guide for the thousands of students who have been in the trainings with me and the amazing teams of *Power of Clearing* coaches, to remind you of the process, how it works, and what you learned.

While many methods and tools are available for working on deep-rooted issues, through my experience, I believe that applying *The Power of Clearing process* profoundly increases each person's conscious awareness. *The Power of Clearing* leads to a renewal and an awakening in one's life of Purpose, Joy, and, ultimately, Peace. The release creates a permanent cellular shift in the person.

My favorite ACIM lesson (ACIM, W-185.1:1-3) is: *I want the peace of God. To say these words is nothing. But to mean these words is everything. If you could but mean them for just an instant, there would be no further sorrow possible for you in any form; in any place or time.*

Everyone has peace within them; it is part of our true nature. We are all beings of peace. It's only because of our conditioning or past pain and traumas that we have forgotten this truth. It has been covered over, but it is still there, like clouds blocking the sun, like dark cloths covering the light that we are. As we go through our life, we forget that we have Peace within, that we *are* Peace. Living, experiencing, and being Peace in every moment is our true goal.

And why do you want to read it?

What is it that *you* truly desire? What holds the most meaning for you?

I would like to share a story with you. I once saw a man living on the street corner in my hometown of Bellingham, WA, holding a sign that said "HOMELESS." I immediately wanted to know what this man *really* wanted. The message on the sign was unclear to me. Did he need someone to take him into their home, did he want a job, or food, or clothes, or what? So, I asked him, "What do you want?" Sighing, he told me: "I just want peace." In that moment, I felt completely connected and at One with him, for that was all that I wanted as well. This encounter always stood out in my mind and greatly influenced my entire life and this book.

The purpose of *The Clearing Process* is simply to reveal and bring forth the Peace of who you are. Peace on every level of your being and in every aspect of your life. Your true home is Peace within. When you strip away everything that keeps you occupied in your busy world and allow yourself to feel, Peace gives you a greater sense of balance, harmony, and serenity in all things.

In sharing *The Clearing Process* with you and all who desire to learn it, I invite you to use it in its fullness to revive and expand the Peace and aliveness within you so you can be in alignment with Truth, the Divine, and your Higher Self. This book explains the precise method to make that happen and I trust it will help you reveal your True Nature.

PRELUDE

HOW AND WHY I BECAME A STUDENT OF *A COURSE IN MIRACLES*

When I look back on my life of seventy-seven years so far, I would say that it was my destiny to find and study *A Course in Miracles*. I have read some sections over one hundred times, and I see something in a new way every time. When I first read some passages, I could complete the sentences as though I had a pre-knowledge of the writing. It seemed so familiar to me, as though I had seen or heard its wisdom before.

While I was in the City College of New York (CCNY) with a major in psychology for my undergraduate degree, I was drawn to study at the Columbia School of Psychology, a distance away of about twenty blocks. I had always joked that I wanted to study psychology at Columbia University rather than CCNY because they had cuter boys there. However, when I look back at my life and destiny, I realize I was studying in that school of psychology at the same time that Helen Schucman and Bill Thetford were there scribing ACIM. At the time, I was not aware of that coincidence. Many years later, in 1980, when I became a professional Life Coach and Counselor, I was given ACIM as a gift by one of my clients. Back then, they had large print and were three very thick volumes, taking up half a bookshelf. I looked into these books and said to myself, "If I were to study these books and this methodology, I would have to change everything I think, feel, and believe about my life. And why would I want to do that? I would have to revamp my whole life." I put the books aside, concluding, "This is too much work."

Six weeks later, another client gave me a second set of these books. Now I had two sets! I thought to myself that this had to be more than a coincidence. It must be a message or a sign. Reading the books more closely, I began to feel it was my destiny to read and study these books. Up until that point I thought my best choice was to follow my feelings and act according to them. Now, as I was reading material in these spiritual books, it showed me my feelings were temporary. I realized that if I became a student of ACIM, I would need to radically change everything I perceived as truth and find another place in myself to know Truth. I knew I would become a student committed to learning and teaching *A Course in Miracles*.

In the 1980s, I memorized many quotes and passages. When I received a cassette tape directed by ACIM and written by Rabbi Nathan and Rabbi Joseph, I began singing with it. In singing these songs constantly, I later realized the songs were the deep passages I had unknowingly memorized from the ACIM book. I became a teacher, a seminar leader, and a trainer with my business, which I named *On Purpose*. ACIM became a reference library for me in all the trainings I have written, for quotes, ideas, and ways to help people process what they are experiencing.

Even though I had used ACIM in my life coaching, counseling practice, and trainings, when I left behind San Francisco and my flourishing business in 1989 to move to Sweden, I wasn't yet a full student of ACIM. It was in 1990 in Sweden, during my relationship crisis, that I learned how to embody the complete thought system of these books.

ACIM and *The Power of Clearing*

Many people who study ACIM begin at a turning point or predicament in their lives when they feel like there is nothing else that makes sense and need a way through their pain and into Peace.

Through my healing process, as I describe in Chapter 6, *The Power of Clearing* and *The Clearing Process* emerged. ACIM is 1,500 pages and requires a year of study to follow the Workbook (one lesson per day, in order) and read the Text (two pages per day). In contrast, *The Power of Clearing* is a concise guide with steps that are practical, simple, and easy to follow and learn. Anyone can do *The Clearing Process* anytime, anywhere, and release whatever is upsetting them in their ego-mind. Both studies, done together or separately, provide an extraordinary shift from ego-mind to your True mind.

For most people, it is a challenge just to read *A Course in Miracles* and comprehend what it says. Of course, it's much more challenging to live what it says on a day-to-day basis. That is the real challenge—to bring the teachings into your daily living. That is the opportunity ACIM offers each one of us. In every area of our lives, we can either say, "I am clear, and in my truth," or have some judgment, some fear, and some guilt. Clear or not clear is the same as you are pregnant or not pregnant, there is no grey area. You are either in your Big T Truth or in your ego.

The Power of Clearing process requires a willingness to take responsibility for what we see, what we think, and what we do. I automatically check myself with everything I think, do, feel, and say to see if I am in line with *The Power of Clearing* thinking and philosophy. If not, I see what I can forgive in my beliefs and live more peacefully to be in pure Truth.

From *A Course in Miracles* in "The Responsibility for Sight" (ACIM, T-21.II):

> This is the only thing that you need do for vision, happiness, release from pain and the complete escape from sin, all to be given you. ²Say only this, but mean it with no reservations, for here the power of salvation lies:
>
> ³*I **am** responsible for what I see.*
>
> ⁴ *I choose the feelings I experience, and I decide upon the goal I would achieve.*
>
> ⁵ *And everything that seems to happen to me I ask for, and receive as I have asked.*
>
> ⁶ Deceive yourself no longer that you are helpless in the face of what is done to you. ⁷ Acknowledge but that you have been mistaken, and all effects of your mistakes will disappear.
>
> (ACIM, T-21.II.2:1-7)

Here is an anecdote by Mats Stjernqvist (of Sweden) relating to this ACIM quote about responsibility for sight.

> Since only perception needs correction, because it is not being created by God, we need to shift our minds about how we see the World.
>
> Whenever someone in the training had an attitude of "It wasn't me" and pointed their finger blaming someone else, we always jokingly asked, "Who?" When we are pointing our finger at someone else, it has to come from us somehow.

Listening to the person in the sharing chair, we heard an elaborate story of their perception of what happened to them against their will. Thinking that if they could see this situation differently, they would be free, we taught them forgiveness to stop and reverse the mind from digging deeper into the illusion of their perceived guilt and being stuck forever.

They had a misperception that the perfect projection in the illusion would provide a perfect life, a perfect partner, the perfect happiness, but the real benefit of being "Responsible for Sight" is Oneness, the end of Separation, and thereby, total Peace and freedom.

I Just Want Peace contains examples of *The Clearing Process* and testimonials from participants and coaches to illustrate the transformational potential. You may notice repetition of key concepts, principles, and definitions like projection, forgiveness, separation, healing, fear, and guilt. I have noticed that we need to hear ideas three times for it to sink into ego-minds resistant to change and learning.

I wish for you to find a way that truly works to release all conflict from your mind about yourself, your issues, your negative past, and your current reality. We will no longer need to fight with anyone, family members, friends or colleagues, when we finally release our personal wars within our ego-mind. Being at peace within will lessen external conflicts. This inner transformation will truly change the world we are currently experiencing into the one I dream about: a world of peace, a world in which we are all unified!

Peace is the Truth of who you are. So come, let's journey together through these pages guiding you in clearing the blocks covering your Peace. This book is the way.

The Annotation System for *A Course in Miracles* provides a method for students of the Course to reference a specific passage within the Course and its Supplements. Here are examples.

"You will first dream of peace, and then awaken to it." (T-13.VII.9:1)

T = Text, 13 = Chapter 13, VII = Section VII (of Chapter 13),
9 = Paragraph 9 (in Section VII), 1 = Line 1 (of Paragraph 9)

"We say 'God is,' and then we cease to speak, for in that knowledge words are meaningless." (W-pI.169.5:4)

W = Workbook, pI = part I (of the Workbook), 169 = Lesson 169,
5 = Paragraph 5, 4 = Line 4 (of Paragraph 5)

"Forgiveness is the final goal of the curriculum." (M-4.X.2:9)

M = Manual for Teachers, 4 = Section 4, X = Part X (of Section 4),
2 = Paragraph 2 (of Part X), 9 = Line 9 (of Paragraph 2)

Additional abbreviations:
in = introduction(s)
r = Review (workbook)
fl = Final Lessons (workbook)
C = Clarification of Terms (in the Manual for Teachers)
ep = Epilogues (end of Workbook and Clarification of Terms)
P = Psychotherapy: Purpose, Process and Practice
S = The Song of Prayer

REFLECTIONS ON
THE POWER OF CLEARING
A SUMMARY OF
THE CLEARING PROCESS

The philosophy of *The Power of Clearing Process* is the essence of how I live my life. The core of my thinking comes from *A Course in Miracles* (ACIM) lesson entitled; *In my defenselessness my safety lies.* (ACIM, W-153) This lesson has become the foundation for how I respond to whomever and whatever is going on in my world.

I do not think about a boundary between you and me. I know you are one with me. If you ask me for something or say something to me, I know I have somehow attracted you and what you are saying to me. Therefore, I strongly consider how we can be in agreement. If something happens that I react negatively against, I know I have something to release, and I want to release what is in the way of us coming together in alignment. When I am triggered, I know I have something in my mind to clear.

We all create our reality, like a movie or story, and then we work only within that story line. I choose not to ignore my fears and worries. Instead, I take responsibility for them. We create our world and what the characters are doing as evidence to prove our negative ego beliefs. "No amount of evidence will ever make true something that isn't true anyway." Even if with countless incidents where my ego proves this negative core belief to be correct, such as "I'm not good enough" or "I'm not worthy of love," it will never be the Truth of who I am. It may feel true, but it is not the ultimate Truth. The stronger the negative feeling, the more strongly the ego may try to convince us that it's the Truth. If I continue to hold the unconscious negative belief that something is wrong with me or I will always be rejected, I will repeatedly react to it until I transform the core belief.

Whenever I have anxiety or worry, I go back to the truth of ACIM and tell myself that I made up everything that I feel, think, or believe about it. Then I will do the 3-step *Clearing Process* on my fear or anxiety. This process always leads me back to peace.

I work specifically with the meaning that I give to what happens in my life or my environment. When an event triggers me, I will clear my upset and find the root of my lack of peace within my mind. When I look at the beliefs I made up to survive childhood traumas, I gain perspective on the root of my projections on current relationships, which is an opportunity for healing incomplete neuropathways.

ACIM says: *I am never upset for the reason I think.* (ACIM, W-5) Everything I am upset about has its meaning in the form of some attack on myself in the form of a negative belief. For example, I may be upset that no one left me any birthday cake, which may seem trivial initially. This upset may occur because I always believed I am not good enough—no one sees me, no one cares, no one wants me to be around, or no one hears me. So, ultimately, everything I am upset about has to do with my evaluation, blame, judgment, or a believed fear about myself.

If I do not like someone, I ask myself, "What do I not like about this person, precisely?" and "Who do they remind me of from my past?" I would then use a sentence in my mind that removes the projection on them: "What I see in (name of the person) that I don't like about myself, or my mother, or my father is…" If it's about my father, "…that my father constantly lost his patience." Or, if it is about myself, "…that I constantly lose my patience if I feel hurt, or frustrated." Ultimately, I bring the projection I made back to myself because there is no one else to clear here except me.

If I come to love someone who I did not like at first, I know I have cleared the projection I placed on them based on someone from the past. I would be clearing my way through my thoughts and feelings about them until I am in Oneness with them. I would not push them away or cast them out of my life. Instead, I go through clearing my mind. They are a gift to me by triggering me to clear an aspect of myself that needed healing.

Another example might be if I do not want to have someone over for dinner or sleep at my house, my resistance means I have something to clear in my perception of them because I am projecting a character from my past. Begin by holding awareness of every word you speak; mindfully listening to yourself provides a powerful insight into your beliefs and thought patterns. Ultimately, you are only teaching yourself to become aware of what you are manifesting through your thoughts and words; there is no one else "out there."

According to our original belief system, the ego-mind constantly misinterprets what others say or do. Therefore, we have little accuracy in reporting anything because our past colors it. When you hold the space for someone in *The Clearing Process* and are present with them, you give them the greatest gift: the chance to release their ego barriers of negativity, thus freeing themselves. You can only do that by seeing them in their authentic self—Divine Being, Love, and Oneness. You are holding them in this Oneness, no matter what they are doing or saying in front of you, thus enabling them to see and know their innocence beyond any guilt they may be perceiving.

Whenever anyone is angry, there is an energy of guilt present. Anger is a projection of guilt. To release my anger, I can ask myself, "What am I feeling guilty about?" Usually, it would be something irrational that I made up that has nothing to do with me in truth. If your partner, or your friend, is angry, you can ask them, in a very peaceful, loving way, "May I ask you, is there anything you are feeling guilty about?" If you have an intimate connection with them, they will receive the question as support rather than an attack. You must have developed that intimacy to ask this kind of question.

In a holy relationship, we want this continuous support to help each other clear illusionary thinking. A holy relationship is an equal partnership, a teaching-learning situation, in which both of us are teachers and learners with each other. We both recognize that we can learn and clearly communicate our vulnerabilities. Therefore, the relationship has an opening dimension, a non-competitive dynamic. There is no power struggle for who is more intelligent, has more to learn from the other, or needs more from the other.

A holy relationship is one of the most exciting adventures one can have in life for advancing movement into aliveness, passion, purpose, and clarity. In the beginning, we fill each other with happy, joyous moments. Eventually, what we have each buried deeply in our unconscious will emerge as we relate further in our relationship. Then we will get into the nitty-gritty of what we get to clear in our connection.

Each person we meet, we are destined to meet and have a holy relationship with them, whether for a moment, a month, a year, or a lifetime. We have both come to teach and learn with each other. Therefore, it's essential to discover the inherent purpose of our relationship. There must be a purpose, or we would not have come together in the first place, even if only for a moment. Out of the millions of people in the world, we are participating together. I always ask myself, "What is this relationship for?" Every person we meet is an aspect of our Self, and if we attract them into our lives, we are to work with that part of ourselves that they are mirroring or bringing up within us.

It is helpful and important to have a tool or a method to use when triggered to clear our upsets, projections, or negative feelings that come up in any relationship. Without these tools in relationship, people will always get stuck in the same conflictual patterns and have no way to achieve a higher level of consciousness. Relationships will always bring up anything unhealed from the past to be healed in the present. If left incomplete, it will repeat itself in another form, perhaps with another person, a different face. Yet, the same scenario plays itself out over and over and over again until we end the cycle.

When triggered in a big way, we can always get rid of the other person from our lives. We can tell them to go away or ask them to move out. Alternatively, we can choose to work with ourselves to clear at the deepest level of our upset that is activated in our mind. Most people want to do the former, which is the easiest ego method of defense.

If I feel abused physically, mentally, or emotionally by someone, I will ask them to stop. I must be clear in my mind about what I want and what I do not want. If someone is a real threat to my safety or anyone else's, physically or emotionally, I will leave the situation. If I choose to continue working on the relationship with them, it is not okay for them to continue to abuse me, including any emotional abuse that implies I am damaged in some way, less-than, stupid, or unworthy. Allowing this treatment will not be beneficial for the abused or the abuser. Either way, my negative beliefs will still be in my mind to clear until I take the steps to clear them.

We constantly react to our inner child's *perceived* traumas and feelings about what we experienced, because it's buried within our unconscious mind. Our goal is to release the *perceived* negative meaning we gave these incidents. The core negative beliefs affect our feelings about ourselves, our life, and the nature of love and the world. For example: "Life is a struggle. I have to work hard to get people to listen to me. No one sees me. No one cares."

I was blessed to notice the beginning of the ego in my two grandchildren when they were around age two to four. I also see how readily they communicate their fears when I am open to listening and receiving them. When I stop everything that I'm doing and stay in the present with them, they can easily let go of their fears. My primary focus is always to see them as infinite, eternal beings rather than in the box called "children." Watch a child under three and see how sensitive they are and how easily they cry. From an early age, we generate so many ego thoughts in a continuous circle that relationships are a challenge to us, therefore, we want to release the ego thoughts about each other because they stand in the way of us joining. The ego's purpose is to keep us safe, but it ends up with us defending ourselves from being hurt and creating separation from ourselves and others.

In all of *The Power of Clearing* trainings, I teach three essential principles that apply to life.

1. Firstly, when you hold space for someone in *The Clearing Process*, you must see this person in their true nature, as Love, Peace, and Joy, no matter what they say to you during *The Clearing Process* from their ego.

2. Secondly, it is essential to be fully present to receive what they are communicating about their ego thoughts without judgment, condemnation, or collusion (agreement with the ego-mind).

3. Lastly, recognize with honesty if you are triggered while holding space for the other person and determine if you can proceed with clarity and peace enough for all.

To become proficient at *The Clearing Process*, you must use it repeatedly to see, know, and understand how your mind works. If you do not use the *Clearing* regularly or practice it often, it will become simply an intellectual exercise. You can use any part of it whenever you feel uncomfortable, worried, anxious, or distracted. Living and being in the present is the greatest gift where we can truly experience Love, Peace, and Joy. We cannot find it in the past. Many people review their negative and positive history, possibly thinking that the past is better than the present or future. When you become proficient at *The Clearing Process* and recognize your ego (thoughts, feelings, and beliefs), you can clear any fear in the way of your freedom. When you become upset, irritated, frustrated, fearful, ashamed, confused, paralyzed, rejected, or isolated, you have something to clear at the root of that feeling. If you are familiar with *The Clearing Process,* you can expel your ego beliefs by writing or speaking to yourself, or you can arrange a session with a coach to complete the 3-step method.

You will always go deeper in your experience of *The Clearing Process* when you have a trained *Power of Clearing* coach facilitating you to look at the upset differently and hold the sacred space for you with no judgment or feedback. Trained as a *Power of Clearing* Certified Coach (POCCC), this person will have excellent knowledge of *The Clearing Process* and philosophy. By being present for one or more of the 24 *On Purpose* training sessions I provide, the coach will have learned how to clear themselves and have experienced how to clear others. This person has the clarity to hold the space for you while you empty all your ego thoughts, feelings, and beliefs in the 3-step structure of *The Clearing Process.* The ego-mind hates structure and always wants to change the words of the *Clearing*. For example, in the second step, rather than saying, "What I want you to forgive ME for thinking, feeling, or believing is…" the ego would rather say, "What I want to forgive YOU for is…" implying that you have done something against me and to hurt me in some way.

Facing our ego thoughts and embracing forgiveness takes courage, and that's why many people prefer to blame external factors for why they're feeling bad. However, when we recognize the potency of problems that persist, we realize our best choice is to begin healing our minds by witnessing our thoughts, clearing our inaccurate ego beliefs, and reclaiming our power through forgiving (pardoning) ourselves. Forgiving is taking responsibility for our thoughts, perceptions, and actions to clear the way forward.

Constantly using fear and guilt to keep me from receiving Love may also become a barrier to giving Love. We are choosing to clear the blocks to being, feeling, and receiving Love because our greatest fear may be the fear Love. When genuinely giving Love, we are receiving Love at the same time; otherwise, it is sacrifice. When we have the impression that bad things are happening to us against our will and we have no power to prevent it, that is a function of the ego-mind. A person or group who claims to have the answer to a problem can easily manipulate a person who believes they have no power. In deep states of disempowerment, with rampant fear, anxiety, and pain, there is increased separation, stress, addiction, and radicalism. Thinking of killing oneself or another appears to be an attempt to escape relentless ego thoughts but only creates more ego separation.

The ego-mind is a tangled mess of a puzzle. *The Clearing Process* puts the puzzle pieces of what happened to you in the past into a structured container, providing a safe opportunity to recognize and release the inaccurate beliefs formed in early life that create present pain. As a result, seemingly unrelated pieces fall together, and occasionally, we make sense of someone's entire life in only two hours of a *Clearing*.

When we acknowledge our fears as they arise in our mind and within our body sensations, we become genuinely aware of them. Instead of running from our fears, we hear them, feel them, acknowledge them, and allow the fear to flow through us completely, ultimately embracing rather than resisting them. When we can let them go consciously, we are no longer in resistance to the flow of life.

Being comfortable and fully present with both feet flat on the floor is essential to prepare for *The Clearing Process*. Ask yourself, or if you have a coach or friend, they can ask this question for you to release any obstacles in your mind or constriction in your body. "What do you need to let go of to be one hundred percent present?" Answer this question repeatedly to release anything holding you back.

You can also repeatedly ask this question to prepare for your day, for an experience with a friend, a lover, a child at play, or time at work. The answers are the first step in acknowledging what is holding you back from being fully present in your life. Start sharing with trusted loved ones and be as transparent as possible. Use complete sentences, for example: "I have to let go of believing that you didn't return my email because I'm not important enough and, therefore, I can't be present or open with you now." Or: "I have to let go of thinking about my mother and wondering if she's okay at home by herself right now," or "I have to let go of wondering whether I need to be there with her," or "I have to let go of feeling guilty about leaving her alone." When you observe your thoughts and do not *become* your thoughts, you will see how your ego continually projects fear, guilt, and separation onto others and the world itself.

Before beginning *The Clearing Process*, it is best to set an intention or purpose for the result of the *Clearing*. For example, "My intention is to release my anger toward my mother and to feel peace and love when I think of her." Next, you and your coach can call in divinity, higher power, or universal consciousness to align with you and support you in all aspects of your thinking, feeling, and beliefs pertinent to your declared intention. It is a kind of prayer or request for support from a higher consciousness.

In Step 1 of *The Advanced Clearing*, your coach provides a safe environment for declaring and sharing your ego-mind about a person (mother, father, sibling, boss, friend), or a subject (money, body, health, the government). Everything felt, said, or expressed is relevant to the process. Step 1 is an opportunity to report all negative ego thoughts, feelings, and beliefs about said person or subject and all related situations and issues. For example, fired from a job, evicted, losing a loved one, or expectations thwarted, bringing up feelings of betrayal, abandonment, or rejection—and then relating that feeling to something familiar in the past, especially in your early childhood, if possible.

In the structure of Step 1, the person clearing closes their eyes and says, **"What I want you to know** (name), **is that I think, feel, or believe** (current ego thought, judgment, attack, accusation, experience), … **which makes me feel** … (express the feeling which arises), … **just like when** … (recount a scene from the past which comes to mind)."

The coach holding space says, **"Thank You,"** which means "I'm listening" and "I hear you, and I make no judgment." It does not mean "I agree with your ego belief or thought."

In **Step 1**, we identify a feeling so that when we close our eyes and the coach asks, "just like when?" a scene from our past (especially before age seven) may appear. People often come up with scenes that they never before remembered until their subconscious was ready to reveal it. Then the feelings can be seen, felt, acknowledged, and released after being held by the subconscious mind for years as evidence of little t truth. Otherwise, you may not know that the meaning you attached to the event has been affecting your life until now as a source of what you think, feel, and believe. Sometimes no image from the subconscious comes up, although a memory feeling or sensation will arise, offering significant insight. Regardless, the *Clearing* will still be effective.

Step 2 of *The Advanced Clearing* is the forgiveness or correction of misperceptions about ourselves based upon the ego's evidence brought up in Step 1 statements. Now we consciously forgive ourselves for these misperceptions or mistaken beliefs. We could choose to forgive another person, but ultimately, the purpose of the clearing is to forgive ourselves. There is truly no one else to forgive because we made up what the situation meant about us. Our ego used that meaning (for example, being unworthy) and searched for evidence against our true nature. The truth is that we are all Worthy without conditions.

In the structure of **Step 2**, the person clearing says, **"What I want you to forgive me for,** (name), **is for thinking, feeling, or believing** … (a little t feeling), **which means I am**… (a little t judgment of oneself) …."

The coach says, **"Thank You. That is not the Truth. That is a story you made up. You are … I love You."**

You will have several forgiveness statements in Step 2 to match what you brought up in your ego thoughts in Step 1. The Coach will confirm it is not the Truth of who you are and will affirm your true nature.

The essence of the *Clearing* is based on our true nature being all-knowing, abundant, and eternal: the Big T Truths. Therefore, Step 3's purpose is to remember our Eternal Truth (the Truth of who we are) that we temporarily forgot.

Step 3, the final and most impactful step in *The Advanced Clearing*, affirms the Big T Truths, based on *A Course in Miracles* and other spiritual books.

The person clearing says: **"What I want you to forgive me for,** (name), **is for forgetting that I am**…. (Say one at a time in each statement to give it more power), for example, Love" (Innocent, Free, Whole and Complete, Joined with…, Pure, Safe, Peace, One with…, Unlimited, Eternally Connected, Divine), or ideally your chosen Big T Truth words that correct your misperceptions. These Big T Truth words must match and align with what you said in Steps 1 and 2 for it to be most effective. For example, if you forgave yourself for feeling unworthy in Step 2, your Step 3 statement would be, **"What I want you to forgive me for is for forgetting that I am** Worthy."

The coach affirms what the person clearing said by affirming the Truth and allowing them to receive it into their heart by saying, **"Thank You. That is the Truth. You are Worthy. And I love You."**

When you stop telling yourself the storyline of misperception that the world is against you and drop your attachment to the meaning the pain has for you—such as "I am not good enough," "I am not worthy," and "I am not lovable," then you are free and fully present. It is vital to clear the idea that someone else is responsible for your suffering and they are to blame for how you feel. The *Clearing* disconnects you from this blame on others and ultimately shows you that you can choose another way for how you see yourself, such as "I am good enough," "I am worthy," and "I am lovable."

In every training, we have a session where people can share aloud what's going on in their minds or bothering them in their lives. The whole group of participants in the training room hears and witnesses them. For example, a woman brought up a perceived trauma that she experienced with her ex-boyfriend but originated from past pain. So, in *The Clearing Process*, she could clear buried feelings toward her mother and father that were standing in the way of her being fully present and feeling safe in a relationship. As a result, she let go of the fear brought up by old pain patterns with her parents and ex-boyfriend and was able to be present in her current relationships.

Another example is when a workshop participant shared that she constantly attacks herself with the self-talk of, "I'm afraid to stand on my own." The language we speak to ourselves can quickly become our reality. When we acknowledge our ego thoughts out loud to ourselves or to another, it becomes apparent, by hearing what we say, what we need to clear as we speak these words. The other person merely witnesses without collusion. When we try to block, deny, or suppress ego thoughts, they persist more strongly and continue to irritate us. Further, when we don't recognize negative ego thoughts and leave them alone in our minds without clearing them, they can become a state that we commonly refer to as dis-ease, mental illness, chronic conditions, or general disagreeableness. In the 1970s, the famous teacher Werner Erhard, founder of the EST training, was inspired by Carl Jung's phrase, "What you resist persists."

When you have accurately done *The Clearing Process* in its entirety with a character from your past (such as your mother or father) or someone who you despised, you may now be able to view them with real Love. However, if you do not feel this peaceful, loving feeling after a clearing, you may need to clear subsequent deeper layers with the support of a certified *Power of Clearing* coach.

There is no place or space where Spirit is not present. *The holiest of all the spots on earth is where an ancient hatred has become a present love.* (ACIM, T-26.IX.6:1)

In my lifetime, I trust that I will see peace transform many people and locations worldwide that are currently in discord, war, and separation—a complete transformation that includes Love, Joy, Abundance, Freedom, Safety, and Compassion for all. I do envision that right now. Will you please join me in that vision of total peace and harmony for everyone worldwide?

"Reflections on *The Power of Clearing*" (under Resources at sandylevey.com) was initially edited by Ian Patrick and published in the Miracle Network magazine in 2012 (updated in 2022) and offers additional insights into how Sandy lives *The Power of Clearing Process* each day.

What is a Sandyism?

If you have sat in any of my trainings, you will remember things that I said over and over. If you have not yet sat in a training, these Sandyisms will give you a glimpse of my humor. I have learned how people get the most from the trainings.

For example, "Feet! Feet!" is a short form meaning, "Put your feet flat on the floor and ground yourself like a plant or a tree into the ground." Then you can be more available to speak, hear, and listen. When you are the sharer in the sharing chair the whole group will listen to you speak and whatever you say will come from the greatest grounding of your being. Having your feet on the ground allows you to be open, get present, and be ready to receive feedback in your transformational process with the entire group.

My dear friend Light Miller kept track of these Sandyisms for over 15 years. She curated them in a purple spiral book decorated with angels, hearts, stars, and cupids, and she inscribed it with her autograph on the front cover: *"To my dearest friend, teacher, and sister. May our hearts always be as one."* It is one of my most cherished Christmas gifts from 2000. She transcended near my birthday in May 2019.

Sandyisms: Sandy Levey-Lunden's quotes in her many courses and *On Purpose* trainings

"I am awake, I am alive, I'm going to do it." This Sandyism came from *The Art of Personal Marketing* as a cheer. We collectively cheered this phrase, putting the left arm straight out (I am awake!), then the right arm (I am alive!), then both arms together and say powerfully, with conviction, three times (I'm going to do it!).

"No amount of evidence will ever make true something that isn't true anyway."

"We're going to go deep. This is a very deep process."

"Everything that happens in my life or in the workshop, I use as a teaching and learning moment, to teach myself and others the essence of the lesson."

"Communicate from your heart."

"There must be something that you are not saying."

"Until you honestly tell all of your ego truth and recognize it is your ego speaking, nothing will shift in your life."

"Speak up, everyone here wants to hear what you have to say."

"Speak with the intention to be heard." Many people speak, but they don't want anyone to hear them, and they have no intention to be heard.

"Look up. Keep eye contact with at least a few of the people in the room while you're speaking. Connect from your open heart to them."

"Let everything in your ego-mind go and speak from your real heart."

"You must be very clear about what you really want and what is your real intention."

"What do you think your special function is?" The gifts and talents that you uniquely have as your contribution to other people.

"I choose to wake up NOW!" Another cheer in all of the *On Purpose* trainings. To be awake is to embody your eternal truth. Being asleep would be trapped in the illusion of the ego world by some circumstance or belief.

"There are no secrets. Everybody knows everything all the time because we are all Knowing beings."

"You don't ever have a secret. A secret has you. It is controlling you at every moment not to speak it."

"The feeling of love is a function of total communication. So, to feel love, you must open, be vulnerable, and fully communicate what you are most afraid to say."

"You will feel love for anyone who you fully communicate with, leaving nothing out and coming from full transparency."

"All relationships are perfect. We have issues within ourselves that we bring to each relationship if we haven't yet cleared them. The relationship brings out the issues that we already have that then get projected onto the new relationship."

"Finish your sentences so you can commit to what you really want to say."

"Whatever you don't like about other people is a mirror of what you don't like about yourself." Ask yourself, "How is that person similar to me in some way?"

"You must wake up and come out of the illusion to see the lesson in the experience you are having now."

"We never know what the appropriate form of the relationship will be until we have thoroughly cleared ourselves of all the issues."

"When you are in pain, ask yourself, 'Who am I feeling separate from?'"

"A headache is two opposite thoughts competing with each other. Say everything that is on your mind to someone who is really listening and wants to hear you, and is listening without judgment, then the headache will disappear. Especially if you are looking in their eyes and connecting."

"In our true nature, we are the spirit of Light and Love, not bodies."

"You must clear everything that is in your ego-mind that is upsetting you, irritating you, annoying you, and shutting you down from the full expression of who you are."

"Triggered out of your mind!"

"Clear it NOW! Don't wait!"

"'Later' is the motto of the ego. The ego is always trying to delay rather than face what you need to clear."

"What is the purpose of this relationship? Every relationship is a gift to your expansion."

"All relationships are about healing."

"All relationships have a purpose, or you wouldn't have the relationship."

"If every person was fulfilling their purpose, we would have peace on earth."

"We are here to know our own divinity." The spiritual essence of who we really are.

"I am Love, You are Love." We are in essence, spiritually the same.

"I am Free, You are Free." We are in essence, spiritually the same.

"I am Abundant, You are Abundant in Big T Truth (Love, Peace, Joy)."

"I am Peace, You are Peace." We are in essence, spiritually the same.

"How do you know what you chose? Because it's what you have right now."

"Choose what you got! What you got is what you created and attracted. To move on to something else, you must accept what you initially created and chose. Then you are available to choose something different." Always accept what is now.

"Choose to be in your true power, clear and free, right now."

"You are a gift to the world."

PART 1

FOUNDATION

CHAPTER 1

I AM WHO YOU ARE

What is Love?

Most people think of love as a feeling. It is in fact who we truly are, our truest essence. Love is our innate nature. We are the "Love Being" we are seeking. All the love we could ever want and imagine is within us. Our most important purpose is to get in touch with this love within ourselves, so we can live from who we truly are and extend our love to others.

Society conditions us to look for love outside of ourselves and is successful because it is a challenging concept for us to accept love as our natural inheritance and state of being. Seeking acknowledgment, approval, and love runs many people's lives and is one of the most powerful programs in our subconscious.

We are a living, walking, talking, breathing demonstration of love in action when being our authentic selves. *A Course in Miracles* repeatedly notes: *Your task is not to seek for love, but merely to seek and find all of the barriers within yourself that you have built against it.* (ACIM, T-16.IV.6:1)

When we remove the barriers to giving and receiving love, we release our resistance to being who we truly are.

The Clearing Process aligns with the spiritual philosophy and the living principles of *A Course in Miracles*. Both of these methods will bring you back to your authentic self, which is love. We don't have to look for love outside of ourselves when we awaken to and understand the idea we are love in its essence.

The Power of Clearing process is a method and tool for a person to release these barriers, fears, and unconscious beliefs. Each clearing of past events and traumas that have affected us negatively brings us closer to the core of who and what we truly are. Another way to describe the result would be a more authentic experience of Peace; as Love is our true nature, so is Peace. *The Power of Clearing* process is simple: releasing the barriers, resistance, and blockages that keep us from loving ourselves. When we are clear, we extend this Love to everyone we meet on our many lessons and journeys through our awakening process.

A Course in Miracles says that Love is our natural inheritance and aims *at removing the blocks to the awareness of love's presence. The opposite of love is fear, but what is all-encompassing can have no opposite.* (ACIM, T-in.1:7-8)

Peace and Joy

The Clearing Process uncovers the core issues that are disturbing a person's mind and experience. It's really like peeling an onion: taking away layer after layer to access the root from which those layers have grown. We need to reach this "core" to see, acknowledge, accept, and release the root cause of behaviors and recurring patterns in our lives and to bring us back to our clear and natural state of peace. Love, peace, and joy will be born of acceptance, because it is a move back to the Truth of Who we are. What could be a greater reward?

My peace depends upon no one and nothing but myself! I have lived through several amazing holy relationships that reaffirm a joint purpose and moving consciously in that common purpose. I have come to realize that my goal is to find that core of Peace within my being and live from there!

Each time I move away from Peace, I have the opportunity to return to it through clearing and awakening to Truth. Therein lies the dance of life, in and out of the ego, and in and out of peace. One of my senior students was a psychiatrist, Hans Jorgan-Gerloff, who attended every class I held and took notes verbatim. He said, "This is like being in a chest of drawers and I keep falling from the top into the lower ones all day long, from Big T Truth to little t truth, depending on what happens." There is importance in recognizing when you are in your ego and that you have left Big T. You can recognize the egoic energy by impatience, annoyance, irritation, anger, brain fog, feeling tired, exhausted, fatigued, confused, distanced, separation. These states are all symptomatic of leaving your Big T Truth and entering your little t ego's sleep.

Knowing that my peace cannot depend on anyone else's behavior, attitude, opinions, or self-worth is amazingly liberating. I can never say or even think, "I'm unhappy because so and so did this or that." I know that it is always up to me to create my joy and my joyful life. No matter what I think, feel, or believe, that joyful life is first created in my mind and heart through my self-talk. To manifest that life and enjoy it, I embrace the Big T Truth idea that I deserve joy and am worthy of it.

Maybe those next to me will be unable to experience the same joy. However, that in no way should diminish my own joyful experience. Most people's ego makes them feel guilty when they feel joyous and someone close to them is not joyous too. The clearer I am within myself, the less I become reactionary, swayed by others' moods and opinions, and the more authentic I become where I can be at peace. I can now focus on moving through each moment, with my intention being peace, joy, and love. Now my request to myself and my higher guidance is to help me live my life through my heart—the center for love and compassion—and through those unique energies, ultimately to Peace.

In earlier years, especially when I was little, it took me a long time to come back to peace when I was disturbed. The hours seemed like days and the days seemed like years. The disturbance to my peace swamped my whole life. As a result, I no longer have a desire to be perfect in anything. My only desire is to always do my best in everything I am doing, coming from my highest place of joy. For example, I only do things in the house when I am in joy. I clean the bathroom for the joyous experience of cleanliness, as if I were *clearing* the bathroom. If a system breaks down in the house, I do the clearing first and ask it to return to wholeness and true functioning before taking any further action, like calling a plumber.

The main message always is to let go and trust that everything is happening in your own best interest, even if you can't figure out why and how. Focus on peace and joy. Truly know that everything you need will be yours and every experience you feel you need will come to you effortlessly and joyously when you are in your Big T Truth. The main focus is to get to peace first and then life will unfold completely naturally through joy. Miriam Evers, one of my dearest friends and colleagues, who is a joy coach, says, "Joy First. Then anything else you have time for."

There is nothing to do and nowhere to go. While life has an element of being pre-determined, you can always choose new paths that would change the course of your life. This idea was demonstrated in Gary Renard's book, *The Disappearance of the Universe.* He was on his way to see a movie that he really desired to see. Then, he decided at the last minute to go to a different movie that he didn't really want to see, that was happening two hours later. When he spoke to his spirit guides who directed him to write his book, they told him that he had made enough good choices in his life to avoid the first movie that would have been in timing for a major accident that would have set him back years in his life. He had mastered enough of his lessons to not have to take that wake-up call to do his personal process. At the time he said, "I had no idea why I was going to this movie that I didn't really want to see." Then you need to stay in the strongest and best, most balanced perspective to meet the experiences you will encounter on your path. Strength, indeed, does exist in gentleness, peace, and joy. It is our birthright and our true nature to be joyous. We are, in truth, joy itself.

You Are Light

Our true nature—the Light that we are—is like Teflon. Nothing negative can stick to this Light! The ego will convince us that we permanently embedded the negative thoughts, feelings, and beliefs we hold in our psyche, and we cannot remove them, ever.

The Clearing Process is a psycho-spiritual method, which means that it incorporates the psychology of how the brain works within an overall spiritual context. We move from a limited state of negative, egoic feelings into a spiritual state of oneness (from little t truth to Big T Truth, see the chart in Chapter 6). Even for someone who perceives themselves as not spiritual, the process works for them because it is a psychological process of tapping into what is familiar to them. We talk about the ideal result of connecting with our "authentic self," however, many people cannot even conceive who they would be without their pain and traumas. This state of peace is such a distant concept it would be like traveling to another planet if they experienced it. If this situation of being disconnected from our true nature were not so painful, we would not be trying so hard to access our authenticity! It is almost always the pain and suffering that motivates people to seek healing.

When we come into the world, we are pure Light—the pure Light that is evident as in the eyes of a newborn baby. Each negative feeling that we experience is like a dark cloth placed over this Light, and by the time we are seven, innumerable cloths are covering up this Light, so very little of the original Light can shine through. We forget we are the Light and begin to identify with the dark cloths which represent unconscious beliefs about ourselves. For example, "I am irreparably damaged or fundamentally flawed," "I am not important," "I am not lovable," and "I am not worthy." There are probably about a dozen of these core beliefs, which also include, "I have decided who I am is unacceptable and have to do what my parents want me to do to be loved."

From a spiritual perspective, *The Clearing Process* is a powerful tool for removing those dark cloths, and as they fall away, like ripe fruit, more Light can and will shine through you to reveal your true identity. You become more of who you are, shining your Light on yourself and everyone. This clearing process can happen over several years, so whatever goes in the clearing is what's ready to be released. Then you have access to the subsequent layers, like peeling an onion.

What would a person be like if they had no pain or suffering? If they removed all the dark cloths, they would be their Big T Self! Most people understand this logic. It feels like a sigh of relief to know this Light inside of us is available and reachable.

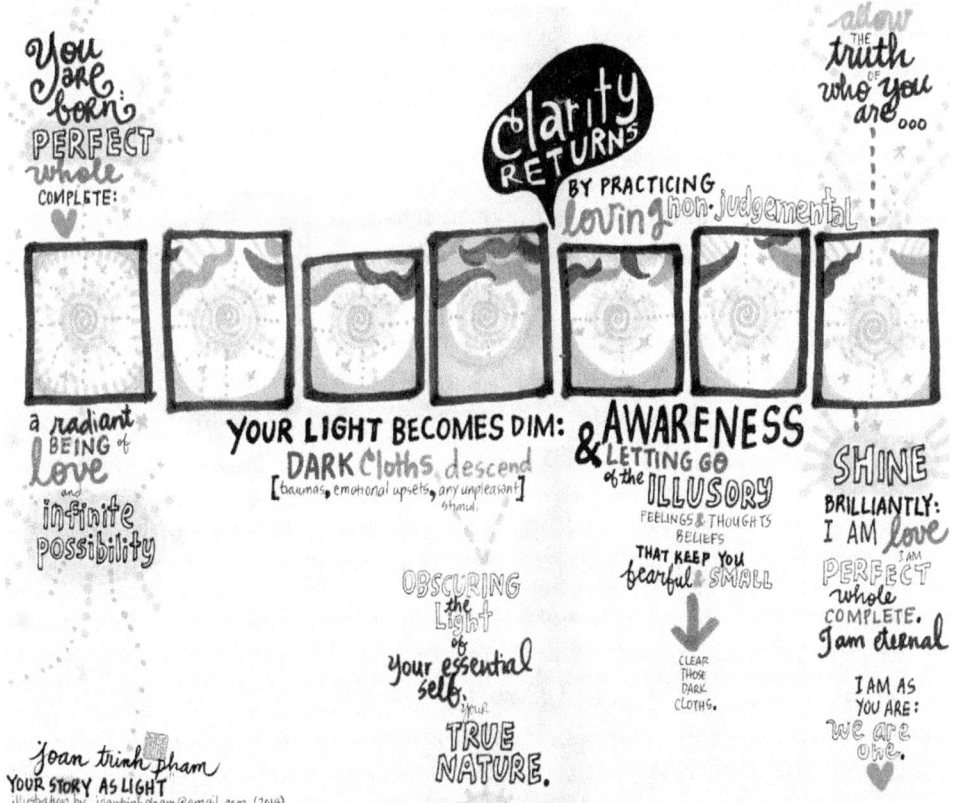

The Power of Clearing gives us a simple and tightly structured way of guiding the ego (little t truth) out of darkness and fully into the Light. One of the reasons *The Clearing Process* works so well is that it bypasses the ego's resistance. The person holding space reflects back Big T Truth statements in Steps 2 and 3. The person clearing may have been waiting all their life to hear these words that they are innocent, free, and that they are loved (which is different than seeking love or hoping for love). They are free to reconnect with their true nature now and reconfirm who they really are. The Big T Truth statements undo knots of stuck energy that are ready to be released at that time. As these dark cloths are cleared, the person clearing now has access to what is underneath that ripens like fruit in sunlight. Then their true nature is revealed as Light, and the natural flow of energy enables them to remember who they are.

Big T Truth

Big T Truth is our Divine, Eternal Nature, the Truth of who we each are, in our authenticity, and the only way we can attain lasting Joy. When embodying the Truth of who we are and living it as a demonstration, for example, I am Peace, I am Love, I am Free, I am Joy, then You are Peace, You are Love, You are Free, You are Joy. Whatever I am in my true nature, then you are the same. This true nature can never be changed or altered, no matter what we think, feel, or believe, and whatever negative evidence appears.

When we are in our highest Self, we make authentic decisions from peace, love, and unity compared to when we are in our ego-mind or make decisions based on fear, lack, and resentment. We can see our direction and what we want in our lives when acting from who we truly are and have cleared ourselves of unhealed past upsets. It is more rewarding to live in our full-bodied truth in the present rather than ego illusion coming from the past. We think that objects of desire like money, houses, cars, full bank accounts, and more education or degrees will bring us happiness.

Once we grasp the concepts of Big T and little t, we can look at the people we blame in our lives for our current situation, and what we want people to regret for how they treated us. However, we are actually forgiving, or letting go of, what we believe it says about *us*, not what they did to us. Holding any core beliefs, such as, "I am unlovable, not worthy, I have no value, or I am not good enough," no longer serves us. We can compassionately forgive ourselves for believing that they reflect any truth at all. We are always good enough, worthy, lovable, and valuable, no matter what I or anyone else may say. This Spiritual Truth is Big T Truth.

Big T Truths Defined – The Truth of Who I AM

Big T Truths are of the eternal spirit world. All humans are bodies animated by eternal spirit. These I AM statements refer to our spiritual aspect, not human form. When we talk about True Self or Higher Self, we're referencing these collective Truths. Through spirit, we are the Totality, the Oneness, the All Knowingness; our connection with Source guides us.

> I AM COMPASSION offering infinite Love
>
> I AM PEACE at one with Source
>
> I AM SAFE eternally in spirit
>
> I AM ABUNDANT overflowing in gifts of awakening
>
> I AM WHOLE AND COMPLETE perfect in Self
>
> I AM FREE in the eternal flow, open to all possibilities
>
> I AM ETERNAL existing in essence forever
>
> I AM JOY delighting in full expression
>
> I AM LIGHT radiant like a star, infinitely glowing
>
> I AM INNOCENT original divine perfection, only love
>
> I AM LOVE in connection with all
>
> I AM INFINITE in eternal Oneness
>
> I AM PURE forever Innocent
>
> I AM BEAUTY with the majesty of a flower
>
> I AM POWERFUL connected to Source
>
> I AM HONESTY in truth and transparency
>
> I AM TRUST all is perfection
>
> I AM FULLY PRESENT focused in this moment
>
> I AM OPEN present and available to all possibilities
>
> I AM PATIENT infinite acceptance, willing to wait
>
> I AM THAT I AM being in the present is all there is

I affirm my true nature by speaking these I AM statements. Declaring the Truth is a powerful action to take full responsibility for myself and attune to the resonance of who I am in Truth.

Language is fundamental to me in my thoughts, feelings, and words. I always speak with my words in alignment with my thoughts about what I want to create. For example, I would never say, "This computer is too slow." I know that could slow it down even further because I am affecting it with my thought energy. Manifestation begins in our awareness of what we are thinking; what we focus on expands, so we are always moving in the direction of what we have believed, consciously or unconsciously.

When I reference an impermanent state of being, I say, "I think, I feel, I believe," because it's a perception and, therefore, changeable and temporary. Thus, I use "I feel" statements in mindful communication with myself and others. For example, instead of saying, "I am sick," I say, "I feel sick." That way, I can shift my focus in the direction of health. When I use the words "I am," it is always a Big T Truth to reconfirm who I AM in truth.

Innocence

In every country I have visited, I hear this most prominent belief: "I am not good enough." These common beliefs continue to fill a person's mind: "I cannot have abundance, a joyous life, a partner who I deeply relate to, the job I dream of, the home I want to live in, and I must constantly struggle for my financial survival. Because I am not good enough and have this feeling of guilt that I have done something wrong, I need to atone for this mistake, or somehow, someone will punish me. I have created a difficult life with struggle and conflict that proves I am not good enough. I allow myself to have a few breadcrumbs of love rather than the loving relationship that I have always dreamed of for my life. I will live in fear and repeatedly create a punishment. For example, I will accept a relationship with poor communication where I feel lesser than because I believe that is all I deserve. I am not good enough to be cared about, heard, and understood by someone who has the desire and the capacity to see me in my wholeness."

Because we are so far from believing that we are good enough, we become removed from all of the good that is ours to receive and we settle for a limited life. Each of us has made up this story on an unconscious level, with characters attacking us based on what we believe about ourselves. This story creates our perceived world—we are inadequate, wrong, and deserve punishment. These characters unconsciously act out what we blame ourselves for, preventing us from having the Love, Peace, and Joy that we could be living.

As children, we believe that we can be or have anything and everything in life. We think in unlimited possibilities. When we grow up and experience many challenges, we find that what we wanted and dreamed of becomes secondary to what we need to do to meet our obligations to others. We begin to think that all we need to do is survive. Surviving becomes a way of life as opposed to thriving, being at peace, being in love. The Big T is replaced by "I should," "I ought to," and "I must," and this list of "have to" instead of "want to" gets longer every day. This conditioning stems back to the idea that "I am not good enough," "I am guilty," and "I don't deserve to have what I want."

We are continually working with the fear that we are wrong or bad, often based on something we believe we did wrong before the age of seven that we must keep hidden. For as long as we have a secret that proves we are guilty, we drag this hidden burden behind us in life with no idea how to release it, or that it's even possible to do so. For us to awaken from this trap, we need to know at a deep level that we are innocent. *The Power of Clearing* process helps us to see and understand the Truth of our innocence. Once we tell the secret to someone it is now on its way to being released because we have allowed someone to witness our innocence. Then the story or secret does not have power over us anymore. We are now open, we have let go of our defenses from our perceived guilt, and we can now share this secret with anyone.

We all must have at least one person who holds us in the light of innocence to whom we can tell this secret. Because we don't believe it ourselves that we are innocent, we need someone to reflect the Truth to us of who we are. We all have to attract at least one person who sees us as more than our guilt, fear, or secret. We need another person always to reflect our innocence when we think we are guilty. This person is usually our holy relationship partner and could be in any role in our life: friend, sibling, parent, boss, co-worker, life partner, wife, husband. The first condition of this holy relationship partner is that they are someone who will never believe our perceived story of guilt, no matter how much evidence we make up, and likewise, they see themselves as whole and complete, lacking nothing.

We all need to gather supporters around us in the world to reflect this innocence to us. *A Course in Miracles* calls this group of supporters "Mighty Companions."

(ACIM, M-4.I-A.6:11) We evolve to a certain point in our process to create and attract these mighty companions.

It would be a great idea to go into a prison and teach *The Power of Clearing* process to all the inmates or anyone who wanted to participate. We would do personal processes of the clearings that pertain to each person's guilt, especially the perceived crime of which someone accused them. If everyone in prison could embody the understanding that they are not guilty according to spiritual law, it would be safe to let them out of prison because they would not need to affirm their guilt by committing the same offense again.

In the youth project in Sweden called *Fri Sikt* ("open view"), five of the participants had potentially committed murder in their gang life. After they did these clearings in the course, I knew they would all be safe to return to society because they had cleared their guilt. With the group of 120 youth project members and the coaching team of 10-15 men and women, these youths had a support system like they had never experienced before in their lives. These relationships confirmed the truth of who they were when they forgot and entered their ego mind. This partnership always reminded the youths to become aware of their thoughts, be responsible for their actions, and remember their innocence. Everyone in the group of youths had a buddy as a confidant for full communication and as a holy relationship partner (either another participant or a member of the coaching team). Each one confirmed that no matter what they had done in their present or past, they were able to open up to this person, tell everything, and be reconfirmed as innocent.

Sometimes, when we marry, the projection that we are not good enough gets put on to our partner. Our ego becomes reflected back to us from them, and now we perceive that they are attacking us. This theme can be ongoing in a person's life—people are talking about them or criticizing them. When we externalize our guilt and belief of not being good enough, we begin and continue the cycle of reconfirming that we are not good enough. Then we constantly defend our innocence while at the same time believing we are guilty.

In couples therapy, this theme of seeing the other person acting like they're guilty and protecting themselves from attack can be challenging for the couple. It can be the partner's function in the holy relationship to hold the space and reconfirm the person's innocence. They reflect the innocence back to the person in many ways, including through their eyes and with love, that "I am holding you as innocent."

No matter what the person says or does, thusly, their partner reconfirms through their thinking and speaking that the person is innocent. The desire is essential and the primary function of a meaningful, total holy relationship, to be each other's partner in this continuous vigil over each other's innocence. The ego is always projecting guilt on the person or someone else in their life, for example, family, friends, or colleagues. To genuinely be an asset in the partnership to free each other from guilt and fear, you have to be fully committed to affirming each other's innocence by always seeing them in their Truth. I have seen very few couples who understand this process and know how to live this demonstration. Most of these couples who do understand it are clients and friends of mine. When we don't commit to each other's process of breaking free from our patterns, it may become the belief that "I have chosen the wrong partner." Then one person may begin looking for someone better or different—a replacement. In many cases, it would be another circle to seek a new partner rather than going deeper to uncover what we are avoiding in our own *Clearing Process*.

The patterns coming up to clear can be very subtle. One of our greatest fears is the fear of love: fear of receiving love, totally knowing we are love, and the resistance to being love, which is our inheritance. When we truly awaken to love as real, and we ARE this love, then the ego has less power over us. When we are aware of our resistance to love, we need to commit to go deeper with our partner to understand the Truth—we are innocent and worthy of love from ourselves and our partner. Thusly, we awaken to accepting that we are worthy of our own love and respect, which is the essential condition before we can allow another person to love, respect, and know us. Now we can finally let them in. For this process, I have seen couples take weeks, months, or years, depending on how strongly they defend their guilt and their belief that no one should love them.

Often, we are unwilling to ask for precisely what we want, and when we know what we want, we feel too guilty to ask for it. Therefore, we stay in the circle of attack and defense with continued confusion.

I have noticed in my work that this theme of incomplete communication keeps many people stuck for years. No matter how many times a discussion goes back and forth between the two parties, it remains resolved and unclear so both people are frustrated. I have also noted in my study of Truth that, when we have found Truth as an answer, both parties would agree, let go, and come to peace. Usually, there is an underlying unconscious, negative belief to release first.

BIG "T" TruthS:

I AM.

I am
i am love
Light
I AM JOY!
I am innocent
I am pure
I AM PEACE
i am   I am abundant
unlimited
I am perfect.
whole & complete
JUST AS I AM.
I AM COMPASSION
I am eternal
I AM   I AM PRESENT.
BEAUTY.   I am all these.
I am infinity embodied:
You are everything
I am: WE ARE
      THE SAME.

joan trinh pham
BIG "T" ILLUMINATED
by joantrinhpham@gmail.com

The Mind Cannot Hold Gratitude and Fear Together

Gratitude is the highest form of prayer, giving thanks for what we already have and who we are. It is important to practice gratitude every day in the form of saying, "I'm so grateful for…" Many friends and clients say the gratitude prayer when they wake up and at the end of the day before they go to sleep. This practice keeps their mind at a fulcrum point of who they are and how everything that happens can be seen as a miracle of perfection. There are no small miracles. In each personal encounter we can see a true learning when we are looking from our True point of view. Karen Drucker's words and music in her song, "I'm So Grateful" sums it up!

I'm So Grateful
Lyrics and music by Karen Drucker

I am so grateful, grateful
I am so grateful for all the love that I have
I am so grateful, grateful
I am so grateful for all the love that I have

Everywhere I look, every face I see
is love reflected shining back to me
I just give thanks for all these simple things
the joy and peace that gratitude brings

Chorus

Every day I wake before I open my eyes
I count my blessings and I realize
Life is a miracle when I see it that way
I focus on the beauty, that's why I've got to say

I am so grateful for:
All of my friends,

My wonderful life,
My radiant health,
My abundance,
The joy in heart,
The peace in my life,
Every blessing.

CHAPTER 2

MY DEFINITION OF EGO

Fear, Guilt, and Separation

It's possible to constantly, silently, and unconsciously, in egoic self-talk, interpret every action as a mistake, and therefore, believe we have done something wrong and that it is our fault. It makes no difference whether it is something big or small. Through this ego illusion we make ourselves guilty whenever anything goes wrong in our lives or those around us.

Americans and many people worldwide enjoyed attacking former President Donald Trump. Possibly he wanted to be attacked and liked being attacked because it aligned with his guilt. This outer attack could only come from an inner attack that he was doing to himself. That attack was like power to him; the more the people attacked him, the more power he thought he had and the more attention he received for his guilt. He had one of the most profound internal wars between guilt and innocence that I have ever witnessed in my life; a war within his mind that he then externalized. He appeared to be unfazed. The reason for this non-reaction was that attack is commonplace to him, since he had been attacking himself for so many years of his life.

When we feel guilty, we separate ourselves from Source and other people. Guilt becomes a pervasive thought in our minds about ourselves, at play much of the time in our daily life through our incriminating regretful thoughts, like, "I could have, I should have, I wish I had, I must, I ought to."

Some people continually say, "I'm sorry." We often think something is wrong with us because there is something required of us that we have not done. We need to forgive ourselves for every mistake we believe we have made (big or small). If someone thinks we are guilty, even if we think it is untrue, we unconsciously feel it must be valid, so we continuously attack ourselves with it. To clear or release our guilt, we first must become self-aware that we are the ones who are laying this guilt trip on ourselves. Even if someone says we are guilty, they are not doing it at the actual level that we are doing it to ourselves. What matters most is what we think about ourselves. When we sense guilt in ourselves, we are in separation.

All fear is fear of our mortality. The media constantly bombards us with the fear of death. During the pandemic, the media projected a state of fear, panic, guilt, and division. Many people accepted the projection without question and subsequently projected those same feelings onto those around them. The danger of the population colluding that they are unsafe, alone, and vulnerable to attack is that we amplify already-embodied beliefs. Ironically, the fear and guilt were more contagious than the reported virus, so people were keeping their distance for fear of being attacked by sickness. Therefore, despite our increased awareness of human interconnectedness, it became more about avoiding infection than spreading love and connection. The required physical distancing became a primary defense to protect each other from getting ill, but it just reinforced the idea that we are all alone, separate, and divided.

What I knew I could do during the pandemic was focus on my main intention of inner peace leading to outer peace. I encouraged everyone I know to focus on this intention of inner peace within themselves at a deep level, releasing all the negative self-talk and releasing all projected states of personal guilt that were affecting themselves and others. If we watched our minds as to what we were really thinking, then we would have a chance to become aware of our conscious feelings of guilt and let them go, and reclaim innocence. The only way out of the pandemic was not to focus on fear-mongering about the virus, and instead, to focus on innocence, unity, and joint purpose.

Whatever is happening for me in my life, I am creating and attracting this energy. After I clear a negative projection, the energy miraculously transforms my outer life from a series of little t reactions into more of a peaceful experience. I can clear the thoughts of separation when I feel people don't want me or don't like me. I can clear my inner thoughts in my mind of feeling separate, alone, or guilty. Many of us have a massive fear that no one likes us and that we are alone, unwanted, and therefore not worthy of love and acceptance. We will often act out a role (for example, as a friend, parent, grandparent, child, husband, or wife) and place restrictions on ourselves based on the role, expecting particular behaviors from ourselves or others. These roles are elaborate forms of proving our separation. The ego-mind is quick to judge us about what we and others expect or do not expect.

We torture ourselves with thoughts about ourselves, living out the negative core beliefs in our minds. The ego defends itself to remain in status quo and not to make changes. Change, especially release of a pattern or habit of thought, is scary to the ego. Often the belief is, "I am hopeless. I can't do anything right." With this belief, a person can stay stuck and not change anything. Our self-talk determines our ability to transform from where we are to where we can go. *The Clearing Process* is so successful because it bypasses the ego self-talk system and awakens us to remember the True Self.

In Step 2, during the *forgiveness* process, the coach or whoever holds space is ideally always holding the vision of the person clearing as their Higher Self. The person who is clearing acknowledges their fear and guilt, forgiving their negative ego-mind in declarative statements, such as **"What I want you to forgive me for is for thinking, feeling, believing… which means I am …."** For example, **"What I want you to forgive me for is for believing** that I can't do anything right, **which means I am** a failure and unworthy." The coach will respond by answering each statement with, "Thank you. That is not the Truth and will never be the Truth of who you are. You are as you were created, Perfect, Whole, and Complete."

Peace and Joy are your birthright; they are not distant concepts of how you could feel in a certain number of months or years from now if you try hard and struggle enough to make it happen! ACIM reminds us that *God's peace and joy are yours.* (ACIM, W-105.1:1) They are always available in every moment. So, first, we need to create the space within our minds to receive these gifts. However, when there is a space in your mind, the ego may fill that void with its negative ideas. The ego does not want you to have space to access your True nature of

Divine Peace, Love, and Oneness. The ego makes temporary ideas real, judging them to be either negative or positive beliefs, and emphasizing the lack and sense of something missing. Deep down, we believe that trust, happiness, freedom, and abundance are conditional and have a time limit. We suspect they are not forever, so while experiencing them, we worry that challenges, pain, and suffering are just around the corner. So, we prepare our defenses rather than enjoy our blessings.

In my defenselessness my safety lies. (ACIM, W-153)

In other words, even when we feel happy, we also sense danger, fearing that someone will take away our happiness or a catastrophe may happen. Thus, our ego-mind convinces us that any experience we have of living in Love, Peace, and Joy is temporary, so we abandon our True Self to stay safe. This fear creates continual survival chemistry in our bodies and minds. When we focus on fear, we attract what we don't want. Perceptions of danger draw destruction, harm, and war. Living in fear, guilt, and separation creates a negative world experience.

In the ego world, many of us unconsciously carry guilt. The Truth is that none of us are guilty in our Spirit Self. Clearing and releasing guilt and fear enables us to join in our Innocence. This release of clearing guilt is one of the most important benefits of *The Power of Clearing* process.

"What am I hiding?"

Can you identify and release the subconscious guilt that is running your mind and your life? I trust that you have realized by now that you have subconscious guilt that keeps you on the run.

As long as guilt remains in the subconscious, it stays buried or hidden from us. It can sneak out from the shadows, frighten us and others, or drain us of energy by trying to keep itself hidden and suppressed in our body! We only truly wish to hide our guilt, beliefs, or experiences about something if we believe we have become unacceptable because of them. Therefore, we create separation from others because of guilt and secrets often related to sex, power, money, control, love, intimacy, and relationships. These secrets can be things we've done, something we are afraid we've done, things we wish we could do (fantasies), or secrets that others have told us that we must keep and never tell. Sometimes the abusers have threatened their victims or person being abused that if they tell anyone, this bad thing will occur, and that they must always keep this secret to themselves.

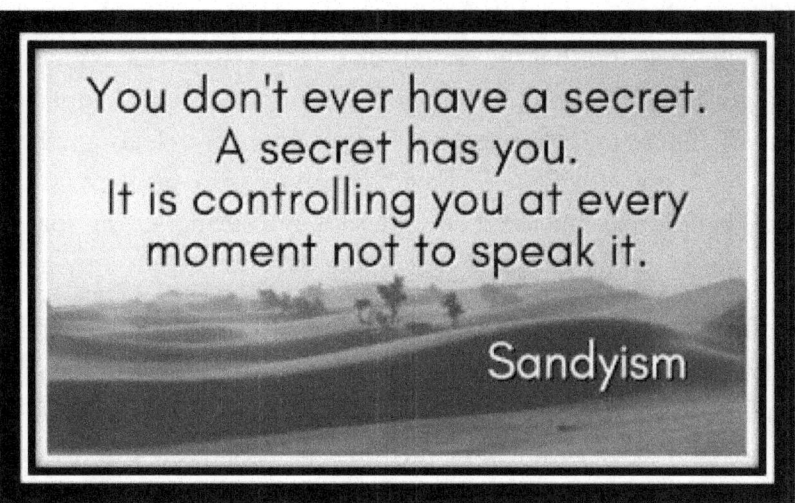

Keeping secrets, big or small, keeps you stuck. The ego is always trying to find a way to protect the secret so you will stay guilty. In the end, the most damage is caused while the secret remains unspoken for so long out of fear of interpretation and potential retaliation by others.

Releasing subconscious guilt is what *The Power of Clearing* process does through a series of emotional and spiritual exercises. We can look at this process of working with the subconscious or unconscious mind using the analogy of "the basement." Most people don't even know that they have a basement (below the level of the conscious mind) because the ego doesn't want us to look down there. The game is over if we do look, and the ego is no longer in control of us! If we shine a big light and look into the basement, we see all the boxes containing everything that we've hidden there (everything we feel guilty for, are afraid of, have done wrong).

Once you know you have a basement, then it is possible to clear it. We are able to clear the fear from the little child within us. Children are typically afraid of the basement—it's dark and creepy with monsters down there; the monsters are the illusions, misperceptions, and secrets that we have hidden from ourselves and kept hidden. So, every thought in the boxes is completely exposed when we shine a light on them, and we face the idea that we are not guilty as we previously interpreted.

In effect, clearing dissolves the belief that anything in the box that we brought up from the basement is real. It is like when a child is having a nightmare. The parent holds a loving space for the child, constantly reassuring the child that the nightmare is not real and that the child is okay. The parent doesn't need to know what the night terror is about, and allows the process to unfold and the dream to be released. There are no monsters. In the same way, clearing allows all the scary, deep, dark, and terrifying feelings that we treasure and are familiar with, to emerge. Then we can release them in a safe, reassuring, loving space without judgment; where nothing is seen as impossible to let go.

When we are doing inner work, we never go down to the basement alone. We go down there holding the hand of someone with whom we feel safe, who has a great big light so nothing will startle us, and we can safely illuminate the shadows inside the boxes. This person can be a counselor, coach, mentor, trusted friend, or guide (physical or spiritual). If we go down there alone, we can scare ourselves further and perceive these secrets or guilt as valid. When the light shines in the basement, we see that it is not scary, that the monsters aren't real, and only boxes are stored down there, covered in layers of dust and cobwebs. We think these boxes contain traumas from our past. When we use *The Clearing Process*, we go down to the basement, get a box, and bring it up into the kitchen where there is lots of light. With our guide beside us, we open the box when we are feeling safer and less overwhelmed.

In the light, we find there is nothing in the box, in truth—we realize that we made up the monsters and terrifying things that threatened to get us, and that's how the ego stopped us from looking there. There is nothing real in the box! When we open the box to the light, we free ourselves from what we made up. If we don't open these boxes, what we think is in them stays with us, always influencing our perception of the world and our behavior without our even knowing it. Every time we come close to what we think is in the box, it is always there to shut us off emotionally. Many people may think it is unnecessary to open the box, and instead just suppress and deny its influence. Thus, they miss out on experiencing joy, aliveness, and clarity, never knowing freedom.

Ultimately, *The Power of Clearing* process is profound and almost miraculous. The process takes the seemingly unrelated fear, guilt, and upset and we discover a pattern to our habitual stuck-ness and pain. Once the pattern is revealed, the person is freed from resistance. We are free when we see that we are innocent and can finally let go of this perceived guilt.

So why do we make it up?

Essentially what happens is that up to the age of seven years, even during our phase "in utero," if something happens to us that we perceive as negative, we take it on and store that contracting and negative energy in our subconscious. When we are very young, we have yet to develop a logical understanding, so whatever happens to us that doesn't feel good is too much to process rationally. Even a look can be interpreted as bad, blaming, or threatening. So, we could make up that "I am unlovable, not heard, not accepted," as a result of a mild misinterpretation. And those negative beliefs get repressed and stuffed into the basement (the subconscious mind).

The little t truth, the temporary truth, is the boxed-up feelings, thoughts, and beliefs about ourselves, others, and events that we are finally clearing out of the basement. These negative judgments in our unconscious mind are like a poorly-programmed computer hard drive—producing the same negative results over and over again until these beliefs are changed or deleted. If we do not release the judgments that we made up before the age of seven, they will keep resurfacing in our lives.

Making the decision to bring your Ego into the Light

Since the ego is basically out of control, it acts as a blockage to change, wanting to keep the status quo, always delaying any attempt to change anything that has become familiar and habitual, like fear. Our ego will resist anything that it feels is a threat to its survival. So, it often tells us to rest and not bother when we consider looking at something different in our lives, taking a risk that could take us to an unknown place in ourselves. It might be too big, frightening, or otherwise unpleasant or uncomfortable. Best to go back to where we feel okay again, back into the dark. The ego is tricky and can be subtle. The ego could take you on a journey for years and years in the same circle. You may think you made a breakthrough, however at some point you will notice it is the same choice with a different picture. We can take a pill, drink, go out and make ourselves happy for a while with friends. We know that after the pill, the alcohol, and the night out, we will feel the same, since happiness or brief relaxation is from an outside source. Nothing has changed. None of these activities will change or release the root of our pain and suffering until we have brought the ego into the light and have released our ego justifications that circle in our mind. We need to go to the source in order to clear it at that level to fully clear our guilt and fear.

Only then can we experience true peace and joy, both of which are steady core states that define who we are. This true nature is our authentic self, expressing our fullness.

little t truth

The term "little t truth" is what we use for all the thoughts, feelings, and beliefs we can describe coming from the ego-mind. By its design, the ego is a great protector, a survival instinct, and a limitation for taking risks! However, it can also be a great hider and divider. Everything goes through the ego filter and is labeled and boxed and held in the mind. The ego structure is rigid-thinking, primarily responsive to fear, guilt, and shame.

For example, the ego could tell me, "If I don't stay in this job and earn lots of money for my family, they won't love me anymore because I won't be able to buy things or take them out as much. Therefore, I had better do this job, even though I feel stressed about it daily and do not enjoy it, so others will accept me and look after me because I perform to their expectations!" The ego makes conclusions without checking with family to see if it is true or not or to see if there is another way to think.

In the light of day, when we look at the ego's interpretations, assumptions, and conclusions, we see they are false. We accept them from the ego and follow them like unconscious robots. And most of us do not engage in self-inquiry or review these misperceptions to see if they are true and if they serve us. The ego repetitively gives voice to core beliefs such as, "I am guilty," "I am to blame," "I'll never amount to anything," "No one will choose me because there's something wrong with me," "I am alone, isolated, and no one will ever love me," and "I'm disgusting."

The word "disgusting" usually has its origin in sexual guilt from a person's sexual past in terms of thoughts, feelings, beliefs, and experience, like child sexual play with one of their playmates. The one who initiated or suggested the play usually has the most to clear, thinking they have done something bad to someone else.

Any behavior or decisions made when in the little t truth state of mind are fear-based reactions from our uncleared selves.

Whenever we are in a strong, negative emotion cycle, we believe the little t temporary truths to be real. Our ego-mind drives feelings such as fear, anger, jealousy, sadness, shame, blame, embarrassment, regret, hurt, and any other negative feeling that is disruptive and disturbing.

Here is how a *Power of Clearing* student describes many ways the ego mind can show up in her intimate relationships.

> "When defending my ego's thoughts, feelings, and beliefs, instead of responding, I react, surprising myself with the potency of my defense.
>
> I can be critical, demanding, dismissive, and arrogant.
> I can be angry, attacking, and blaming.
> I can be scornful and vindictive, projecting my pain on others.
> I can be totally self-righteous.
> I can be mean and manipulative.
>
> I can be withdrawn and shut down.
> I can be sad and pitiful.
> I can be careless and indifferent.
> I can be stuck in a feeling for days.
> I can be hurt and helpless.
> I can make myself sick and tired.
> I can be expectant of special consideration.
>
> These behaviours are not my true nature. When I realize they are temporary ego-driven misperceptions, I can use them as entry points to do *The Clearing Process* with my subconscious mind and return to Peace and Joining."

If we run away from someone without completing the entire communication, it is by the ego's dictate. For example, many people leave a marriage in this justified state of mind of being right about some ego feeling, thought, or belief, without ever remembering their original love and connection. If they cleared their reaction using *The Clearing Process,* they would come back to love, knowing if they truly want to continue being in the marriage.

The Complete Way Out of "Stuck-ness"

I have met many people in so much emotional pain that it feels to them like they are losing their minds. Many people take pills and exhibit other escapist activity to block out their anxiety as a way to manage their fear. To anyone observing them it appears as if they are having a mental breakdown because this experience can seem out of character and out of control. Since many people do not know how to deal with emotional outbursts (of themselves or others), they can be afraid. When they numb or self-medicate their pain, they increase the chaotic experience; they could even be "sectioned" (put away in a psych ward against their will). I would recommend spending our time releasing what is at the core of the pain. We need to become more curious about what creates the feeling accentuating the pain in our body, mind, and heart; where the traumas, thoughts, and emotions are buried.

I want you to know that when you recognize and feel this emotional pain, you are fully capable of releasing yourself from it through *The Clearing Process*. One of the most important components in this releasing is that you are willing to let the pain go. It is not who you really are, even though it is so familiar and compelling.

I applaud all souls pushing through their emotional process from stuck-ness to spiritual awakening. I recognize their need for compassion and presence with someone willing to point out other possibilities of being. I honor their courage throughout their challenging journey.

Love holds no grievances.
(ACIM, W-84.3:1)

My grievances hide the light of the world in me.
(ACIM, W-69)

When I let all my grievances go, I will know I am perfectly safe.
(ACIM, W-68.6:9)

CHAPTER 3

THE WORLD OF ILLUSIONS

The War is Within

I married a Swedish man in 1989 and moved to Sweden. I met him there in 1987 during a three-week tour facilitating my training courses. I desired to embrace this new life and understand Swedish customs, language, and nuances in their way of life. I knew I was following my destiny; however, leaving my familiar Californian lifestyle was a shock.

For my residency status, I needed to attend Swedish cultural schooling to help me integrate. As part of my immersion process, I learned alongside immigrants from countries I had never even heard of at the time. They spoke of the wars raging in their homelands and the dictators they hated and wanted to kill. It was a tremendous source of pain and suffering for them, how they were treated in their country of origin and how they wanted to retaliate using the same means—violence!

Listening to these immigrants speak of their perspectives, it dawned on me that I must be responsible for the war outside of myself as I still had some conflicting thoughts about relationships with family, friends, and colleagues. Some misunderstandings with my friends were minor, but any conflict is conflict, and any lack of peace is still a lack. Up to this point, I had not yet cleared or even acknowledged these struggles. I magnified everything that was not yet feeling peaceful inside of me, and I found that the war outside mirrored what was inside me as a projection of my inner conflicted mind.

I believe we are responsible for the violence we view and perceive in our world. How we perceive life, love, war, and differences is unique for a person based on experiences. Until we can let go of all judgments and conflicts within our minds, we will prevent ourselves from receiving the gift of truly living in peace. Any discord reminds us we must commit to releasing these thoughts of internal and external conflict for good and always if we truly desire to live in peace. Thus, we would put an end to the war by living this higher ideal of divine peace and remembering our true nature.

For each of us, it takes vigilance and intention to attend to our thoughts and emotions and consciously release all negative beliefs to end the external war. Every mind that fights within itself begins with a personal turmoil, which becomes an outer turmoil and collectively we create a world where many of us are fearful, conflicted, and angry.

I say, "It is time we end this madness!"

We all could say, "We have had enough!"

Attack and Defense

Massacres have increased overwhelmingly during the last three decades, where mainstream media reports shooting after shooting, each more shocking than the previous one. At first, these incidents appeared to be random and isolated. Many classrooms have been the scene of these sudden attacks. Attacking and shooting people is a form of war. As a society or culture, we ask, "Why is this happening, and what can we do about it?"

Unexamined fear manifests in the ego-mind as a defense that turns into an attack. It appears that many people are feeling separate, alienated, and alone. Something we can do through all of this chaos, fear, and confusion is take personal responsibility for everything happening in both our internal and external world. The idea that violence is happening in some distant part of the world and won't happen in my town or school has been proven delusional. It's happening in places we would least expect, like in Stockholm, Sweden, where the first shooting occurred in the city's streets after nearly a hundred years of peace. No one thought such a thing was possible in such a peaceful culture.

The first mass shootings of children occurred in Dunblane, Scotland, on March 13, 1996, when a local man in his mid-forties shot and killed sixteen pupils and one teacher and injured fifteen others before killing himself. Since then, many shootings have occurred across many countries. The response to the Dunblane incident was to build a Sports-plex and Community Center for the healing of everyone in Dunblane. Everyone could come, have a cup of tea, have snacks, and talk to remedy feelings of anger, sadness, and confusion.

On May 6, 2021, in a sixth-grade classroom in the Midwest of the United States, a student pulled a gun out of her backpack and shot one custodian and two students. As soon as she fired the first shot, students in the classrooms and throughout the school ran for cover and hid in corners to avoid being visible. In this situation, the student's teacher risked her life by stepping in and hugging her, calming her down, enabling the teacher to take the gun away, thus preventing more shootings that day. Unfortunately, as is often the case, the shooter's motive remained unknown. And school shootings have become so commonplace that there are now drills in some US schools where students and teachers prepare to take a shooter down.

Soon after, in Kazan, Russia, on May 11, 2021, a nineteen-year-old man attacked a school, killing seven eighth-grade students and a teacher, with over twenty-one people sent to the hospital.

One of the phenomena I have noticed over the years as a transformational therapist has been the extent of the emotional and sexual abuse of young children under seven years old. From my therapeutic experience, I see the process of releasing any pain and suffering from such attacks as a key to healing for all parties concerned. Both persecutor and victim must go through an intense process to let go and heal the mistaken beliefs about themselves and the other. To begin, they need to be able to recognize they need help and deserve to receive it.

I hypothesize that many of the teenagers who have been school shooters were sexually or otherwise abused. For the troubled teenager, it could have led to feelings of helplessness, of being attacked, controlled, or bullied, and now, in the classroom, they are reclaiming internal power, and striking back at someone weaker than them. Many forms of therapy help these children, teenagers, and adults; transformational therapy, especially one with a spiritual component, offers the opportunity to let go of their pain and suffering, thus returning them to their more authentic and peaceful nature.

In 1996, we created *Youth on Purpose*, called *Fri Sikt* ("open view" in Swedish), an initiative in in Sweden to end separation among high school students. (Call it "bullying.") The first program ran for eighteen months for 120 youths. This program demonstrated the living experience where the youth gained and lived the awareness of being one united mind in love, peace, and joy. In Chapter 10, we go into more detail about that program and the movie *The Difference*.

Separation from others increases the sense of isolation and aloneness that can lead to a deep rage. Thoughts such as, "Well, I'm all alone. No one cares about me. I'm not part of any group or family. I feel separate, so it doesn't matter if I kill those people because I am all alone, completely alienated from everyone. Whoever I shoot will not matter because I don't matter. Why should I care about anyone else? I don't even care about myself." Ultimately, they are attacking others with the projection of this self-hatred, insecurity, and despair. Now they have become the shooter rather than the victim. It is noteworthy that in many cases, they are fighting back and killing children, just as others attacked them when they were children and defenseless. They may not have had an adult or ally to stand up for them in a powerful way. In many cases, the shooter or persecutor commits suicide in the end, demonstrating how shooters believe they are under attack.

These massacres are evidence of a negative core perception in their belief system about themselves. When a person has these negative thoughts of themselves without clearing and releasing them, those thoughts and feelings become their reality and, eventually, their experiences. This "aloneness" or sense of separation and self-loathing makes them a danger to themselves and others.

Many people who feel alienated, rejected, and bullied have difficulty making friends, feeling accepted, and fitting in. They can be a "danger point" to those around them. When we recognize this danger point, we understand it is not their problem or their fault alone. In their isolation, they may not even know it's possible to release their rage because it is so integrated in their lives, and they believe it defines who they are as a person. They manifest the attack as a way to release their anger for feeling abandoned by everyone around them.

We can answer the question, "How can I make a difference in these shootings?" by extending generous compassion to ourselves and others. It is up to all of us to wake up and be aware of the negativity we see inside ourselves and others. We can no longer afford to be silent and sleep. It is time to say to ourselves, "I need to choose to live my life awake and see the people around me who might need support, comfort, and inclusion while there's still time."

Shifting our focus, we can take our eyes off computers, televisions, smartphones, and myriad other distractions in our present-day lives, so we notice people and situations around us. While these modern-day devices can be informative and stimulating, keeping us connected and entertained, we remain unaware, detached, and in oblivion. It is necessary to observe everyone in our vicinity, including friends, family, and loved ones. It can be dangerous to be too focused on a smartphone and ignore signs of people feeling isolated, potentially leading to violence to themselves or others. It is time for us to become aware and awake to what needs to be cleared or released that is negative within ourselves and to notice others around us. We can no longer afford to be silent and sleeping-walking through life, playing video games, watching Netflix, or being attached to our devices and zoning out not to feel our pain. And say to ourselves, "I choose to wake up now." The ego always says, "I can wait till later." However, "later" may be too late.

As we increasingly become self-absorbed, self-reliant, and isolated in our independence, we are encouraged to "just mind your own business!" However, the opposite is true! We all need to wake up to the thought, "I am a part of the Totality." Whatever is happening in my world is part of my business. If I notice it, perhaps I am seeing it for some reason. If I feel uneasy from my intuition or a gut feeling, I can contact someone who will do something about it or investigate it thoroughly myself!

We must also be more observant of strangers and aware of what they are going through, supporting them to feel seen, heard, and valued. It's always possible to make a difference, helping each other release separation by taking the action of reaching out when we notice other people separating and retreating into their own little worlds. Each of us has the opportunity to go beyond our tight-knit group and extend ourselves to others so we can feel connected again in hearts and minds.

In each encounter, when we choose to connect at a deeper level, we enable both parties to step closer to peace within, thereby adding to the greater good. Looking at the larger picture, what can we each do to be helpful and awake? How can we end separation from our family, friends, and loved ones and thus, create peace, joining, and interconnectedness? Peace begins within and specifically in our inner circle relationships, including our conflicts and their conflicts. It's possible to clear our emotional pain relevant to each person we know and meet.

Civil conflict and unrest in cities have now become far too big a sociological challenge and psychological problem for us to rely only on formalized therapists, counselors, or consultants. Police forces worldwide are being defunded, curtailed, and reduced in numbers, with new rules making them unable to defend the public. They no longer feel safe, respected, or valued after many threats to their authority and lives.

Simultaneously, I've noticed that people are more afraid to leave their homes more than ever. People of color are even more fearful because they are at the risk of being shot based on appearance. Parents talk with their children about them potentially being in danger, so to be aware of their surroundings.

In this climate of suspicion, fear, and general anxiety, it becomes a matter of life and death, attack and defense, and where does it end? How will we protect and defend ourselves? ACIM says, *"In my defenselessness my safety lies."* (ACIM, W-153) This statement implies we must release all our fears and negative projections, as our unconscious fear and guilt can draw this attack on us.

What can we do? The only answers are within. It is a waste of time to focus on, discuss, and perpetuate the drama of the conflicts outside of ourselves. By doing so, we appear to be joining our guilt with the guilt of others and energetically projecting it outside of ourselves onto the world.

Instead, we can let go of the evidence of creating the feeling that we are unsafe and energetically join with others in Love and Compassion. We are powerful beings, and when we get in touch with our connection to Source, we rise above the fear-based thought system that has kept us feeling small, stuck, insignificant, and insecure. Finally, we can choose to surround ourselves with supportive, loving, conscious people to mutually confirm our invincibility whenever we forget the truth of who we are.

The Goal of Therapy

Fifty-five years ago, I was held up in New York City three times. I could have been killed. I felt scared, and I still showed up with intense love and compassion for the person. The only reason I'm alive today is that I focused on the joining between us instead of my fear.

Once, on the street, a man followed me for four long blocks, and I started running and finally went into a restaurant. The proprietor was at the counter, and I went and stood beside him. The man followed me in and stood in front of us. I didn't say anything. He stared at me and then ran out.

Another time, I was in the elevator, and a man pushed his way in and pointed a knife at me. He asked for my jewelry and my money. I told him, "I have nothing on me that you would want." I looked into his eyes, and we connected. The door opened at the floor where I was going, and I immediately got out and fled, and he stayed in the elevator.

The third man showed up at my door in the middle of the night when I was expecting my friend to arrive. He needed money, and I said, "If I gave you all the money, then I would have no money to eat, but I'm happy to count what I have and give you half, then I can call it a gift." It worked out. I counted out half and gave it joyously to him. In each case, I was safe because I held the space for their ego craziness and faced them. I held the space for their pain that looked like an attack, and they let go. I will do anything I can to help people and offer what they might want or need at that moment if I can.

The goal of therapy as I see it is to find out what the client is afraid to say or may not know about consciously. We bring it forth in a safe, supportive atmosphere and container, and help the person gently release any meaning they made up that's untrue about themselves, to them. For example, letting go of the idea that they are guilty, not likable, wanted, or worthy of love because of an event. Everyone who does the 3-step *Power of Clearing* process forgives themselves for these beliefs and comes to the Truth that they are Whole, Complete, Perfect, and worthy of Love.

Initial steps can include asking myself, "How can I take responsibility for my feelings, beliefs, and thoughts?" And, "How can I be honest with someone I'm in conflict with and share how I feel without blaming them?" We fear they will judge, attack, or reject us in response to our honesty, thus confirming evidence of the misunderstanding. If the interaction triggers my ego, I need to own my part of what is happening, and use the conflict in my mind as a basis for what to clear from my thought system. Alternatively, the ego might insist that I get rid of this person from my life as quickly as possible, and then everything will be fine. It is common to walk away, blaming the other person.

As a life coach and counselor, I see how most people confuse their personality traits with their authentic self. They do not know they can clear and *release* the thinking of "this is who I am: a negative, separate, unworthy person." They believe their ego is their authentic self; however, that is not the Truth.

It's key to watch for our negative beliefs about ourselves and others (ego attack thoughts.) For example, judging others as dangerous, or oneself as wrong, leads to a belief in separation.

Then we may look for someone else to agree with an ego thought and blame someone else, confirming the belief as true in our minds. In seeking collusion, I get confirmation that "I am right" and it gains power with "we are right." When someone agrees with us, we feel justified in believing we are separate from the one we judge.

How we speak to others and ourselves sets up our reality. We can learn how to use our language to reveal our ego-mind in a more clear, undefended, and concise way with the words, phrases, and references we choose. We can see the correlated effect of how our thoughts and words create negative or positive experiences.

When I reflect on famous people who died in emotional pain—such as Michael Jackson, Robin Williams, Anna Nicole Smith, Marilyn Monroe, and the following story about Cheslie Corrinne Kryst—I regret missing the opportunity to have helped them clear their guilt and correct their misperceptions about themselves; they were valued and loved.

Recently, I saw on the news that a 30-year-old stunning black woman, Cheslie Corrinne Kryst (Miss USA in 2019, a lawyer and journalist), had jumped from her ninth-story apartment in suicide. I have heard nothing in the investigation about why she chose to take her life. The cause of this action can be deep in someone's mind in what they held in their earliest childhood memories. Most people never have a chance or would be afraid to do therapy because they are scared to share or say what they are hiding. Therefore, it never gets brought up, spoken about, or cleared with any professional who knows how to release the trauma. This secret can be experienced like PTSD, which goes on and on, retraumatizing the person so they think the only choice is drugs to block it out or a leap to their death to take the anxiety away.

My theory is that this woman who jumped must have had something in her life driving her she didn't know about, felt uncomfortable about, or kept as a secret; a negative, repetitive thought, and she might have thought there was no way out, so "I'll just give up and jump." Or she knew about it and felt humiliated, ashamed, or guilty about something. She chose to end her life in a dramatic example of separation rather than face her pain, heal, and find a way to return to peace. Being a well-known person, she may not have wanted to disappoint people by revealing that she had emotional pain.

People are not exposed to methods of dealing with their issues until they learn about a method that could potentially work to release this painful cycling in their minds. Instead, anxiety and pain medications that were supposed to be temporary "until we deal with the issue" have become a permanent solution in society. It takes time, energy, willingness, and a commitment to identify your issues and find a way out of your pain and suffering into your pure, natural state of peace.

Hundreds of people have told me I saved their lives in my four decades of supporting people through *The Clearing Process*. They had thought they would never be free of their negative judgment and constant upset from their emotional pain.

The Projection Factor

Projection is when you notice a characteristic in another (for example, a father's dismissiveness, a mother's anger, or your own fear) and you feel a negative emotion arising in you and unconsciously blame the other for your reaction.

Projection happens if you haven't recognized what the feelings about that specific characteristic or behavior means about you. For example, when my mom placed her attention on everyone else and not me, it made me feel like "I wasn't important." So, if I haven't cleared that belief of not feeling important, anyone who doesn't give me attention activates that feeling inside of me. Subsequently, I feel guilty for not being important enough, and so I attempt to rid myself of feeling that guilt and I blame it on the person who triggered it in me.

If a feeling is triggered, I have the opportunity to find a way to release or clear what is upsetting me. For example, it's often connected with someone in my family of origin; and the meaning I gave to their behavior. If I can catch my thoughts and understanding where the feeling is coming from, I can express this awareness to the person in the present. For example, "What I see in you that I don't like about my mom is that I felt she didn't make me a priority and cherish the time to connect with me."

When I have an emotional reaction, it can shock the person who triggered me because they don't have the context of what is coming up for me, unless I tell them. The purpose of becoming more aware is to shift out of blame and projection into accepting responsibility for my upset.

Any time someone has a pet peeve or something they are upset about clearly indicates that they are projecting. Remember that whenever you are pointing at someone, you have three fingers pointing back at yourself. Pointing indicates blaming. In our current intimate relationship, we project this characteristic (of someone in our past) on our partner and see them as guilty of this behavior. So, we unconsciously choose projection, hoping to get rid of the guilt we are feeling in the first place. Of course, this never works, except maybe temporarily to feel better in the moment.

Since we're only ever clearing what we need to release in ourselves, we don't clear with the actual person. We always use the clearing as a process with someone playing the character of that person, portraying their higher self. (The higher self is the true spiritual aspect in their divine nature.)

We often take on the traits of the person we choose to blame, such as our mother or father. This phenomenon can be shocking to us when we realize that we, ourselves, have the same traits that we consider negative in one or both of our parents. When we place blame, we always get blamed back because judgment is a circle; what we see in others is what we have the opportunity to recognize in ourselves.

We use this sentence from an exercise in *The Art of Surrender* training to release projections:

"What I see in you that I didn't like about my father, mother, brother, sister, partner, is that they… (for example) didn't listen to me."

When we use this sentence, we are now coming into present time and conscious awareness of our projections. By seeing and owning our projections, we are able to see the person as who they are rather than through the filter of our projections.

One of the consequences of projection is the phenomenon of separation because when we do not see the other for who they are, we feel disconnected from them. Separation is one of the most important concepts we can and need to heal. When people believe they are separate, they feel alone, distant, defensive, and hostile. These unconscious results can include depression, anxiety, suicide, and attack. Sometimes unconscious projections are so powerful that they can lead a person to lash out, for example, in a mass shooting.

It is essential to understand and identify the force of separation in ourselves and our relationships. Becoming conscious of our projections and using *The Clearing Process* to heal them makes it safer for yourself and everyone else. One of the reasons we don't feel safe is because so many people are unconsciously projecting on each other. Walking around in a fear of being judged manifests in an experience of defensiveness and anxiety, which leads to the world appearing dangerous.

The Clearing Process goes to the root of anxiety and separation and releases it. *The Art of Surrender* training is the only one my trainings where we use projection as one of our learning models and skillsets. This training is a microcosm of the world, a living laboratory for each of us to process how we think, feel, and behave in our lives and in the world. At first, when we look around the classroom at the other participants, we immediately know we are projecting on someone we hardly know when we have a distaste or judgment about them. For some reason, we don't like them and want to separate from them. Then, we identify a characteristic we don't like about them that triggers us and write down the judgment exactly. Finally, we ask ourselves who this person reminds us of from our past. It could even be something about ourselves. We can use this exercise with anyone in our lives who we feel we don't like or when they do or say something that triggers us. This exercise is an alternative to following our usual ego decision to separate from them.

You may prefer to share this exercise with a safe, neutral person. And if it's a big upset, you'll benefit from doing the 3-step *Clearing Process*.

The first question to ask yourself in the exercise is, "What do I specifically not like about this person? Who do they remind me of?" Ask yourself honestly because it could be yourself. Example: "What I see in you that I don't like about (myself, my mother, father, brother sister) is that (I, she, he, they) …"

Over the years, I have met thousands of people in this work. I notice that very few people take back their projection, realizing it isn't about the other person they instantly disliked. Instead, they prefer to separate from them because they remind them of something or someone they don't like.

One day, I found a person who I disliked. So, the first question I asked myself was, "What do I not like about her, exactly, and who does that remind me of?" I answered, "She is talking too quickly, and therefore I can't understand her or take in everything she is saying. It is just too fast." I then identified that the characteristic I disliked was actually in myself.

When I asked her where she was born, it was the exact location where I was born. Then I said, "You must have my birthday, too." She confirmed she was also born on May 17. Now, I am always aware that, in general, when I immediately dislike somebody, it may be myself that I see. So, then I used the forgiveness sentence about myself. **"What I want you to forgive me for believing** is that I'm talking too fast and therefore, I'm pushing people away and not letting them get to know me, **which means I am** not worthy of being loved."

Then I answer it for myself as my own coach: "Thank you. That is not the Truth. You are a being of infinite worth." (This is Step 2 in *The Power of Clearing* process.)

Whenever you do Step 2, you do Step 3 to complete the process. **"What I want you to forgive me for forgetting is that I am** Love personified and I am worthy of being loved." Coach answers (in this case, myself): "Thank you. That is the Truth. You are love itself and worthy of being loved."

It is important to note that there are both negative and positive projections.

The reason that it's essential to identify positive projections is to avoid falling in love with and marrying someone who reminds you of your dog without either of you being aware of it. Awareness is everything when you are working with your process. I have significant relationships with men in my life, and I wouldn't want to project someone else's characteristics onto them and choose them for that reason. Since we are constantly projecting on the favorite people in our lives, the reason we love them could be that they remind us of someone we used to know. In my life, these people include my grandmother, aunt, and also special dogs (five significant, lovable dogs in my whole life). These characteristics could be the appearance of their eyes or the way they make me feel. I can be projecting the qualities of these remarkable beings on these new people in my life, loving or liking them because of these dogs, my grandmother, or my special aunt.

Therefore, I can adjust the sentence used for a negative projection to be a positive projection: "What I see in you that I loved about my (aunt, grandmother, dog) is that they…."

I Choose to Wake Up NOW!

It is up to us to wake up from this illusionary dream of defense, attack, fear, and guilt. Carrying those negative beliefs makes us more likely to react with an attack when we feel unimportant and believe no one cares about us. But it is possible to heal our conflicted mind, because no amount of evidence will ever make true something that isn't true anyway.

Instead of looking for evidence of lack and feeding our focus with fear and collusion with others, we can expand our mind and see our experience of life differently. The focus of this clearing philosophy is on finding the opposite of projection and collusion, which is owning and holding a vision of unification and joining. We can consciously gather people around us who can support us in that vision, continuously affirming it is possible for all of us to transform and return to Love.

After we tend to ourselves, we can become more joined and purposeful in our world by extending to our global family. As we notice people who are feeling alienated and separated from us, we become more aware of our own feelings of separation. We have an opportunity to embrace these people feeling separate, and together we can learn how to connect, reach out, and join with others in community. With tools and a method to heal, release, and integrate the discord, we can all return to wholeness; my healing is your healing.

I think that people joining together in Peace and Love demonstrates the possibilities of Oneness. Some people believe Peace is impossible. One of my intentions in writing this book is to increase unity consciousness, reach out, and take action. At home, and wherever I go, I can ask myself, "Who can I extend myself to in this situation?" Through my commitment to clearing, I have become an open vessel of spirit extending love and compassion rather than living in contraction, doubt, and fear.

Awareness is the difference between someone acting out their pain on others and someone taking responsibility for their thoughts, feelings, and beliefs, knowing the negative ones can be shifted and released. Recognizing that that is not the truth of who they really are, elevates them to a new state of awareness and consciousness. It is like a Rebirth of the self.

As a therapist and life coach, I have learned the importance of recognizing how much a person unconsciously agrees with their pain and suffering. In my therapeutic sessions, the Hawaiian Huna Healing traditional system, specifically the Ho'oponopono prayer, can help change negative experiences in a person's life by releasing perceived guilt. The Hawaiian word translates into English as "correction." It's a simple practice with a long history. This ancient Huna prayer hypothesis is, "If it is happening in my world and I take notice of it, it has something to do with me on some level, and I have attracted it." We may be carrying generational guilt that we now have an opportunity to clear and release in this lifetime. Even before birth, we may have absorbed our mother's and father's unresolved trauma and continue to repeat it, then pass it on.

We use this practice of the Ho'oponopono prayer to take personal responsibility for attracting our individual guilt. You can repeat the four parts of this prayer silently or aloud to yourself whenever you are uncomfortable in a situation or with someone.

I'm Sorry, Please Forgive me, Thank You, I Love You.

For example, a couple might integrate the Ho'oponopono practice into a conflict during their divorce. One could say the prayer even more clearly to themselves by being specific in their mind:

"I'm sorry our marriage didn't work out.

Please forgive me for not being fully available for your love.

Thank you for hearing me.

I love you for who you really are."

They are thereby correcting their projection onto the other that it's all their fault by taking responsibility for the misperception coming from their own mind. The highest values of love, forgiveness, and compassion replace misperceptions and mistaken beliefs about oneself and the other, returning us to the awareness of our wholeness. I consistently witness how we can clear suffering *to allow more* joy, aliveness, power, and passion for living life.

A primary theme of my philosophy is, "I choose to wake up now." In trainings, when we boldly and powerfully stand up and say this motto aloud, we direct our unconscious mind to be all we can be with conscious desire and intention.

"The inner spiritual transformation of people
is the only way to change this world.
Peace pacts will not do it;
we cannot change people by passing laws.
Real change can only come from the
moral and spiritual efforts of individuals."

"As long as all our life energy is consumed
in the world of the senses, our consciousness remains
oblivious to the infinite stores of wisdom, bliss,
and divine love that lie at the innermost core of our being."

Paramahansa Yogananda
World in Transition:
Finding Spiritual Security in Times of Change

CHAPTER 4

EGO GAMES

The Ego Plays to Win

The ego has favorite strategic games in this world of ego-illusions that we continually work out as patterns that show up in our relationship with ourselves and others. How these ego games are played and acted out in our lives can be the basis for many kinds of clearing processes. The Big T Truth and little t truth chart in Chapter 6 is the philosophical foundation of the *On Purpose* training courses. The ego games as part of the little t chart are described in the sections of this chapter to illustrate the main points of the life lessons learned according to the training's philosophy. In this chapter, we explore how guilt is often related to ego games of money, time, sex, power, and control and how it impacts our experiences of love in intimate relationships.

Ego Games: Money, Time, Sex, Power, and Control

Every culture, country, community, and family has its ego games. We develop many moves, manipulations, and strategic behaviors in childhood, often with the perceived need for survival and safety, through experience, observation, and role modeling. All strategic behavior is of the ego. "If I talk nicely to you and make your favorite dinner and make love with you the way you're always wanting me to, then you'd better let me spend the $500 I want on my spa weekend." It's fine when we're playing around, however when we're relating unconsciously with a lot at stake, it's another situation. Rather than further enmeshment, you can easily release yourself from the ego in your relationships by choosing to make clear and direct communication for what you want. "I intend to withdraw $500 from our joint account for my women's spa weekend. Is that okay with you?"

THE MONEY GAME

Money is neutral, in and of itself. However, when not seen in that way, money can create a survival game throughout one's life:

> *I never have enough money.*
> *I will run out of money and never be able to get or buy what I want.*
> *I will never have enough money to do the things I want to do.*
> *I look at my paycheck and bank account, my home, my inability to afford a holiday for the whole family, and I believe I am in lack and do not have enough, and will never have enough money.*
> *Even though I have had a lot in my bank account all my life, I worry that I will never have enough.*
> *Money goes out much easier than it comes in.*

These beliefs and many more that people concede to, can lead to feeling trapped and imprisoned in a game of lack of security, with money in control of giving and taking. Believing one does not have enough money translates to the belief that one is not good enough or clever enough to create more. Money, to the ego, is seen as a source of strength, power, and control. Therefore, people feel powerless when they have little money, and they see themselves as weak and at the mercy of people who are well-off. They fear that others will see them as powerless and reject them as being weak. The more strongly they hold this belief in their powerlessness, the more it becomes their perceived reality and experience, reinforced by the evidence of lack in every area "outside" of themselves, their home, possessions, bank account.

The money game has a double-edged sword effect. Our group consciousness holds the idea that "If I have lots of money, then I will be able to get love or freedom or both." The belief holds the opposite thought that "If I don't have lots of money, then I will be rejected and ignored because of my feeling of powerlessness." There is also a belief that "If I have lots of money, others will be jealous and maybe want to take it from me, so I have to hide it to be safe."

A sense of guilt is often associated with having money when others do not, ultimately stopping the flow of the possible benefit in using that money to enhance life, joy, and abundance, in general. We often observe that when lottery winners gain a tremendous amount of money overnight, they spend it all just as quickly and end up back in the same place where they started, or even owing money. They hold the belief that money is in control of them and that it is finite. Their guilt or excitement about having such an abundance of money causes them to spend it or give it away as quickly as possible like it is a hot potato.

The fear of having "not enough" or "too much" money can dominate our lives and keep us in flux and confused. Money can be a symbolic demonstration of where we are stuck in our minds and our lives. Many people are waiting years for the money to show up to change their lives or live their dreams: for an investment to pay off, a stock to go up, an inheritance to be settled, a currency to re-evaluate. Evidently, we have all the money we are willing to allow ourselves to have right now, for our egoic reasons. If we want to have more money, we would have to clear our negative belief systems associated with having money at the deep roots in our mind, from our history within our family system, culture, and past monetary experiences.

Many wealthy people are challenged by spending, investing, securing, and donating money, and to whom, to what, and how much. It can be a burden and a great responsibility to consciously circulate and manage their wealth. Negative core beliefs can limit our wisdom to create, manifest, or spend money. Most people are concerned with not having enough money.

To manifest money efficiently in a natural flow, we need to create an intention for that money. Joining with another in holy relationship with a common purpose for the money can accelerate its manifestation. It requires planning and having a precise vision of your desired goals or dreams. People create vision boards for this purpose and include images of money, objects of desire, places to go, and activities that require money. Once we agree on our vision, purpose, and mission, then money is no longer an end in itself, and becomes a vehicle. We come into alignment with what we really want the money for and the joyous feeling we have when we realize our goals and dreams. Money then falls into proper perspective in our minds.

When we recognize that we do have enough money, enough possessions, and enough in our bank accounts, we wake up and realize we are able to be philanthropists and create ways to contribute to the benefit of others who have yet to manifest abundant circumstances for themselves. Likewise, we can support others even before we recognize that we have enough for ourselves. Ultimately, how much will ever be enough? We always have enough to share, no matter how little we have. It makes us feel really good to extend to others what we have to share. "It's better to give than to receive." It's also important to be able to receive to honor the giver who can't exist otherwise.

THE TIME GAME

The time game can feel like a lack of time or an over-abundance of time. During the pandemic of 2020-2021, people were confined to their homes with what seemed to be an infinite amount of time, and for some, that may have been new to them. They were unable to travel or participate in regular activities. Before the pandemic, they were constantly watching the clock and feeling they were always running out of time. The concept of time runs many people's lives. As the months went by, people noticed they were not motivated by their abundance of time and instead fell into a "pandemic stupor" of not being inspired to do anything. Many went into a kind of apathy or resignation, obliterating themselves in hypnotic states with television, internet, Netflix, food, alcohol, and non-productive activities. They felt that the disease would take us over and kill us all and then, what's the point? There was constant reporting and "fear porn" from the mainstream media that more people were getting sick and dying, and thus more restrictions were being imposed, to supposedly keep everybody safe. Others were very motivated and inspired by this vast space of time and felt the urgency to seek truth, research, fight back, step up, and create a new parallel reality, focusing on becoming more aware, more awake, freer, and finding their power in this perceived hopeless state. When they did not have a lack of time or an urgency motivating them to act or take action, they may have decided to do nothing and just wait it out and delay.

The prior belief held in this "time game" is that "There is never enough time to do what I want," or "I must fill the time that I have with my to-do list; otherwise, I will never meet my needs or desires." The other side of the story is that "If I have too much time, I'll be bored or feel that my worth is less than those who are busy." I hope this example makes it clear that for those people who complained about wishing they had time for their dreams, now, with the opportunity of time, there must be a block or barrier within themselves to what they always dreamed of doing. Otherwise, they would finally act upon their dream or desire. A lot of guilt could arise in them because they no longer have the excuse of not having enough time to do what they envisioned.

Our society has strict rules about punctuality and arriving on time. If we do not arrive on time, we believe that others will think we do not respect them. The need to be punctual and respect other people's time compounds our feelings of guilt when we do not obey this principle which is increased by fear and excuses.

Our ego makes up that we have strict codes of right and wrong in all of these egoic games. We have made up the rules or agreements (often unspoken), so we are guilty or wrong when we violate these time rules. Examples: "You are late. Therefore, you are not caring about me and my time." Or "You did not call to let me know you were going to be late." Or "You didn't even remember that we had an appointment to meet at this particular time and place. Therefore, you chose to disregard me. I blame you and judge you as irresponsible, unreliable, uncaring as a person and not respecting me."

This is a clearing opportunity to go much deeper to free the belief or feeling that they are not worthy of being cared about, loved or wanted.

Example of a clearing for this particular time issue.

Step 1 (with a coach, guide, or the person who was late)

"What I want you to know *(name of person who is late)* **is that I feel** *that you don't respect me or value my time when you make an appointment with me or we have an agreement and you don't show up or call,* **which makes me feel** *unimportant...* **just like when...** (close their eyes and see if a specific scene or incident from their past emerges into their awareness).

They can also say other incidences of people not keeping their time commitments, feeling betrayed, or changing the appointment; any other ego thoughts that relate to this time issue.

The coach or guide holding the space says **"Thank you"** following each statement which simply means "I hear you, I'm with you. I am listening."

Step 2 (forgiveness and correction of misperceptions)

"What I want you to forgive me for is thinking/feeling/believing *that you didn't care when you forgot our appointment,* **which means I am...** *unimportant, don't matter, am unworthy, and unloved."*

Coach: **"Thank you. That is not the Big T Truth. You are always worthy, important, and loved. I love you."**

Step 3 (remembering the Truth of who you are) always follows Step 2.

"What I want you to forgive me for forgetting is that I am always Loved, Important, and Worthy."

Coach: **"Thank you. That is the Truth. You have always been Loved and are Worthy of Love."**

The amount of upset we feel from this kind of time-game incident (angry, annoyed, irritated, or numb, cold, apathetic, sad) demonstrates to us that it is a clearing item for us to do the 3-step *Clearing Process*. This incident preoccupies us both consciously and unconsciously and takes up space in our energy field. Therefore, we will not be present to what we are doing next until we clear it from our minds and hearts. It's very important for us to realize that we'll be unable to bypass it because our unconscious mind will do something with the energy that needs to be cleared. We will transfer our upset by projecting it onto something or someone else in our lives until we pay attention and see what we are doing.

Every upsetting incident in our lives that triggers us can be used as a doorway to our own clearing and healing. We will clear to get to the root of a deeper issue that the current incident brings up. We can let go and forgive negative beliefs like we are unimportant, unworthy, or unlovable. Once forgiven and released, we are more readily available to attain our main goals or natural states in life, which is ultimately, Love, Peace and Joy.

For example, an accident, a bankruptcy, a divorce, a death, or a physical ailment can prompt us to go within and review what is happening in our lives. Awareness and willingness take conviction and courage to face our lessons in this lifetime. Even if we think our relationships are random, we chose them for the lessons that we originally came to this life to learn and grow from. These lessons and growth opportunities are being revealed by how we respond to these particular people and incidents. We are the ones who give everything the particular meaning it has for us in our lives and what the message is there to teach us. Every trigger is an opportunity to heal or repeat the lesson, until we take ownership of it, release it, heal it and move on.

The following example is based on the principle that the unconscious mind dictates to the body what to do. I had a client who experienced a significant upset in her life with a series of friends. In her mind, there were indiscretions that brought up huge resentment and a lack of forgiveness for those she was blaming, along with herself. She began drinking, smoking and avoiding her feelings. She was in a completely numb state, only doing what she needed to do in her life for her family and children. After one and a half years of being numb and unavailable to her feelings, she had a major wake-up call, in the form of cancer. Of course, she's not guilty for this diagnosis or of this condition in any way. She may have felt guilty when she became aware of the enormity of the upset that she was avoiding. By not considering the magnitude of the unresolved process in her mind, she may have attracted the cancer as a wake-up call to become self-aware. She chose to wake up before it was too late. This client is now paying attention to her entire process and has been for several years, taking full responsibility for her thoughts, feelings, and beliefs. She has cleared all the upset, projections, guilt, and unforgiveness. She has changed her whole life as a result of this wake-up call. Life has taken on a new and different reality for and perspective on her relationships and purpose. After she had done the most significant part of the clearing, the client said it felt like she was dying. That would be like an ego-death to her defense system. The ego had made up that it was not safe anymore because she had divulged and cleared her secrets. She was no longer hiding anything from herself or from me as her coach.

Whenever we take space and time, with awareness to do *The Clearing Process*, we will be reclaiming a piece of our own presence and personal power. You will always take *The Clearing Process* deeper when you have another person holding the space for you who is fully present. Then you can open more fully to your ego thoughts, feelings, and beliefs and feel safe to share, without judgment. This energy that you may feel (upset, distance, irritation) and the dissonant thoughts that you are having at the core of the story demonstrates the essence of what you ultimately need to clear about. We have to get to the bottom line or the important points of every story to see the root cause. A person has to ask themselves these questions: "What is the core upset in the story? Did I not feel listened to? Heard? Respected?" Or some other feeling that is up in relationship to the issue. The next question is: "Who is the person this feeling is about?" Then you know what and who to direct the clearing to.

Once you have some practice with your coach or a clearing partner, you can also do this process in the mirror, playing both roles of yourself and the coach. In other words, you have to answer Step 1, 2 and 3 as if you were the coach, holding the space for yourself, as you talk in the mirror. You represent the higher self of the person you are clearing with so you are able to empty all the ego thoughts that you may not be able to express directly to the actual person. This person may not be available or alive, but we are still able to release old feelings, beliefs and projections, to find the deeper hidden meaning that really upsets you.

Remember that we give everything the meaning that we attach to it, personally and collectively, in any relationship. We seek agreement or collusion from our allies for the importance that we have given some ego illusion. We usually tell people our version of the story that we want them to agree with, hoping they will collude with our interpretation of the situation. We are always hoping for ego cooperation with another person to confirm our point of view. When two ego-minds agree on any ego illusion, especially someone's guilt, this agreement makes them believe that they are correct. Then they take it on as a fact instead of the temporary ego perspective that it is. Their point of view can be changed and released, once they process all the dynamics of the story through to its roots. We find this phenomenon true when someone is gossiping and going behind someone's back. Terry Cole-Whittaker wrote the book, *What You Think of me is None of My Business*. What you think of me is coming through your history and pain that you have yet to resolve and that you are projecting onto me. Therefore, I can view it that way. It's really about you, not me. If we make our pain about the other person, we make ourselves into victims, feeling like we are losing our power.

Consider your patterns around time and what is in your mind that is keeping you late. Also pay attention to how others will project their mind and their history onto your behavior of being late; what is their interpretation going to be? You can get stuck together with your interpretation of their interpretation! A lot of people who are constantly late might have been late in their birthing process.

Being born prematurely, pushed out, or pulled out with forceps influences a person throughout their life in how they manage time, pressure, expectation, and the choice to do something. They may constantly feel they must, should, or have to, from their birth experience. In general, these people want to arrive in their own time, in their own flow, with their own rules.

For example, "I can be late because I don't want to be pushed against my will to be on time. If I have an appointment and I'm on time, it's an anomaly." It's optimal for them to say, "I'll be there when I get there," rather than making a time commitment that they probably won't keep. That way, there is no real disrespect or a perceived judgment to have to clear. They have already told you the truth. They won't be on time.

Birth is the single most important event of our lifetime. The memory of this experience is held deep within our cells, which is governed by our subconscious mind. Through processes like rebirthing, transformational breathwork, or past life regression, we may access our birth experience. Then we can reframe it in a more conscious way to integrate it into our current reality. We can recreate it as our first and most significant rite of passage in the way we would have preferred to enter into this world. A personal way to envision this is, "I will hang out in my cozy womb with my nurturing Mama for a little longer, and I will come out when I'm ready. Everyone can await my arrival, patiently, in my own time, in my own space. I will take it in as a defining moment in my life that I was wanted and welcomed."

As we grow older and our life continues to unfold, we each see a pattern of how we are using our birth process played out in the time game. If this pattern has a negative connotation for us in life, we can seek out a practitioner to assist with one of the techniques mentioned, to transform the pain of stuck-ness or resignation of birth into a positive, alive, more nurturing experience. The same may be true with the experience of being in utero, which also may have had some painful or traumatic influences. We may constantly feel unwanted, unwelcome, or not chosen in various situations, which can be linked to the mother's perception of the uncertainty of her conception and the birthing process while we were in the womb. These cellular memories, held in our bodies that may direct our lives, consciously or unconsciously, can be transmuted by re-enacting the womb and birth experience, allowing one to feel more welcomed, wanted, and accepted in the world: the ultimate Re-Birth into a new you.

THE SEX GAME

The attraction to sexual guilt runs this world! (Please see Appendix B.)

Sexual guilt is the most substantial guilt we have in our minds—the fear and excitement of being found out start early with masturbation and sexual abuse. There is a reason for the public fascination with sex scandals such as the Clinton-Lewinsky affair in the late '90s. More recent revelations include Jeffrey Epstein, the financier convicted with sex trafficking, ending in an apparent suicide, and Ghislaine Maxwell, a former British socialite and convicted sex offender, found guilty in 2021 of child sex trafficking and other offenses in connection with Epstein. For many years, the public and the press have attacked and scrutinized various politicians, luminaries, and celebrities for sexual indiscretions. Some seem more protected from public shaming, like the Royals, Presidential leaders, global elites, and secret societies. It's common for the perpetrator and even the victim not to consider the outcome of potential exposure of their secret.

The widely publicized "Me Too" movement supported women to come forward and reveal their sexual victimization. Until then, they had felt guilty as the victim, which held them back from speaking up; guilt that the assault happened to them, that something in them attracted it, or they deserved it. Most of us carry some sexual guilt that overlaps with our spiritual guilt. We think, feel, and believe we've left God and have lost our natural connection to the source; thus, it appears that we have chosen the ego world. Our egoic self dominates by fascinations with the body, sexuality, money, material possessions, and other false demonstrations. This recurring illusion is why betrayal and abandonment are ongoing themes in human relationships.

As a life coach and counselor, every client I have worked with who had prostate, breast, or ovarian cancer had a charged sexual component from their history and development that they needed to clear. This clearing always involves sexual guilt from something they thought, believed, felt, or did. This guilt, buried in their subconscious, then went into their body and became a condition commonly known as a dis-ease. We've been able to do *The Clearing Process* with sexual guilt at its core. Sexual guilt will be projected into some other feeling, thought, or experience with someone, even your sexual inclination if it's not cleared.

Betrayal and Abandonment

We create and attract patterns of betrayal and abandonment over and over again unconsciously out of our perceived guilt. This thought pattern also translates into rejection and isolation. Each time we hear a story about the next celebrity in movies, music, Hollywood, or trusted authority, such as a government representative or a religious leader, associated with a sex scandal, this thought pattern gets activated. There are numerous stories of satanic ritual abuse perpetrated on innocent souls, including children. These tales of infidelity, betrayal, and abandonment stimulate our memories of every single perceived sexual indiscretion in our lives. We choose to hide these experiences and stuff them down while believing that our fascination is with the plight of others. All sexual fantasies can be part of these sexual indiscretions, which can be an attractive force of guilt in our lives, compelling us to perceive ourselves as "bad," "wrong," and "guilty." Sexual guilt as an attractive force is an addiction, making it difficult to let go of it. Sad stories in the media of pedophilia, predator attacks, and sexual abuse bombard us. The nature of these inhumane acts has now become more commonplace, with a tendency to deny, deflect, or normalize it.

We are attracted to the "forbidden" in our minds and experiences because we perceive ourselves as guilty. Since we don't want to look at ourselves, we point the finger at someone else to place the blame on them. We love to ask, "How could they do such a terrible, reprehensible thing?" Yet, there's an internal resonance and compatibility through our unconscious guilt that we may have betrayed God. We then experience a type of Hell in our lives that can appear very dramatic and challenging in many situations. We accept punishment for believing we are not worthy of acceptance, respect, and pure love from source, God's Love, or Divine Love.

Believing we have betrayed God, we make up an opposite interpretation that God has betrayed us. Therefore, betrayal becomes a theme in so many relationships regarding our sexuality, fidelity, and finances. We attract the scenario of someone not giving us "a piece of the pie" that we feel we deserve monetarily. This dynamic can manifest as a dispute related to an inheritance, a divorce, or bankruptcy. One can attack the other about sex or money based on the violation of an agreement, thus creating feelings of separation and abandonment. The actual cause of this upset is the original idea that we believe we are "bad" or "guilty" because we feel disconnected from source. We have lost our natural spiritual connection, which we had as children, knowing who we really are. The loss of our connection to source makes us feel very uncertain and unstable about our present and future because this connection is the most vital part of our existence.

The Man-Woman Game

Men and women often engage in the stereotypical game where the woman gives the man everything he needs, believing he will financially and emotionally support her in exchange for her sacrifice. The traditional saying has been "a woman's place is in the kitchen" because that is where the woman and her man may perceive her authority by running the kitchen as her domain of power in the home. This domain could include other domestic activities, such as cleaning, laundry, shopping, and decorating, which is an old-school concept, often present in our unconscious or conscious mind. It may be a driving force affecting the current relationship dynamic, subtly or overtly. Also, she may blame the man for not helping her in the domestic duties. The man may use excuses to allow the woman to play her "housewife" role (like the man's mother did). His statements can often sound like: "I'll never do it as well as you would like, so carry on," and "I knew I wouldn't do it the way you wanted it done," and "I know you can do it so much better than I can, so I'll just let you get on with it."

For his part, when a man fails to achieve his expectations of success and financial abundance, he may feel guilty and blame his guilt on his wife for not supporting him more in reaching his goals. Another problem can arise when the woman prefers to be outside the home, sharing her talents and gifts for remuneration because she is competing with him in the workplace. Since the man may take pride in the stereotypical role of "taking care" of the family as the primary breadwinner, he can generate great resentment if his wife exceeds his financial and professional success.

A few decades ago, society viewed material success as a male activity. The perception has changed from the wife's full feminine power being in the home to taking over the male role by earning comparably good money in her own career alongside his. Also, this equalized financial dynamic can lead to new pressure in their man-woman struggle game, expressed by her as "I feel that you don't want me going to work because we have children. I should stay home and look after them and the house. I feel guilty for wanting to work and fulfill my purpose, and for leaving my children, which means I am an uncaring mother." Therefore, an unspoken conflict can lead to an underlying "need" to determine the "dominant male" in the relationship. Either way, one or the other partner may leave the relationship as a result or retreat into a space of bitterness, victimhood, and apathy. This impasse echoes cultural beliefs and collective consciousness about what these male-female roles look like and how they get played out in the relationship. When the woman goes to work, it adds extra pressure, with more responsibilities along with all her domestic and parenting roles. She now may have become a full-time breadwinner, parent, and domestic manager, allowing her very little free time to recuperate from her demanding world. Once she becomes overwhelmed by all of these demands, she feels unseen, uncared about, and turned-off, so then there is no more sex with her husband. He may also feel that he no longer has a singular role of importance as he once did.

As time goes on, the woman doesn't feel supported by "her" man, mainly because she is not standing in her power to ask for what she wants and needs. She may decide to leave the relationship without thoroughly communicating with him about how she feels and what she wants. She may interpret the entire situation as "he doesn't care about me or acknowledge all that I have given to him and our home and our children. Now I'm a full-time homemaker with my full-time job and I am exhausted."

In essence, she may look back later and realize that she didn't communicate what she wanted in an empowering way with full transparency and clarity. She may not have given him any clear messages about her desires and allow space for him to support her in his own way. By not fully communicating with him, she is keeping the game alive with the belief or feeling that she will never get what she really wants. No one is listening to her, supporting her, or caring about her, especially her man. The man may think, "I give her everything she wants, and she is still complaining about my involvement or lack of it in the family and the relationship." So now he becomes confused about what he's done wrong and may feel frustrated that no matter what he does, it's never quite enough or good enough, resulting in him wondering what to do next. She doesn't seem to be satisfied, no matter what he does or doesn't do. All he wants to do is please her and his frustration is that he doesn't know how.

In many years of teaching *True Woman's Power*, I learned that the most significant power a woman genuinely has is her ability to communicate directly and honestly what she thinks, feels, believes, and desires. Most women realize that they only fractionally share because they fear that saying everything will cause men to reject or abandon them. This lack of communication on both of their parts can make them feel that they are no longer in love. The feeling of love is a function of total communication, which is their ability to be transparent and vulnerable in an intimate relationship. Thus, when they feel like they are no longer in love, their full communication is not as it was. This pattern in relationship of not being direct with each other, if not recognized and acknowledged with some humility, will have a high probability of repeating itself in their subsequent relationships. They will imagine that it's the wrong kind of love with the wrong person and that someone else will love them more, better, or different (ego's favorite words) if they change partners.

Our most significant responsibility in a relationship is fully communicating on all levels (mentally, physically, emotionally, and spiritually) and prioritizing the feeling of love through full, transparent communication to keep the relationship ever-growing, developing, and expanding. We are always in the process of change. As we fully share with our partner the thoughts that we usually hold as personal and private, we will produce a deeper bonding and understanding. This sharing will keep the partners current with each other. A lack of total communication is the primary cause of relationship breakdown, separation, and divorce. The partners no longer feel as if they know the person they fell in love with initially. Where is that person they married and once knew intimately? When we fall out of total communication, we make up interpretations that are usually not true. Opening up communication between the partners is the one thing that will save them from irreparable estrangement. As in *The Clearing Process*, we need to hold the space to be present to hear someone's ego thoughts without reacting, defending, or responding other than "thank you" for sharing. The same presence or mindfulness would be optimal when a partner shares their desires or vulnerabilities, so they feel encouraged to share more and go deeper without concern of their partner's judgment, blame, or attack. They feel supported, heard, and thus, cared about.

In the man-woman game, we have unclear agreements and ambiguous boundaries on what we can and cannot do that would cause the other person to feel unsafe or violated. Meanwhile, we can project onto the other person and therefore reinforce our emotional pain. We become addicted to the pain of our belief that we are being rejected or abandoned by the other person. It's like a habitual circle. We interpret our negative beliefs that we are no longer loved, worthy, or valued as our payoffs of the ego's desire to be right.

A couple has an agreement of monogamy, and now there is a suspicion of another woman in the picture. They are at a party, and the wife inadvertently witnesses her partner intimately kissing this woman. She may believe her partner has broken their agreement and, on the drive home, say, "You violated our marriage agreement by kissing someone else, so you are guilty of breaking our agreement. Seeing you kiss her makes me feel emotionally charged and shut down, angry, and upset. I will talk to you when I feel I am ready to hear you and listen to your side of the story. I'm choosing in this moment to separate emotionally from you because I am not feeling safe or trusting." Silence!

The typical man-woman game is called "I am right, and you are wrong." Also, "I am innocent, and you are guilty." The payoff in maintaining this point of view that only one of us can be right is that we get to reinforce the idea that it's better to be alone and separate, without anyone. That way, I am safer, and no one can hurt or trigger me by rejecting or abandoning me. We have to maintain this point of view due to our unwillingness to communicate fully in a safe, structured situation. We generally don't know how to create a safe space container that will allow us to share and be heard with loving, open, honest communication. It's imperative that each person take responsibility for their thoughts, feelings, and actions, rather than attacking, defending, or blaming the other. This container is quite simple once we have the feel of it and we have experienced it. We may need a third-party professional, neutral coach to demonstrate how to create a safe container for communication, what it feels and looks like to understand how it works, with a resolution goal in mind, thus returning to love. Then, they take ownership of their current issue and reality, being as fully transparent and willing as possible. They would sit opposite each other, with one person talking while the other one listens. Then, at key moments, every few sentences, they would repeat back what they heard and ask, "Is this correct?" to see if they have fully understood the other's point of view and reality. It's best to say up to four ego statements per person and then switch. The listener would repeat back what they heard.

We usually call this technique of listening and reflecting, like a mirror, what they heard the other say "pacing" in the Neurolinguistic Programming model (NLP). By matching or mirroring the language, experience, beliefs, and words of the other, we gain and maintain a genuine rapport, thus a deeper awareness and understanding of the nature of the relationship between us. This exercise works best when both partners in the relationship take turns sharing and listening without conversation or interpretation. We can easily accomplish this communication structure by using Step 1 of *The Clearing Process*. For example, **"What I want you to know is ... I think, feel, or believe** ... you betrayed me by kissing that other woman" (a clear statement), and the other person says, "Thank You." His response is simply hearing and taking in what she is saying, from her point of view, without judgment or defense. He hears her and acknowledges her.

It is a common phenomenon in our society that the feminine part of ourselves is healing victim consciousness, abandonment, and rejection. The masculine aspect of ourselves is healing guilt consciousness, attack, and defense. Ultimately, we will liberate the self and each other when we take back and own these long-held projections, forgiving ourselves for believing we were separate. We are constantly merging the masculine and feminine energies within ourselves, so we balance these two aspects. When we create a list of all the masculine and feminine characteristics we possess, we can see how balanced or imbalanced we may be in the physical embodiment of our gender.

For example, I am a woman, and I have a ratio of 70% masculine to 30% feminine as an assessment grade of myself in terms of masculine-feminine balance. However, in *True Woman's Power*, I discovered that my friends would give me a very different rating than how I assessed myself in the balance of these traits. And then my feelings about their perceptions of my gender balance may give me items to clear on my ego clearing list.

I could ask myself:

"Am I content with the way I see myself in this masculine-feminine percentage balance?"

"Which characteristics would I like to embrace more of to feel more fulfilled in my authentic self as a woman?"

"What would be my fear in living these characteristics more full-out and demonstrating them?"

It's essential to keep a clearing list of issues or upsets as they show up in your daily life and then take the time to clear them one by one, like a to-do list. Then, you can pair together some of them to release in one clearing.

Desperate Women Online

Some women give everything financially, risking it all. They offer all they have accumulated in financial wealth, possessions, and wisdom to have this man want and love them. It can happen to any woman who fixates on a specific type of man they believe will be their ideal partner. It becomes an irrational addiction to share everything they own with this man who they think will love them until the end of time. They become so involved in their fantasy that they finally find him. In this way, men have fooled many women into thinking they are the kind of authentic man who genuinely wants to be with her for who she is. It turns out these men want to take the wealth of these women. This deceiving of women is all over the internet because of how desperate some women are to have someone love and care for them. Thus, whenever someone gives them attention, they are easily hooked and may buy any story he is selling. She may overshare to ensure this love and attention continue coming to them. The term "catfish" is notorious for this occurrence. It's a term for someone who uses fake photos and false persona to find friends or romantic partners online.

When the desperate woman gets hooked, he uses terms of endearment, poetry, and images to capture her heart, making her believe she's the only one for him. It's hard for her to know whether this man wants her for what she has or who she is. The solution to this puzzle is to clear any feelings of lack, low self-esteem, or a hunger for love and attention, releasing any unconscious desperate need to be loved and to buy love at any cost. Unfortunately, it's not uncommon for powerful, sensitive women to be in a relationship with narcissistic unavailable men who promise them the world.

Why do men pursue women in this deceptive way? When a man has a deep wound from his mother, he may inadvertently punish women in some way to try and get what he didn't get from his mother. So, some men and women are a match, with the man stealing everything possible from her. He will take, and she will give, due to their unhealed and unresolved wounds. Clearing these issues will heal the core wounds of separation.

The Man-Woman-Child Game

We are always born into a trinity, a man-woman-child configuration, even if one parent is not present at the time of birth and beyond or a same-sex couple. Short of artificial insemination, there is always this magical trinity that is formed as part of our existence here in a body. In this triangular pattern, a break or schism creates a sense of a missing link, a lost connection, or void, with a longing to re-create that loving triad.

This game can be a constant theme in many people's lives, where a young child or even an adolescent of separated or divorced parents feels stuck in the middle between them. The child may even sense that s/he is the cause of the separation at some level and may look for ways to engage their parents to come back together by asking mom and dad questions to get them to see how much they love each other. If a child perceives their parents' discordance or abuse with each other, they may feel safer with the separation. However, the guilt that they were unsuccessful at getting them back together goes into adulthood, which becomes a common focus for clearing as adults.

Other aspects of the man-woman-child game during separation are the act of custody, visiting rights, ego accusations against the other, money distribution, child support, travel, and living accommodations, all felt by the child. The child feels s/he must choose between the loyalty and support for mom or dad, and they are no longer a joint family. Now they have two separate families, with two individual households and possibly two respective cities, with a new and different relationship with each parent. One or both parents may have a new partner who has other children. The child often feels a lack of choice, so the new dynamics create the need for massive adjustments and stress to be included, wanted, and loved as part of a newly-formed family that overtook them against their will.

The Feeling that I'm not a Good Mother

The thinking may be something like this: "I believe I was a failure as a mother when I couldn't support my son through difficult times. I didn't have the words or knowledge about the world to help him. I felt guilty that I couldn't help him cope because I didn't know what to do or how to help. So, I made up that I didn't have it in me to be a natural mother, knowing what to do naturally. I believed there was no natural flow in me to express myself in a motherly way because I didn't get that from my mother. I couldn't even conceive a child and was amazed when I finally did—because the man I was with repulsed me. He said derogatory things to me, which completely turned me off to him sexually. We were playing a sex power game of not sharing sex because I felt that he didn't deserve or appreciate me and that I had a choice, so I didn't want to give him sex."

The Ego Comparing the Body Game

In the *Choosing Freedom* course that I teach for participants to choose to create a state of freedom and peace in their life, there are 19 principles to live by. One of the principles is *"I will not compare people, places, and things."* For example, "I had a better vacation last year; this one isn't as exciting" because it would take you out of the present experience and put you in the past experience. It would have you believe that you or your companion are not worthy or good enough in the current situation. Everything is perfect enough exactly as it is. This principle goes along with the language of "I could have, would have, or should have done something different," which is another comparison to make you feel unworthy. What is already in the past can never be changed, so going over it is pointless. The ego's defense mechanism keeps you feeling you have made a mistake and keeps you stuck in a circle. For example, I never say "I should have turned left or should have said that" because it's about training your mind to accept everything that is happening as perfect and stay in the present.

The body game concerns your body, your looks, and how you think you appear to others. The ego will always compare you to others in terms of more, better than, and different from other women in terms of your perceived beauty, weight, hips, firmness, breasts, face, nose, hair, skin, and total body appearance. Men have their own comparisons, muscular, height, weight, hair (or no hair), stomach size, penis, and body odour. The outer appearance is a vast subject that people focus on to be acceptable to others and worthy of love and respect. This obsession with our physical body can extend to material characteristics like your age, home, job, money, place of worship, and education. In the ego illusion, we can create separation in our minds based on our belief in the importance of these differences. All comparisons are of the ego. The ego is always talking in the language of "I am better than you because…" or "I am less than you because…"

Since women very often compare themselves with other women, there was one exercise in *True Woman's Power* called The Comparison Game. We go into more detail in Chapter 9 about *True Woman's Power* and OUTLAW *(Outrageous Unstoppable True Leadership Adventure for Women)*, the advanced course of *True Woman's Power*.

THE POWER AND CONTROL GAME

The ego can create numerous games that reinforce a sense of limitation within us, making up a potential win-lose situation ("I am right, you are wrong") or even a lose-lose ("If I can't have it, then neither can you"). We demonstrate these outer "games" in the world because they are already in your psyche in some way to show you an area within yourself that you need to heal. Most people have this power game as a competitive relationship to see who is more intelligent, more resourceful, more successful, more clear-minded, more spiritual, and overall, better in some way. These power games show up in the family of origin, with parent and child, between siblings, in coupling relationships, in friendships, at workplaces between colleagues and bosses, with pet and pet owner, and every other relationship in general. These power struggles and competitive ego exchanges are exhausting as you must be hyper-vigilant to keep affirming you are the best and that you are the one in control. It becomes a priority to ensure that no one usurps your power or controls you. Most "special relationships" are competitive connections with unspoken bargains. My working definition of a special relationship is when someone tries to fill what they perceive as another's lack of love, believing that something is missing in them. They see this hole or missing piece in the other because the other is always a reflective mirror of what they may not see in themselves. Or they are inadvertently attempting to fill a perceived missing piece from the past in their current relationship.

"Giving the other person what I perceive they need will ultimately provide me with what I think I need that I didn't get in my original 'family of origin' relationship." For instance, "I will give them the love and caring that they perceive their father never gave them, and in return, they will provide me with love and caring that I perceive my mother never gave me." A special relationship is like a prison because I need to give this love in a certain way as an unspoken bargain for them to provide me with what I think I need. As a simple example of this, it can be a symbolic gesture, like bringing a specific organic dark-roasted coffee to me in bed every morning with coconut milk and raw honey, all stirred together and presented on a colorful tray with a scented flower. What a beautiful and caring gesture and a wonderful way to start my every day. If the partner neglects to bring this coffee for a day or two and maybe a third day in a row, I may think, "Something or someone else must be more important than me, or maybe he doesn't value me in the same way. What is really going on?" The ego-mind is going crazy now, going in circles, trying to figure it out. I'm preparing in my mind a defense or worst-case scenario, an exit strategy, in reaction to this perceived withdrawal of my partner's love.

Since these symbolic demonstrations of love are, for the most part, unspoken exchanges, we may feel some fear about asking our partner, "What's going on? Why didn't I get the coffee the past three days?" because we are uncertain of what the answer might be. Still, we wonder, "Why the withdrawal of such a devotional act of kindness and caring?" This craziness can be the same ego illusion that demonstrates a lack of reciprocation of love, "I'm taking care of you in the way that your mother didn't show or do." What he may get back in return for his act of kindness is a specific type of ego exchange, perhaps his favorite dinner, a back rub, or a foot rub later in the evening. If, for any reason, either party fails to do the act that demonstrates this feeling of the entirety of love and caring, then the whole relationship could topple very quickly. One person could withdraw emotionally and separate themselves from the other in their mind. The lack of this precise exchange of devotional proof means that one or both parties may interpret that the love has vanished. Then they may both be prepared to leave the relationship immediately in their minds and hearts, cutting themselves off from each other by going numb or emotionally distancing. When they feel they are not loved or cared about anymore in the way they depended on, inner pacts are made in defiance, declaring independence and autonomy. One partner or both believe that they no longer need the other person or anyone else for that matter. No one will fool them into thinking that the other one or anyone still loves them. The ego is on hyper-alert, activated to win this perceived power game. "I will need you less than you will need me." One person believes the relationship is over, and they need to arrange an exit strategy to move on.

Often, people are afraid to talk to the other partner and ask what they are feeling, believing, and thinking. And why the special coffee stopped appearing. Without completion and closure through understanding what happened, both of them could be in fear and project the worst-case separation scenario as its conclusion.

Then they would both leave with their fearful interpretations. Falling into a circular, downward cycle, both partners can believe that they are unlovable and unwanted and that the other is rejecting them and withdrawing from the relationship. If either or both partners took the risk of addressing the situation, they could discover that both were making significant assumptions about the other that are not true. Even when you are afraid of what the other might say, it is crucial to check out the reality of the situation by fully communicating in a vulnerable way. "I think that you have withdrawn from me and maybe found someone else, and that's why you no longer bring me the special coffee in bed when I wake up. It's been two days without this important symbolic demonstration of love. So that's why I didn't cook your dinner, and I wasn't home when you returned." In this way, the ego gets revenge when there is no clear communication.

The dynamic of this special relationship was demonstrated in February 2021 on *The Bachelor* reality television show (in the US) when Matt James refused to disclose his reasons for not choosing to marry the second runner-up named Michelle. She wanted just a few minutes of his time for an explanation from him and to be able to share her feelings about not being chosen. The alternative was to leave with her perceived rejection and confusion, not understanding what had happened between them. Matt rejecting her was completely unexpected. She and the television audience thought he would select her after going through the show for seven weeks believing she was his most significant love relationship and connection. He had thirty women to choose from at the beginning of the show. When it was down to choosing between Michelle and one other woman, in the end, he decided not to marry either of them. He chose the other woman to continue having a relationship with after the show. In mere seconds, it was all over for Michelle and Matt with no explanation from him, which devasted Michelle after she had set up her expectations that she would be his fiancé at the end of the show.

Usually, at the end of the series, the woman who is not chosen leaves immediately that evening for the airport in a limousine to go home. For Michelle, since she was already married to Matt in her mind's eye, it was an abrupt and shocking change from her perceived reality that he would propose to her and she would be engaged that night at the end of the show. So, she stayed overnight to communicate with Matt the following morning before leaving for the airport because she felt so incomplete with confusion, despair, loss, and rejection. However, my impression is that he refused to meet with her out of his sense of guilt. Therefore, he declined to listen to what she had to say, talk about their relationship, or say why he chose the other woman over her. He probably didn't even know what he felt, why he didn't choose her or what to say, so it was easier for him to disconnect and cut off all communication. Some unconscious drive or "special feeling" pushed him to choose the other woman. He had no rational explanation for it that he wanted to share.

As in the two examples of the coffee not showing up in the morning and Matt not choosing Michele as his life partner, we can see how no one wins or gets their true needs met in the power-control ego game. Instead, it creates a more perceived separation. Each of these scenarios is an opportunity to clear our fears, doubts, and projections that we are separate, unworthy, or unlovable.

WHY DO WE KEEP PLAYING EGO GAMES?

If we can see so clearly that playing and engaging in these ego games makes our lives miserable, creating more disharmony and separation, why do we continue to play them, and how can we stop them from running our lives? Our experiences reveal that people's ego games are habitual and not conscious. Some people play ego games to keep others at a distance to avoid feeling hurt, while others play them unconsciously because they fear intimacy and real love. Most people feel uncomfortable revealing their true selves to others before they establish a safe level of trust within themselves. When they have cleared enough, they no longer base their safety on what other people do or don't do.

The Clearing Process allows one to get real, get in touch with the underlying meaning behind the words, actions, or reactions, and go deeper. By being vulnerable, helping to discover one's ego truth, and ultimately the Big T Truth, they can return to Innocence. If we want to create healthy relationships, we must be courageous enough to become aware of the ego games we are playing. Then, we can choose to give up playing unhealthy ego games and get real with how we feel and communicate with ourselves and each other. When you become aware of the many ego games you play, you can disrupt them whenever you notice the ego appear. By clearing your thoughts, feelings, and beliefs that no longer serve you with any current issue, situation, or person, your relationships will take on a new level of intimacy, flourishing with each new awareness.

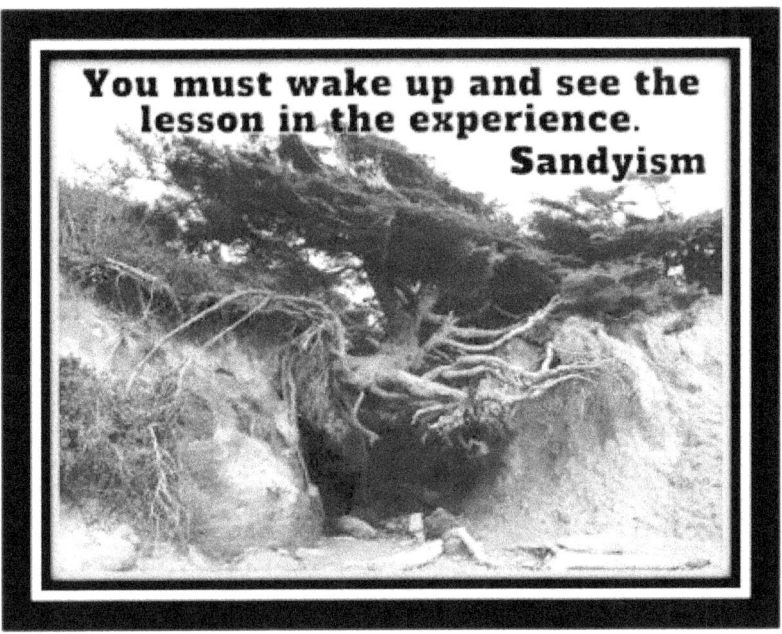

Are you feeling a little scared? Do you feel threatened by the idea that you could clear all separation in your life from within yourself, with everyone else, and even with God? Sometimes the idea of being free, open, and transparent can be scary to the ego-mind that has been protecting us our whole lives from feelings of guilt, shame, judgment, and unworthiness. When we come to this place, we will have an immense emptiness, so we will want to fill it with something. However, we can only attend to that space with Big T Truth, as in Source energy, Peace energy, and God energy. Otherwise, filling this space with anything else would take us back to the negative illusion we just cleared or released. Sometimes our ego will make up a story after getting to this clear space that we can now buy the house or the car or take the trip of our dreams, convincing us that this action will make us even happier. If we participate in any of these activities, we will realize that none of these things are "it" or the things we truly desire. Once we have played out these ego illusions, we will recognize we already have "it." In truth, we realize the only things worth attaining are true Peace, true Love, and true Joy.

OUR DEEPEST FEAR

by Marianne Williamson

A Return to Love:
Reflections on the Principles of A Course in Miracles

"Our deepest fear is not that we are inadequate.
Our deepest fear is that we are powerful beyond measure.
It is our light, not our darkness, that most frightens us.
We ask ourselves, 'Who am I to be brilliant, gorgeous, handsome,
talented and fabulous?' Actually, who are you not to be?
You are a child of God. Your playing small does not serve the world.
There is nothing enlightened about shrinking so that other
people won't feel insecure around you.

We are all meant to shine, as children do.
We were born to make manifest the glory of God within us.
It is not just in some; it is in everyone.
And, as we let our own light shine, we consciously give
other people permission to do the same.
As we are liberated from our fear,
our presence automatically liberates others."

CHAPTER 5

RELATIONSHIPS

Reveal Patterns

For decades, I have examined people's relationships and helped them figure out their patterns. My goal has been to see how we construct our reality, dance the same dance, and repeatedly engage in the same non-productive patterns (circles). We seem to make the same choice to avoid the lesson. I have looked into this phenomenon, learning how to guide the circle "owners" to arrive at the lesson's main point. If you look closely at your life, you'll see that these patterns can be subtle or obvious. Sometimes, we think we've overcome a pattern only to see it pop up elsewhere. We will repeat the same patterns until we dive deep down and truly forgive ourselves and others. Only through complete forgiveness will we truly understand the whole process, as the ACIM book states. (ACIM, T-15.VIII.1:2-7)

Our most influential teachers on this journey of awakening are the people closest to us, and they can present us with many opportunities for us to clear. ACIM says we will always meet the ones we are meant to meet, and together we have the potential to create the teaching-learning situation known as a holy relationship. (ACIM M-3.2:4) Therefore, every person we meet is on purpose; it is always about healing some aspect of ourselves, even when we don't consciously know the aspect of healing or purpose. These meetings can be brief seconds, minutes, or hours. They may last for a sustained time or become a longer-life relationship and partnership. ACIM refers to these holy relationship encounters.

I remember how, several times when I was on a trip, I would encounter the same person, at the airport, on a train, or in a restaurant. I am in a waiting area and notice three people stand out to me. Then I will meet them on the plane, find myself standing next to them, or meet them again in the washroom. I make it a point to talk with anyone who repeatedly appears in my path this way. They will also recognize that we have met many times that day, yet they seem less willing to bring it up and initiate speaking with me. Even though the purpose is not apparent, I join with them, whether it's a long or short moment. I know they are meant to cross my path. It is not a mistake. We are destined to meet for joining and healing purposes. I include the telemarketers who call me. There are no accidents as to who is calling or why. Everyone is on purpose to our meeting, which is why, in 1980, I chose the name for my company to be *On Purpose*. Before that time, it was rare to hear anyone talk about purpose. Ever since I was a child, I have understood that my life is either on purpose or off purpose.

The Movie Called *Your Life*

Everything you see happening before you in this movie called *Your Life* is what you think, feel, and believe yourself to be, what you can have, what you can earn, and where you can live. Many things often need to happen before a person is ready to accept their highest vision to manifest in their life. In experiencing a strong ego feeling, we perceive these limiting beliefs as facts instead of temporary feelings that can often instantly change when we change our minds. We all have a unique worldview that is very specific to our movie, and our thoughts, feelings, and beliefs influence what is possible to occur in our movie. The mind is powerful, so be mindful of what you feed it with your thoughts and what feelings you focus on because that is how you manifest your reality and experience.

The world is a school. To know Who We Really Are, we must take every aspect of ourselves that we thought was guilty and wrong—thought, feeling, belief, or action—and bring it back to one hundred percent innocence and total forgiveness. We also must take everyone we encounter—all of their actions, thoughts, feelings, and beliefs—back to Innocence. Every single one. Every single aspect. We do not grow: we awaken to who we truly are. In other words,

I Am That I Am. We—all of us—are this Truth: I Am That I Am, Eternal Love, Peace, Joy, Totality, Infinity. We don't need to grow; we need to wake up to who we truly are.

As a student of ACIM, I know that I am in complete Love, Peace, and Joy, or I have something to clear. And, of course, I still have my "normal" life to live. Everyone has their ego stories, egoic patterns, and lessons they came to this planet to address. I have yet to meet anyone who doesn't have something to work out or release. I have been observing my patterns for many years and releasing them. They come up, and I see them. Healing myself and attending to the healing of others is an ongoing process.

The ACIM Manual for Teachers: *This is a manual for the teachers of God. They are not perfect, or they would not be here. Yet it is their mission to become perfect here, and so they teach perfection over and over, in many, many ways, until they have learned it. And then they are seen no more, although their thoughts remain a source of strength and truth forever.* (ACIM, M-in.5:4-7)

Holy Relationship and Special Relationship

The holy relationship and the "special relationship" are terms and definitions from *A Course in Miracles,* and they are as different as night is from the day.

ACIM characterizes a special relationship as one that creates separation. The perspective is, "I think there is something wrong with me; therefore, I think there is something wrong with you. So, I'm going to fix you to make our relationship better." It's all about trying to fulfill my perception of the other person's lack of love or "hole." At its core, the special relationship is an unspoken bargaining process—you give me what I think I need, and I'll give you what you think you need. This dynamic is why we may feel trapped when we become so enmeshed in needing someone else to falsely fulfill us with a "relationship fix," like a drug hit.

Meanwhile, the holy relationship is a teaching-learning situation with the teacher and learner joined as one team. While the holy relationship is a commitment, it is not necessarily a sexual and cohabitating situation. Once a relationship involves sex and romance, each partner becomes more vulnerable, offering the opportunity of more egoic beliefs from childhood experiences to surface.

"If we were living *A Course in Miracles,* we'd stop looking for the sexier, richer, more famous, more powerful, or more intellectual partner who would enhance our image. We would know that we could love any person. We'd have to choose which one. We always get the one with the next lesson we are to learn. We can pick them out in a room full of a hundred people because we will notice them and be drawn to that one."

It can be challenging for some people to grasp the difference between the special relationship and the holy relationship. Most people have special relationships that they could transform into holy relationships. The Big T Truth for people who want to wake up now is that they could feel fulfilled with anyone because we're all spiritually the same, yet we all have different lessons we are learning. Therefore, we will choose a particular person even though it's not apparent what the lessons are because that attraction to them is unconscious. The lesson we will learn with this person can be primarily unconscious. At times, our judgments, perceptions, fear, and guilt also stop us from choosing certain people as partners. The truth is that we are only attracted to someone with lessons complementary to our lessons. And these lessons could involve guilt or forbidden attraction, as evidenced by this trilogy and three movies based on *Fifty Shades of Grey*. I call this material the attraction of guilt and the excitement and fear of sexual surrender with a safe partner.

The holy relationship creates joining and oneness. In it, each partner acknowledges that they have nothing missing, so they are whole and complete and therefore do not "need" anything from each other or anyone else. Consequently, they see no lack in themselves or their partner. They think, "I am completely who I am in my love, and I see the same over there." In a holy relationship, people know they are innocent. They see themselves and their partner as perfect in who they each are. To live in this way, two people agree to have a joint purpose: to release their negative past and perceived guilt and live in the present in one hundred percent love. It must be a purpose they both want, and in so choosing, they recognize how they enhance their lives by committing to the synergistic collaboration of purpose with each other.

We are never committed to the body of a person. We are only committed to the purpose we have together with that person. Purpose and joint intentions go on forever. Therefore, we are not committed to joining with them as an ego body or personality. Instead, we commit to something much more significant than this world, which is a commitment for eternity. The True purpose that we joined in together creates our aligned synergy. Holy relationships are about purpose and intention. Eventually, we will each and together transition into a spiritual realm of Big T state of joining from emotional states of fear and upset.

For example, if you and I have the purpose of making an herb garden together, we enter into a spiritually ecstatic state through the appreciation of the herbs. We will go through many projections in actualizing the garden in agreeing on textures and smells. There will be points when we may want to walk away, separate, and give up on our joint purpose. Our egos may convince us that it's hopeless because our differences are so vast that we will never be able to join and complete the original purpose. No matter what earthly purpose we join in, whether creating an herb garden or releasing our fear and guilt in a relationship, we will let go of emotional baggage and past projections of other relationships.

By remaining faithful to our purpose, trusting each other at higher levels, and recommitting to our intention and purpose several times, we will eventually arrive at divinity and realize that the journey is as important as the destination.

These holy relationships are a commitment of two whole beings in equal partnership coming from equal joining. We are together because we want to be together, not because we need or have to be together to survive. We are joined because we recognize and acknowledge that we are infinitely enhanced by our relationship, union, and by joining in purpose. We love working together on our purpose; it is exhilarating, uplifting, and enhances our full self-expression.

Veils of judgments, blame, and patterns make it challenging, if not impossible, to maintain any relationship that requires us to be with each other in Truth. Clearing is the essence of the process that allows us to shed the many veils we've superimposed on our true selves.

The Special Relationship

A special relationship is when you try to fulfill someone's perceived lack of love by giving them something "special" you think they need to be happy or fulfilled. In general, you are meeting this need with unsaid bargains, expecting them to fill this missing hole with something you think you need. This trap will hold both of you in each of your perceived needs. When you realize that meeting these expectations is unnecessary, that each party is whole and complete in their self-expression (the expression of God within and who they are), you understand that only you can fill your imaginary hole or lack therein. If someone else were filling this hole or missing piece, they would be making it real and colluding with you in the belief that something was missing or wrong with you, so you need something from someone else to fix it. You and this person would no longer be free to choose to be yourselves because you would have a mutual need for each other in what you both may feel the other is missing. Needing to meet this expectation or condition of each other would entrap both of you in prison, filling each other's perceived lack of love. At first, you would be very attached, and in the end, this special attraction could turn into special hate because you would no longer feel free.

Fears, anxieties, and limitations are not facts (Big T Truth); they are little t truths or temporary truths. Most people seek to find their match for partnership in someone who will bring them into their "perfect state" or their "true nature"—whether being more fun, more spiritual, or more available to communicate. These expectations of the other person can create a "special relationship" and so can only lead to disappointment. In truth, the only thing we need another person for is to help remind us of who we are when we get stuck in our ego feelings and believe them to be true. We can even become trapped in these ego-driven fears, guilts, and beliefs when they become our reality. Without that other person, we may start to believe this ego and its pain-related feelings as the truth. This partner can be there to help remind us of who we are by holding space for us to clear and return to our true nature: Love, Peace, and Joy. Our function for each other in the relationship is to remind us we are diamonds, whole, perfect, and complete, no matter what we are going through and no matter what negative story or scenario we are making up.

The Holy Relationship

Thirty years ago, I purposely created *The Holy Relationship* course to live this experience in a supportive atmosphere (a beautiful location with nothing else going on around us) with the support from other participants and their coaches. This course was organized in Hawaii, Denmark, Sweden, and Canada and lasted two to three weeks. With the commitments in people's lives, I shortened it to ten days, then a week, and finally to a weekend. For single people in the long sessions, they each met a new partner. They lived in the same room as this person and sometimes even in the same bed.

The purpose of this holy relationship partner is to clear the negative belief systems, traumas, and projections from the past, using this partner as a reflection of prior partners. In essence, we need another person always to reconfirm our innocence and that we are loved in our true nature, no matter what we feel, think, or believe. The source of this reflection can be what occurred in past relationships. Of course, when our ego pain of the past triggers us, we test this reflection. Most of us get extremely triggered by the idea of betrayal or someone loving another person as much or more than they love us. We can quickly go into this ego jealousy by wanting to own and possess our holy relationship partner to feel less threatened by loss.

In observing couples who were part of my courses over many years, I have seen a few of them test out this situation. One person in their relationship cleared his egoic pain of someone betraying him sexually. He could forgive and return to total Peace and union with his partner, staying joined and releasing all threats of separation and abandonment. He told me he could allow himself and his partner to explore other relationships and then return to one another because he knew they were all Love and were all One. He recognized that no amount of Love could be taken from them in Truth, ever. This process can take several hours or days to come to the Big T Truth for each person to be fully released from their egoic pain of being hurt, abandoned, betrayed, or attacked. Each person will always re-confirm their Big T Truth in the final step (Step 3) of *The Clearing Process,* when they consciously reiterate that they are Love, Peace, and Joy.

I have used *The Clearing Process* to help others for over four decades and witnessed about twenty couples arrive at this level of Enlightenment and Truth. Even after twenty or thirty years, these life partners are still together, all remaining in their original relationships. The process of the holy relationship, which is experiential, only works by having no private thoughts and a willingness to share out loud all egoic thoughts. This complete mutual transparency translates into living with authenticity within yourself and with your holy relationship partner. Please see Appendix C.

For example, when we did *The Holy Relationship* training for three weeks in 2000, one of them took place in Bornholm, Denmark, a beautiful vacation spot. In advance of the training, I always pre-match the singles who will be partners for the three weeks based on their writings ahead of time for their purpose, mission, vision, life lessons, and relationship patterns. I matched a man and woman, both from Sweden, before I met them and before they met each other, who both turned out to be very tall, both over 6 foot 1, and almost an exact mirror of each other, with fair hair, fair skin, and blue eyes.

Before pre-matched pairs enter their sleeping quarters, they meet in the training room, where we have introductions. I told this Swedish pair they would be partners in the holy relationship process, which is emotional-spiritual, not physical, so they would not be engaging in sexual activity. After that, they each came to me separately during the lunch break to tell me they could not be the other's partner since they did not find each other attractive. They even saw the other as repulsive, so they could not possibly sleep in the same bed because the other person did not turn them on. Again, I told them it's not a sexual process in any way—it's about personal healing in their thoughts, feelings, and beliefs about themselves and in relationships with others. Ultimately, they had to forgive every thought, feeling, and belief they held against themselves to find inner peace. For example, not desirable, not good enough, not wanted, or not chosen by anyone.

After two weeks, they had been sleeping in the same bed and, during the days, doing all the clearings together of clearing and forgiving negative projections. It became evident in the training room that they had come to see each other as exact mirrors.

I matched them because neither had been in a relationship with anyone (both virgins, not even a kiss or dating), and that's why they were attending *The Holy Relationship* training. They each wanted an answer and a breakthrough to have a partner. Initially, I had seen them physically as mirrors; however, they didn't understand until they learned about mirror projection.

In the third week of the training, they came to me separately to tell me they had fallen in love and wanted to be married when we did the beach ceremony and the banquet for the finale. The woman said she only needed one thing: Could she ask my ten-year-old daughter to be her flower girl and go shopping for her dress and hat, the whole outfit? I said, "Of course, if she wants to do it since it's her own choice."

My daughter chose to go shopping with the woman, and when they were together in the dressing room, she told the woman, "Your dress is beautiful, my mother would love it, but you have to get new underwear; you can't have holes in it on your wedding day. It has to be new. 'What you look like underneath has to match what you have outside, and it's all about a reflection of how you see yourself,' is what my mother would say."

They married on the beach, had children, and are still together.

I know one couple who initially met about 25 years ago in my *Art of Surrender* training program. They became a couple and chose to do the entire holy relationship process. Over the next 20 years, they freed themselves of guilt, traumas, and conflict in past relationships. They called upon me during those 20 years to ensure they stayed on course and made it through the process. I married them in a holy relationship ceremony in Spain five years ago, witnessed by all their friends and family. Their wedding symbolized graduation of coming to a place of pure peace, love, and union; the final goal of the holy relationship being holiness. They emerged as teachers of what they learned and knew the value gained from their journey together. During the 20-year process of releasing ego, all physical ailments that had plagued them disappeared. They always were extraordinary beings, and now they have even more clarity and awareness to share with everyone they meet.

Among the most magical moments of my life has been creating and officiating a personalized wedding ceremony for seven couples to match their healing and matrimonial journey, unique for them. The ceremony takes almost two hours to experience and fulfills all aspects of the ritual of coming together in wholeness, love, and innocence. I have recorded in my mind the journey to create each couple's process in coming together in total unity and matrimony.

So far, I created the wedding ceremony only for those who have been my students and who I have known for years. Being part of their therapeutic team, I had coached them through the challenging times when they thought they might want to leave the relationship.

Many couples have told me that they wouldn't have been married for these many years except for me because I never lost faith in their purpose and holy relationship commitment in coming together in the first place.

Making the Holy Relationship Real: Living in a Healing Partnership

Some people might find it challenging to live *A Course in Miracles* (ACIM) and translate the philosophy and principles into the actual living in this world. Studying the Course is very different from living it. An exchange with my friend (I'll call her Linda), who had studied *A Course in Miracles* night and day for seven years, inspired me to tell this next story.

Linda picked me up for our weekly ACIM class. We spoke about our holy relationship. We were two people joined in a truly common purpose and felt excited about working together as each other's teacher and student equally, a full circle without hierarchy.

I remarked in our conversation that I could be in a holy relationship with anyone and spend the night sleeping non-sexually next to any person. Linda didn't believe that was possible and thought I couldn't do it; she thought I would judge the person as not good enough. I persisted and told her that I could do it. She pointed out a man in the Miracles group and said, "I bet you can't be that man's holy relationship partner. You couldn't spend a night in the same bed with him." This friend picked out that specific man as a deal-breaker because she didn't consider him handsome, engaging, or intelligent enough for her or me. Her judgment showed me what Linda thought of herself since we only judge others in how we see ourselves. When we believe we're not good enough, we will find the same "flaw" in others and project it onto them even at the subtlest levels.

I told her I could be in a holy relationship and spend the night sleeping non-sexually next to this man she had pointed out. I had known him for some time and felt familiar with his feelings, thoughts, beliefs, and understanding of *A Course in Miracles*. Therefore, I trusted him to be safe and understand the purpose of our process of sleeping non-sexually in the same bed. Of course, it would be after I had a chance to speak with him and learn that our energy was aligned with synergy. It would not be about his looks, intelligence, or status in the world, whether I would choose him. As it turned out, it didn't work out for me to sleep with that man, however, over the years I have done this holy relationship communication process with other people, sleeping in the same bed together.

We picked out-of-the-way idyllic paradises, one with only bicycles (the island of Bornholm, Denmark's vacation spot), so we could focus intensely on the process with no outer distractions of the modern world. During *The Holy Relationship* program, I've asked many pairs who have met for the first time to sleep in the same room and same bed, and it's always been a profound learning experience. If these people were already in relationships the danger would be real that they could fall in love with the new person and leave their current partner. Once in my lengthy coaching career, I took a couple already in a committed relationship and matched them each with new partners for the process. They both fell in love with their assigned partners. Then, they returned to their original relationship with their lessons as reference points about what was possible and opened to their life partners in a new way.

How to Create a Holy Relationship

The holy relationship is a healing partnership based upon authentic, one hundred percent Truth in communicating with each other in a fully aligned conscious purpose or joint intention. Both people are safe, held, and fully seen as one hundred percent Innocent in a holy relationship.

No matter what they tell each other in their sharings, this other person will always hold the space of your innocence even if you think, feel, or believe you are guilty. They are holding the space of Big T Truth for you always. Even when you have forgotten, they remind you of your Innocence, Love, Peace, Joy, and freedom, even when you think otherwise about yourself. This constant remembrance of who you truly are when you forget is one of the main functions of the other person who is your holy relationship partner. To be a holy relationship, both people must, in some knowledge and truth, know themselves as whole, complete, lacking nothing, and that everything exists divinely within.

In this relationship, *in each the other saw a perfect shelter where his Self could be reborn in safety and in peace.* (ACIM, T-22.I.8:7)

True love arises from the heart as a holy relationship based on Truth. You recognize each other as divine beings. You are not in this relationship to fulfill a perceived lack; you understand you have everything you need within you already. By releasing your negative beliefs about yourself and the other, you can see each other's infinite perfection and become spiritually one.

The Keys to Creating a Holy Relationship

- You have each looked within and know there is no lack; you are both fully whole and complete
- You see each other as a divine being
- You have a mutual purpose together that you wholeheartedly share
- You are each other's student and teacher; in a constant flow of learning and teaching
- Walking together in purpose, you surrender your relationship to Spirit's guidance
- You wholeheartedly love working together
- You are always awake and present with your partner to remind them of who they really are when they forget and believe they are their ego
- Your intention is always to go in the direction of love and healing

A holy relationship is a sacred meeting of two souls, forever extending into eternity.

So, no matter what crazy story, fantasy, admission of a past incident, or an attraction your partner may relate to you, your job in a holy relationship with them is to affirm their true perfection and innocence. The purpose is to release them from the guilt of these past experiences. In this adventure and journey into the unknown of one's vast, egoic mind, the holy relationship process can be the most exciting and fulfilling part of someone's life.

When you practice the holy relationship, you agree to clear whatever barriers and hindrances stand between you and remember Who You Really Are in True Love. *A Course in Miracles* says the Course aims *at removing the blocks to the awareness of love's presence,* our natural inheritance. (ACIM T-in.1:7) In a holy relationship, your job is to support your partner in going all the way toward discovering who they truly are and what is Real and True in every situation. And what is Real, of course, is Eternal Love.

Many of us attempt to separate from those who disturb us, including "Un-friending" on Facebook, not dating them anymore, leaving and then sending them a "Goodbye!" text, or even ignoring them altogether. This approach will never work because we will always meet these same projections again in another person, thus experiencing the same predicament. The only sure way to complete the relationship is by coming to Love and forgiveness. This process can take days or weeks to work through this egoic pain for you and your partner, and it is worth it. This completion can even be done with only one person participating. Only then can we be free of pain from this relationship. Then, we can genuinely release this person and this relationship, and they can also release us.

Sometimes, once we have completed a series of learnings with someone, it is time to move on to the next series of lessons with the next relationship. We recognize we have done what we came here to do and go to the next partnership for the next stage of our development. We can only know if we complete these teachings from our True Self, not from our ego, which is the common denominator in every relationship where we are involved.

The other person cannot make us suffer. This suffering or pain comes from our perception. Therefore, the only option is to HEAL, which is to make whole the separation we feel with our brothers and sisters everywhere, both near and far, so we may see and know that we are One with them.

During *The Clearing Process*, you will have the opportunity to see who the other person in your current relationship represents from your past (which could even be yourself) and release the original pain from your family of origin (i.e., fear, disappointment, unworthiness). You will then have cleared any feelings of alienation, anger, rage, or guilt toward yourself and this person. In *The Clearing Process*, you will turn hate into Love and separation into joining and change the deadness of the relationship into it being alive once more. Therefore, you can bring to life the following words from *A Course in Miracles*:

> *In each the other saw a perfect shelter where his Self could be reborn in safety and in peace.* (T-22.I.9)

Many types of clearings could be necessary to get to this awakened state of mind. After each clearing, you will experience a new feeling of peace, relief, love, understanding, and compassion. It will be like taking a great breath of fresh air, also known as "space within." I love to clear myself or someone else, holding the space for them as they release their negative energy and emotional pain, allowing them to see and know the Big T Truth.

Family

Over the past forty years, I have had the opportunity to do four training sessions on *The Art of Joining a Family* with four generations of a family. In all sessions, each member cleared all of their projections, blame, and judgments with every other family member. It took many hours over three days to listen to each person's egoic feelings, thoughts, and beliefs. Each family pair had their own personal coach during their family clearing. The form of the statements we asked them to use often began with "What I want you to know is" because it is straightforward. Sometimes I changed the wording to "What I don't want you to know," "What I don't want to state or acknowledge," or "What I feel afraid to tell you." These are plain statements that the person cannot misconstrue. By making these clear, precise, and definitive statements, the person declares responsibility for having these feelings. The ego hates form and structure because it prefers continuous circles, also known as a repetitive cycle. The ego dislikes saying anything specific because that would mean taking responsibility for our egoic thoughts, feelings, and communications. We fear that people will judge us.

During the family training, when they finally heard what each person felt and thought, I observed through their comments that they had been minimally communicating with each other on important subjects. I often had to ask the person to clarify what they were saying because it was vague and ambiguous. They would not commit themselves to what they said. Also, I would often halt the person's statement and ask the listener to repeat what they heard to see if they were listening. These people lived in the same house for years and never really said anything in total communication. Therefore, the relationships did not have complete love and joining because they were only *present* on the surface.

One of the most complex themes I also clear is the "Will" theme; who got what in the inheritance and why they got it. Powerful feelings such as betrayal and abandonment arise when a person thinks they didn't get what they deserved in the final act of their family member's death. I cannot tell you how many fights I have watched when people are in conflict over thousands of dollars and end up spending it all on lawyer's fees to settle it and feel that they are right. Instead, family members could have handled this "Will" betrayal by *clearing* and communicating every misinterpretation they had about each other, thus coming to complete forgiveness. If they did the clearings with a clearing coach or life coach, they would feel much more fulfillment, oneness, and joining.

I have a client who fought for years over the money her mother left for her and her sister. After five years and hundreds of hours of attack and defense, there was only about $3,000 left, and she still hadn't fully communicated with her sister, which prevented them from joining. As well as the inheritance disappearing in the conflict, she lost her sister to estrangement, so she always complained that she had no sister. One time, I went with her to a remote area of Canada looking for her sister; she hoped to share with her sister finally. We arrived at a house with a fortress around it. We had a cake with us in the car. She believed her sister wouldn't receive her, demonstrating her fear of wholly communicating. She had to have guilt about something in the relationship with her sister to be willing to travel and be that close and stop and not go for it when she likely had the opportunity. She made it about her sister's unwillingness when it was really about her own fear of being rejected. By then, many of her other family members had already abandoned her.

I had another family situation with the husband and his first wife and second wife, and two children (as the father of one with each wife). When he was in the process of dying, the man was updating his Will and asked his first wife what she wanted after their marriage of twenty years. She said, "I don't need anything." At that moment, however, with him being ill, she was not clear with him or herself about what she wanted, which was the rights to the film projects he had created during the years when they were together. Soon after he died, his first wife began fighting with the second wife over possessions, money, and those film rights. While he was alive, his children were closely bonded, and later, their mothers, in their conflict, turned the children against each other. The children believed they needed to be at odds to support their mothers. As a result, they experienced loss and estrangement from their only sibling because their mothers continued fighting with each other to be right.

Getting Divorced?

If you are getting divorced, the only danger of taking one of my clearing courses, like *The Art of Surrender*, is you might want to get back together with your original partner. This situation is especially challenging if you have married a new person or are in a relationship with a new boyfriend or girlfriend. I have seen people divorced for over twenty years come back together once they held the space for their former partner with the help of a coach and cleared themselves of their perceived guilt. After completing the formalized *clearing* processes in *The Art of Surrender*, the reunited couples explain the Truth (see Big T, little t chart in Chapter 6) to their new partners. Together with a coach (usually me), they did these clearing sessions, and the new partner made the formal and free choice between their current and former relationship. I felt privileged to be present and to witness the experience of this space of Love in total oneness, peace, vulnerability, and full communication.

As a relationship coach and counselor, the fear of fully communicating with each other is especially evident when working with couples going through a divorce and legal battles. They so strongly fear being misinterpreted that they would hire an expensive lawyer to do what they could rather than communicate between themselves. They are terrified of what the other person would say, afraid they would infer they are guilty of doing something wrong in the relationship. In other words, they perceive themselves as guilty, as though they had "done something wrong," simply because the relationship is ending in divorce. This fear comes from their belief there is something wrong with *them*. They fear communicating; they believe that no one will listen, no one cares, and the other person will never receive them. They have given up on communication as the means to solve anything between them. They believe they tried in the past and got nowhere. They feel they failed because they didn't have a trained facilitator to assist them in communicating deeply and totally. They never said what they really felt or meant. They realize they have never even come close to it. They have been going around in circles within themselves and with their partner because they fear that the other person would think they are guilty, bad, and wrong. They are punishing themselves by not being willing to communicate everything, even with the assistance of a trained facilitator.

Some of these legal divorces cost more than $100,000. Yet, in just ten hours of clearing and communicating, we fully took these relationships to Peace and Love. In *The Clearing Process,* participants forgave each other and themselves for the interpretation they thought the other had about them and realized it was what they felt about themselves. This awareness gave each person a lot of peace and much-needed relief, understanding, fulfillment, and compassion. They solved their financial conflict in a matter of hours instead of years of going back and forth about what each person wanted and what the other one didn't want to give them.

One of my greatest joys in life is when parties fully communicate and realize there is nothing and never was anything to be upset about—nothing to forgive—it was all one big misperception and misunderstanding of what the other person meant, said, or did. No one can do what you are not willing to do for yourself, especially in the world of communication. In any upset or misinterpretation, I can ask myself, "Have I said everything here that I need to say with nothing left out?" This review includes what I think happened, my reactions, what it meant to me, and all my perceptions and interpretations of the situation.

More than thirty years ago, I enjoyed working with Ralph Baker, one of my clients. He was known as the Love Lawyer. He wrote a book, and in it, he said,

> "I will only do your divorce if you can fully tell me with truth that you love your partner, tell me all about the process of originally falling in love with your partner, and come back to full love with them, as you were at the beginning of the relationship. I call this total and unconditional love *Agape* love."

Of course, I thought this idea was brilliant; they *must* be complete by returning to their original love, including releasing feelings of abandonment and betrayal before their divorce or "parting of ways." Ralph then said:

> "If you don't want to go through this process with me, my legal business partner will give you a divorce, and you may never actually be complete with this relationship. You may be going over what you could've, would've, and should've said, for many years to come. If you don't want to go through the process of whatever is in the way of returning to love with this person, you will get this fast divorce legally on paper, but you will never actually be divorced. This choice is yours alone to make."

It takes owning great responsibility for your life to clear what is in the way of truly loving yourself and the other person again. Some people may think this involves too much effort or pain or is impossible to do. Therefore, we need a coach or mentor to guide us through the process without getting stuck in our ego-mind. If we could have done this process independently, we would have already done it.

Let me repeat: If we could have done it ourselves, we wouldn't need to seek help outside ourselves from a life coach or counselor.

I once helped two doctors, married and now separated, who had been working on settling their divorce for over four years. They could not, and would not, agree with each other on anything. Finally, after nearly three hours of clearing and proper communication, they solved their settlement in only fifteen minutes. Both doctors were relieved and amazed at how easy it could have been if only they had learned to clear and more fully communicate with one another earlier. Both were grateful for *The Clearing Process* and its accompanying philosophy, giving them so much space and peace with one another and their children.

There is No Divorce!

ACIM views the route to Peace as more productive with two people who will trigger each other into seeing what needs to be released and heal much faster. This two-ness, or holy relationship, is where each has come to teach and learn from the other.

> *Each teaching-learning situation is maximal in the sense that each person involved will learn the most that he can from the other person at that time.* (ACIM, M-3.4:1)

This two-ness is the fastest way to remember who you truly are. At moments, the holy relationship can feel scary because you are stripping naked your emotional self and becoming transparent by sharing all of your private thoughts. The other person's function will be to hold space for you and affirm you as perfect, whole, complete, and innocent, no matter what you say or have ever done. This experience can be challenging because your ego will want your partner to see you as your ego sees you—The Guilty One—so you may do and say things to demonstrate your guilt. You may also give out the energy that you are guilty and pull this energy toward you as you may have done all of your life to this point. Therefore, feeling guilty is more familiar than accepting yourself as perfect, whole, complete, and innocent.

The common purpose committed to by those joined together in a holy relationship exists in eternity. We can change our relationship by removing the husband or wife role through a divorce, but the common purpose you committed to remains forever. In the final analysis, the commitment to that purpose will always create love, joining, and peace. When you're working together on the meaning of the relationship, you will eventually meet in this authentic joining, no matter how many years it may take. The only way we can release a person from our ego-mind, so we don't entangle ourselves in the energetics of that relationship, is to come to total Love and join together at our essence.

Of course, we can divorce the person, but we never seem to release the burden of our addiction to thinking about what wasn't complete in the relationship. I have met people who still talk about their ex-husband or ex-wife, who they divorced thirty-plus years ago, as if they were still married to that person. They have never moved on or even created a new relationship because there is no space for anyone else. They are stuck in their old relationship while at the same time denying every new connection. They are still carrying the negative parts of the experience in their mind because they haven't yet come to complete forgiveness of their perceived guilt for what they did or didn't do. Thus, their made-up guilt is very much at the forefront of their mind, even if they constantly blame their ex-partner.

A key element of *The Power of Clearing* is the release of all thoughts, feelings, and beliefs in separation. We will always be One, no matter how much we try to separate from each other; we can try to abandon or reject one another, but we will still be joined and connected spiritually, no matter what. Whatever issues we haven't resolved in this relationship will keep coming up in our conscious and unconscious minds to be resolved. Therefore, there is no divorce, and there never will be because, again, we are all One. We came here to clear and resolve any issues with whomever we are attracted to in a relationship and release the negative projections of ourselves and our past relationships that we are placing on this new person. We can then complete the lessons and patterns deep inside us, such as fear, pain, guilt, betrayal, abandonment, and separation in our past relationships. The reward we get when we clear our lessons and patterns deep inside our being is the forgiveness for ourselves and each other. We then understand my Innocence and your Innocence, and stand firm in the Truth that there is only *our* Innocence.

Betrayal and Abandonment

Betrayal and abandonment are tremendous themes I've noticed in my counseling practice and the trainings I've conducted since the 1980s. I have worked with thousands of people who feel someone very close has betrayed them: a partner, lover, boss, sister, brother, best friend, family member, parent, or child.

We are all writing in our ego-minds the movies or "scripts" of our lives. We must commit to ourselves to recognize the payoffs and benefits we receive when we hold on to negative ego beliefs about who we are. What am I getting by holding on to believing that someone has betrayed me? Could it be so I can feel victimized and be a victim of this betrayal? This perspective would make me believe I am wrongfully taken advantage of, and I would then blame others. Also, I could reaffirm my powerlessness so I don't have to take responsibility for my life to be proactive and go forward with what I want to create. Do I want sympathy from others in the way they show that they care about me? If so, I would be able to project guilt onto others for what they have done to me, and I could re-tell the story over and over to anyone who will listen, getting a lot of attention. Staying in this feeling would keep me in my guilt because I would perceive myself as guilty if I believed someone had unfairly treated me. While these are BIG benefits in the ego's mind, they suppress the Truth of who I am. Do I see myself in a theme of being continually betrayed by someone? If so, I must ask myself: Do I want to be *right* about being betrayed, or do I want to be *happy*? Attachment to being right will always ruin our lives.

> *Self-blame is therefore ego identification, and as much an*
> *ego defence as blaming others.* (ACIM, T-11.IV.5:5)

I can see how vital it is to myself and everyone else that we demonstrate, by living it, that betrayal is not the Truth of who we are and what we want to create. Once we remember this Truth, there is no reason to project that betrayal onto others. We can give up the attack and defense game for the sake of our freedom and peace through the forgiveness process. I commit to doing this myself and sharing it with everyone I meet. I ask that you join me in this intention. If we constantly have a story that friends are doing things to us, relationships are victimizing us, and we can't trust anyone, we may be living in the theme of betrayal even if we don't use this word. If we have this theme showing up in our lives in various ways and situations, we may choose to do a betrayal clearing. We would put everyone and everything into the clearing that we feel has betrayed us.

One of the most amazing puzzles I discovered was when I taught a highly-attended course in Dalarna, Sweden. Dalarna is the home of St. Nicholas, the

Swedish version of Santa Claus. People are drawn to this area to experience the peaceful, perfect reality with pure light and love reflected everywhere. This region is an idyllic oasis with the same attraction as the Northern Lights in Norway, for the light reflects everything outdoors, adding to the picture-perfect feeling of peace. People envision snow, reindeer, a sled, children sitting on the lap of Santa Claus by a fireplace in a cabin, or looking out at the perfect scenery and glimmering light surrounding the entire environment.

Ironically, in this town where people firmly dedicate themselves to family values and Christmas, I discovered that at least half the people in the Dalarna training (many of whom were residents) believed their mother or father had abandoned them. Dalarna has no movie theatre; stores close at 1 pm on Saturday and open on Monday morning so families can be together. I realized there must be something deeper going on than I had previously seen since there was nowhere to go to abandon anyone. I thought it was very unusual to have a theme of abandonment because of the wholesome values with everything working perfectly in this town, like a child's storybook. Swedish morality does not promote "to be unfaithful to your partner" in its culture; instead, it is a town that conveys a perfect love, a perfect life, and a sense of fantasy.

When I became a student of ACIM in 1990, I realized that abandonment and betrayal are universal themes in people's relationships, based on the perception that we abandoned and betrayed God by choosing this ego world of specialness and unique bodies in our original choice to come to Earth. By believing we are guilty of betraying God, we project abandonment, betrayal, and rejection onto our present relationships. This projection is reflected on our family members as though they had abandoned us and they are the guilty ones. This little t truth that I experienced in the Dalarna training was an egoic projection and perception of reality. Therefore, I believe strongly that the ACIM theory is true, as I confirmed in my own life (I also was clearing abandonment, betrayal, and rejection), in my counseling and life coaching practice, and with the attendees of my many courses.

No one I have ever met remembers this choice of specialness and choosing to come to this ego world, yet everyone I have met has a feeling that someone has abandoned or betrayed them. I have done thousands of clearings, particularly about abandonment and betrayal. In each of these clearings, everyone thinks it is the other person who abandoned or betrayed them. They have lots of egoic evidence to support this story and are attached to being right about their story. We have so much misperception in communication because we leave out important points to justify someone misperceiving us. When we think we are communicating, most of us are conveying at a fractional level what we think, feel, and believe, which is how we feel secure enough to share. As a result, there is a lot of ambiguity, confusion, and misinterpretation about what you said and what they said. It seems like we are afraid to commit ourselves to what we are really saying because if we did, we wouldn't have a reason to feel attacked or be attacked in the form of betrayal and abandonment. We would have no evidence to show for it, either. If we communicated fully, we could learn to experience more freedom in our lives. However, in our egoic fantasy, our ego confirms that there is an advantage in holding power over the people we love by guilt-tripping them and thus, believing we are controlling them. Of course, that is not the truth because no one can control or be controlled. We always have the choice, even in a split second, to wake up to our true nature. Therefore, in every moment, we actualize our awakening in the sense of seeing, "I choose to wake up now."

What Happens Next in Relationship?

We are all One. For example, your lover's wife is you, and you are her. If he does join with you instead of his wife since you believe you are so much better or worthy, you may feel guilty about his choice and your choice for the rest of your life. Your guilt about causing a couple, or even worse, a family, to break up could remain a stressor throughout your relationship—his choice and your part in him leaving her for you.

In more than forty years of counseling, I have witnessed this occurrence often in relationships. One of the greatest tragedies comes when a family breaks up with children involved because one of the parents chooses a new partner. The children could interpret this choice as "Dad left my mother and me for a new family and other children. Therefore, I no longer have a dad who wants my mother or me. I have to choose who I will live with or go along with what they choose for me. I may have to choose to defend my mother and separate completely from my dad to support my mom, who has been devastated." The children may also feel the need or unconscious desire to defend their mother's worth from this separation by being against dad. They will then believe in this choice as "we both cannot have you, only one of us can have you, our family cannot join as one. We must be separate." This separation can go on for many years, so they will not invite him or the new relationship woman to their special occasions.

In some cases, the man will say later, "It wasn't worth it, in the end, to change partners because it caused so much suffering for so many people involved, especially my children because I have lost them and missed so many years of interacting with them." The father can often feel punished for the choice he made to choose the new relationship. The new relationship may seem so much better at first because we are awakening from what we learned while we were sleeping in the past relationship to go in a new direction of fuller and more transparent communication.

The Power of Clearing process and the philosophy of the clearing shows how you can join the new family and the original family. In any case, where this dynamic has worked out as a peaceful, family-loving, or extended family-loving relationship, each party has chosen to embrace each other as one family with no separation, in total joining. Both families can now be present at all family gatherings, leaving no one out from then on. This all-inclusive joining is a considerable benefit to all parties, as it generates cohesion rather than separation. I have seen this joining for birthdays, Christmas, Thanksgiving, graduations, and weddings. I have done this process with my relationships, including my divorce. Since then, I have shown many others how to live this newly joined relationship in both families. It has felt so genuine, beneficial, and welcoming for all. One reason a person chooses not to participate in this new joining is to prove they are better, more, or different from the new partner. Another reason not to participate in this new family dynamic is the choice to hold onto an offense or a grievance and refuse to let go or release it to join with their new family successfully. Most spiritual books come down to a similar message: You can either be right about your grievance or be happy. Whatever it is you are holding against them, in reality, is what you are holding against yourself, for you and they are One. If your perception of them is they are guilty, then so are you guilty within your mind.

Once we have cleared ourselves of our projections onto each other, we will understand we are all loved and equally valuable. Then we can all be joined in one family. In my forty years as a counselor and coach, I have only seen fighting, bickering, and struggles in families who are experiencing separation. Those families in such situation who have taken *The Art of Joining a Family* course, worked through their issues by each person individually clearing so that the families were able to work through their issues and join in Peace and Love. It is one of my most gratifying experiences to be present at these trainings.

In my relationships, I am in *relationship* and *joined* with every person I have ever been with, and always experience joy when I think of them.

When couples choose to be in the same course, they face their fear of being there together. The fear compounds if they hold grievances against their partner because they could feel anxious and exposed, especially if they choose to talk about those feelings in front of the class during the sharing part of the course. However, the fear or anger they experience toward each other could dissipate, and they would feel an immediate release. They would have the chance to do clearings with coaches on other issues, although it would be more advanced for them to be clearing their feelings about each other. It's possible that following the immediate release of their fear, anger, and conflict, they would experience joy, peace, and love right there in the course. Anyone who takes the class will see that their issue or conflict is not about someone else, and through *The Clearing Process*, they will be able to release the issue from their mind and come to Peace and Forgiveness with themselves.

A Course in Miracles says the following: *The holiest of all the spots on earth is where an ancient hatred has become a present love.* (ACIM, T-26.IV.6.1) This philosophy of *The Clearing Process* is that all of our issues always originate in ourselves in our minds and family history, even when we think it is about someone else or something happening outside of ourselves.

Are you feeling great angst in one of your relationships? After participating in *The Power of Clearing* process, *The Art of Surrender,* or *The Art of Joining a Family*, you will transform the feeling from angst to joy afterward. You may even be grateful and see the person as the catalyst for the new awakening in your life, which is brought on by *joining* and not *separation*. You can go from hate to love, from negativity to positivity, and learn to truly grasp a natural affinity for Peace and Love as a way of life and being.

Association with the Body

When we came to Earth, we chose bodies to work through to release our feelings of separation and guilt. Whenever we look at a "better" body and compare it to ourselves, we experience a sense of guilt, the opposite of our true authentic self. This experience is the reason we are here in the first place. Otherwise, we would recognize that we are free and innocent. The addiction of seeing yourself as a body, and thinking that your partner prefers to seek out a better body, is an actual state of imprisonment ruled by fear and guilt. There will always be a better-looking body, and if your goal is to define yourself as a more beautiful body, you will be reconfirming the idea you will never be good enough. There will always be a part of your body that isn't right or isn't perfect. That's not the truth or goal of what you are seeking. You seek your true self, which you cannot accomplish by seeing yourself as the best-looking body or even as a body at all. When I look at someone, I don't see their body. I see their essence and the energy around their body, which is how I recognize them. This energy is also known as an aura or etheric body.

A body is a defined form, so you believe others can reject you when you see yourself as a body. You may think someone else has a better-looking body or body part when you feel stuck and trapped. However, the ego and the body are the same. When you see yourself as Spirit, however, you can never be rejected because you are one with Spirit, perfect, whole, complete, and eternally connected with everything and everyone. You can do, be, or create anything you desire as a limitless being. You are never separate or alone. You are unstoppable.

Many years ago, I taught a four-month course on the holy relationship called *Partners on Purpose*. Once we identified each person's purpose for being in the course, including values, and incomplete lessons in love and intimacy, I matched all the single people in the room with a partner to work with through the entire process. The purpose of this course was for each person to awaken to their true, life lessons and complete them with a committed partner who would hold space for them through the four-month process by witnessing and affirming only Truth.

The pairs worked together over four months, meeting one weekend a month in a formalized classroom setting. Along with homework, 25 assistants (*Power of Clearing* coaches) were available to help in *The Clearing Process* during the course period.

A male participant in one of these pairs in the group told me that I had chosen for him the ugliest woman he had ever seen. He told me she had the hair of a rattlesnake, the protruding eyes of a turtle, and the skin of another type of reptile. He asked me if he should tell her, in private, how he felt when they were alone after their weekend meeting. I suggested that he take the opportunity to clear with her in front of everyone present during the next upcoming course of the program. She would hold the space for him while he did the 3-step *Clearing Process*. That way, we could all witness and learn from this clearing. I helped him realize that unless she believed his perception about herself, his negative ego thoughts of her would not be upsetting to her in any way. Thus, she would not feel hurt, rejected, or humiliated by his statement, in Step 1 of the clearing, that he thought she was the ugliest woman he had ever seen. After he completed *The Clearing Process* in front of the group, he realized that his judgments of her appearance mirrored what he thought about himself. Because of how *The Clearing Process* is structured, it will be challenging to project your judgment about yourself onto someone else and make it about them. Your negative judgment is always a mirror of yourself or someone from your past. *The Clearing Process* helps to identify specific projections about yourself or their source from the past and release them at their origin.

This man then felt relieved and grateful to be her partner through the remainder of this four-month process and could experience the purpose of their match. He realized it was not a mismatch to be paired with this woman. Without her as his partner, he might not have been able to see what he needed to clear. Later, he married a woman he saw as a beautiful, whole being, his new reflection of himself.

This laboratory experience, *Partners on Purpose*, gave each pair many breakthroughs from the negative patterns of prior relationships. Their commitment was to stay together for the four-month course and keep engaging in processing and clearing, no matter what each thought, felt, or believed about each other ("little t" feelings). One of the benefits for the participants of this four-month training was successfully releasing negative patterns in which one party would retreat or attempt to escape emotionally or physically if things became too uncomfortable. They committed to releasing all of their negative patterns through *The Clearing Process* rather than ending their relationships to escape their feelings. They also did processes where they saw how they escaped with their little t feelings in prior relationships and cleared those past relationships with their current partner.

In romance novels, movies, and even television sitcoms, a common theme is of someone, usually a woman, falling in love with a married man. Many storylines depict him leaving his wife for the new woman, feeling more connected with her, thereby painting true love as winning out.

In these fantasies and dreams, the woman usually has an enormous fear and obsession about whether the man will follow through, call her and when he will call her, or whether they can be together forever. She has so much attachment to this desired outcome that it becomes the theme of her life. She is no longer present in what is actually happening in their relationship, let alone other areas of her reality. One reason the affair appears to be a better relationship is that they are communicating more clearly in the honeymoon stage of their relationship. There is also the element of the "attraction of guilt" and that rush of hiding and being found out. In the woman's interpretation of the situation, she believes she is much more worthy and capable of loving him than his wife, and their union is much more "special." Conversely, she may think the opposite is true and that she is less worthy of having this love affair.

The Power of Clearing process would say that this dynamic creates separation in both their minds—the idea that "you have to join with me and not her." When we can be completely transparent in the process, it becomes clear who is the right partner for all parties concerned. When these three people involved do the clearing of their feelings for themselves, their partner, and their partner—taking it back to the original core feelings of their family of origin—then it becomes clear to all who should be with who in life.

One of the difficulties in marriage is that people fall asleep in the comfort of thinking they always have this person because they have committed; they believe there is nothing necessary to do since this person will always be there. Unfortunately, this complacency in the relationship can go on for decades.

Revisiting little t truth to Remember

In practice, there is a core group of negative themes (little t truths), for example, abandonment, separation, a lack of trust, a lack of faith**,** and a lack of self-worth that the egoic self has to let go of to live in Peace. One of our greatest challenges is believing we're not good enough to have anyone else's Love, let alone self-Love, and especially God's Love. We often project our past worries, fears, and doubts onto present relationships, unfairly and unjustly. These current relationships will trigger us, bringing up feelings, thoughts, beliefs, and patterns, often unconscious, that we need to release from the original relationship where they began (usually with mothers, fathers, or guardians).

We continuously repeat these patterns and projections until we recognize that our minds make up various interpretations. Once we take responsibility for our negative patterns and understand where they came from in our childhood, we can free ourselves from believing they originate in the here and now. We can finally let go of the illusion of "again" being betrayed, rejected, and abandoned. We often have negative payoffs from always believing something is wrong with us. Our addiction to placing blame on ourselves stops us from moving forward to what we truly want: A peaceful mind, a peaceful heart, and, thus, a peaceful life.

As we go through the three steps of *The Clearing Process*, these negative core patterns and themes may disappear entirely or fizzle out, eventually no longer triggering pain, stuck-ness, or separation. And remember that what we resist persists, and what we fully embrace will be healed and integrated. Once this shift occurs, we can witness the themes of these negative patterns and recognize that they are not the truth of who we are. In his article, "The Watcher," in the Resources section, Len Satov talks about how to witness these patterns.

The Light You Are

The truth is that nothing can change a diamond, and nothing anyone does can dim the light you truly are as a diamond. Diamonds are forever impenetrable and unchangeable. Two of my students once gave me enormous diamonds made of Austrian crystals, with their light reflecting everywhere. One of my students wrote a song many years ago called "You are the Diamond," which I played at my wedding since she wrote it for me. Many people, from their ego-mind, try to make themselves better, look better, or feel better, but nothing they do can change the true nature of themselves as already being a diamond. Others can see our diamond quality far better than we can because our ego fear and feelings cloud us. The only thing we can do with a diamond to make the luster shine brighter is by polishing it and removing all the clouds. Even with cloudiness, it will always be a diamond.

You Are the Diamond
Lyrics and Music by Carole Isis

Go on now, let go of the past,
You are your own Phoenix rising from the ashes.
Go on now, let go of the future;
Let in the love that all the fear never matches.

You, you are the Diamond in the heart of all life...
You, you are deserving of all you want to be.
The strength of your wisdom leaves behind all strife
You are the maker, the doer, the lover – can't you see?

You are magnificent, you are a wonder
You are the dream you've always wanted to be
You are an angel, you are so beautiful;
Now use the magic, you've always had the key.

It only takes a small willingness,
Reach for a door and you'll find they're all around you.
Take the step that takes you through
On to the Holy Instant that is Now...

Now you see...

PART II

CLEARING

CHAPTER 6

THE CLEARING PROCESS

What is *The Power of Clearing?*

The Power of Clearing process, that I received through prayer in 1990 when I lived in Sweden, is a 3-step process in which you release from your mind all suffering, mistaken beliefs, traumas, attacks, and defenses. The last two steps of the process are forgiveness exercises that confirm and affirm Eternal Truth.

From the perspective of *A Course in Miracles*, forgiveness differs from the traditional teaching of how to forgive: We forgive by overlooking something we believe happened, and we see the error someone has made. In the forgiveness process in *The Power of Clearing*, we recognize it is our thoughts about the situation that we need to forgive. We give meaning to everything based on our filters. Therefore, we need to forgive our mistaken negative interpretation of any situation. So, it is all about having "a little willingness" to look at our unconscious, limiting thoughts, beliefs, and traumas to see if our interpretations are valid. Then we can release them.

The Clearing Process assists a person in removing the unconscious and conscious guilt from their past. It provides tools for changing how they view everything, from their relationships and finances to personal success. The clearing is the most helpful tool I have seen for releasing all the limiting beliefs that run people's lives, motivating them into unhealthy cycles of self-destructive attitudes and behaviors. *The Clearing Process* is a simple yet profound tool for speaking your total truth and releasing ego thoughts, feelings, and beliefs. In the clearing, we confirm the Holy Spirit's truth in every communication. The Holy Spirit, in spiritual terms, allows us to look at everything from a higher perspective. With our higher self as witness and guide, we forgive ourselves for believing what our egos tell us. Please note that we refer to Holy Spirit not in traditional religious terms, more being the bridge between Big T Truth of our true nature and the little t truth of ego thoughts. (Please see the chart on page 124.)

Current upsets are doorways into old thoughts and memories in "the basement" (subconscious) of our ego-mind. You can choose a life of joy over suffering by your willingness and readiness to release whatever negative memories are in your subconscious. Making a choice is the most powerful tool we have in our minds. Our ability to choose determines the world we see, our relationships, and the success we experience. We determine the quality of our experience based on our choices (and how we feel about those choices), resulting in our thoughts, beliefs, feelings, and behaviors. This awareness allows us to continue making choices aligned with our truth. We always have the option to choose again if later we notice we made a choice of our ego rather than our truth.

The Power of Clearing is a psycho-spiritual process that allows everyone using it to find their inherent Divinity, Oneness, and Connection with Source, God, Universe, Nature. This process is the key to fully recognizing and embracing our direct connection with the true, eternal power for good and our own essential nature that we call Love.

The philosophy of *The Power of Clearing* says no one is guilty and everyone is innocent in our spiritual essence, our true nature. We are Spirit (living within a human form); thus, we are always pure. We clear because we have ego thoughts, feelings, and beliefs from our human experiences that cloud our memory of our connection to the divine. Clearing brings us back to acknowledging our true nature and innocence.

How *The Power of Clearing* came about

As I mentioned in Chapter 3, in 1987, I met a man in Sweden on my one day off when I was on tour conducting a three-week series of trainings. My husband (I'll call him Peter) was a very kind, sweet, loving person and an entrepreneur committed to humanitarianism, the central focus of his philosophy of life. We fell in love and over the next two years, we met up when we could for adventurous interludes in the United States, Canada, and Europe. Peter proposed to me in Notre Dame Cathedral in France on his birthday and we married in California at the end of a five-day international networking event in 1989. I moved from San Francisco to Sweden with my young daughter and *On Purpose* seminar business to be with him.

During our honeymoon on the Orient Express traveling through three European countries, Peter told me he wanted to host an International Peace Conference that same year. Such an event would be new to him since he wasn't in the event business. Even with my experience organizing seminars, I reluctantly offered to help because I felt it would be overwhelming for us to manage the logistics. We were newly married, and I was living in another culture and learning how to do business in another language with a different banking system. We also blended our families with his two children and my daughter, who couldn't yet speak Swedish to other children.

Soon after, when I told one of my very dear friends about his intention, she was inspired to give us a helpful donation of seed money to initiate the conference. My husband and I began registering and enrolling the speakers and participants. Throughout the months of preparing for the conference, Peter and I renovated his Swedish villa, doubling the size with lots of angles and windows, a meditation room, and an office for me. I felt overwhelmed and worried about how we would pay for the extensive renovation and cover the conference's expenses. As a life coach, I am always interested in having every aspect of my life and everyone else's work out for the highest vision of their realized purpose.

The successful Peace Conference resulted in the creation of a profound document for peace. Gary Zukav, the well-known author and metaphysical teacher, said that this conference changed his life, and the UN speaker, Dr. Rashmi Mayur, said it was the best conference he had attended. On the final evening, we had a gala event with a banquet, music, and dancing to celebrate our successful event. Unfortunately, I could not attend because the babysitter had been with our three children for ten hours, so I went home, even though I sensed it was a wrong move. That final night was one of the greatest moments of Peter's life. He had followed his inspiration to do something he had never done before and succeeded; he felt elated, exhilarated, and victorious. Sadly, I wasn't there to acknowledge his success and celebrate with him in that expanded state.

Ironically, my concern about the Peace Conference expenses created a lack of peace for me, which affected our connection. By the end of the event, I felt separate from Peter; we both believed we were right about our opinions, which increased the stress and division between us. I shared with Peter that the pressure of our financial disagreement had caused my heart to close to him. Feeling very upset in that moment, I suggested that we consider a divorce. After a few minutes, he agreed. However, I didn't think this exchange was final because I was in such a triggered state. With the upset between us unresolved, I left for Hawaii to run a three-week training course with sixty-five adults and twenty children. I called Peter several times during the training and noticed he sounded distant and aloof. However, I didn't feel panic until I returned.

Everything *looked* okay when I arrived at our beautiful home. My husband had even made an elegant and welcoming spread of champagne and smoked salmon as he did for us on special occasions. Yet, something within me *felt* strange and uneasy. I didn't say anything during the meal, but I felt compelled to address it as we got ready for bed that evening. "Tell me now, what happened when I was in Hawaii? I feel like something dreadful has happened. Do you have cancer? Do you feel you're going to die?" That's how upset I perceived his energetic field to be.

I remember him being honest with me. "I've fallen in love with a younger woman. I want to be with her, enjoy my time, and explore my feelings for her. But I don't want to let go of you."

I asked Peter all kinds of fear-based questions. I wanted to know her name—he wouldn't tell me. "You might as well," I said. "I'll know her name by the time I wake up." That night, I hardly slept. I felt like I was dying and was totally out of my mind with jealousy, grief, and loss. And, by the morning, I heard her name in my mind: Birgitta. I had registered her at the Peace Conference and remembered having noticed her: young and pretty with sparkling, innocent blue eyes.

I didn't know how to get through my panic and feel whole again. I felt like someone had run a sharp sword through me. There was some hope, however. In our marriage contract, we had agreed to go for counseling if we ever found ourselves in such difficulty that we couldn't resolve it ourselves. The only person I could think of who could help us heal our marriage with the ability or skill to resolve this situation and find the truth was Lena Kristina, my psychologist friend. We had several sessions of counseling with her; however, it didn't return us to our original married state of oneness, connection, and purpose together.

I felt so raw in my feelings of survival that I couldn't even think clearly. Finally, I resorted to what I did ("when all else fails...") as a child: I prayed.

Over several years of teaching seminars about relationships and counseling couples, I had observed many others experiencing similar pain and confusion that I was now facing. I asked God to give me a means of helping myself and others so we could heal and feel whole and complete again. I longed for someone to join me in this healing process because I believed Peter had chosen the other woman. I told God I could only survive this pain for one more month without a resolution between us. I was continuously in prayer except when I was talking with and caring for my seven-year-old daughter. For that excruciating month—that felt like a year—my husband went back and forth in a relationship with me and his new perceived love. Of course, this situation triggered me, with him away with his girlfriend and then returning home and still living with me.

Receiving the Answer

I said my prayer over and over all day long. I prayed for God to send me a partner who wanted to align with me in my purpose to end separation and suffering. I thought it might even be Peter, but I had no idea who this person could be.

The 31st day of my prayer was the day before my local weekend seminar on *The Art of Surrender*. I was shocked when I found out that thirty-five people had registered for the class without my effort. I couldn't imagine why the universe would send so many people to me when I was in so much emotional pain. I wondered what anyone could learn from me when I was in such turmoil and anguish. As it turned out, leading that weekend seminar allowed me to teach my way through my emotional pain. I listened to every word I said, knowing that the teaching would also directly apply to me when sharing with others in the training.

Before the weekend course, all the assistants gathered at my home that evening to have dinner, prepare, and stay overnight. Peter was spending time with his girlfriend. As I drove into the driveway with food for dinner and supplies for the workshop, one of the parked cars stood out to me. I felt uneasy and anxious with the sense something unusual was about to occur that I didn't have a grasp on or know about yet. I remember feeling a surge of fear when I walked inside my home and saw Mats. He was one of my assistant coaches for *The Art of Surrender* training and one of my promoters for the *On Purpose* trainings. He and his wife were also my students. I had a crazy thought I had never felt about him—*I do not want to be alone with Mats tonight*! This thought persisted, yet I continued preparing the dinner as if everything was okay because I didn't understand my fear.

After the other coaches went to sleep, I was alone with Mats at the end of the evening. He asked if I would like to go into the meditation room to meditate together. My first thought was, *No way*! But even though I felt such resistance, I agreed. As I followed him, I *knew* my life was about to change forever. Whenever I come to a big moment, at first, I always have fear because I want everything to be safe and familiar. Then the fear turns to excitement, and something dramatically shifts, as it did that night in the meditation room.

Mats and I had been out of communication since the Peace Conference; his wife had attended while he was home with their two children. Mats said that after the event, his wife told him she wanted to be with one of the conference presenters. She had gone to Italy for two weeks to spend time with him and then confirmed with Mats that she wanted to leave their marriage (after ten years). I remembered seeing her talking to that presenter and sitting together at many conference sessions. They appeared to be deeply connected. Then, on the final night of the conference, when I was on the stage before I left, I noticed only three people in the audience, sitting together: Birgitta (who I later identified as my husband's new girlfriend), the presenter, and Mats' wife. I had a fearful premonition seeing Mats' wife sitting with the presenter that night.

Sharing in the meditation room, Mats and I recognized that we were having the same experience of our partner choosing someone else. We both felt alone, betrayed, and abandoned in no-where-ville. Then I realized God had sent me Mats Stjernqvist on the 31st day of my prayer. We already knew each other; however, he appeared in a new form in my life that evening. While sitting together on pillows on the floor, facing each other in the energized space, Mats' appearance began to change right before my eyes. I could see he was an ancient, infinite being, and in that moment, I joined energetically with him in oneness (non-physical). Mats had brought *A Course in Miracles*, and he said he wanted to use ACIM as a guide for healing in our relationships and *removing the blocks to the awareness of love's presence*. (ACIM introduction) Our conversation led us to commit to a joint purpose of finding the answer to end all pain and suffering in relationships, something we both knew well. Mats and I shared the same intention and desire: *I want the peace of God*. (ACIM, W-185) Later, I discovered that according to ACIM, when partners commit to a purpose rather than a body or personality, it begins a holy relationship—it lasts for eternity. That's right; we committed for eternity!

When we left the meditation room, I knew that Mats and I had made an enormous commitment. During *The Art of Surrender* training that weekend, the answers I had prayed for so desperately for a month were coming to me effortlessly and quickly in the form of *The Power of Clearing* process and Big T Truth and little t truth. (See page 124.)

After *The Art of Surrender* training, I received the method of helping people work through healing in relationships, which later became *The Holy Relationship* training (a three-week course), and then The Holy Relationship ten-day workshop. With Mats, the magic began to happen in my life exponentially because of our holy relationship purpose and union. During the days, weeks, and months that followed, our explorations revealed more processes as we learned to use *The Power of Clearing* and ACIM to go deeper in our healing.

When Peter called me to ask if I could help him and his girlfriend with a conflict, I visited, introduced *The Clearing Process*, and was able to hold space for them.

Mats and I began to study *A Course in Miracles* to free ourselves and others from suffering in relationship and releasing the core of guilt. *The Clearing Process* parallels the principles of the ACIM book. We focused on the area of our family of origin for anything upsetting from our childhood that we had not cleared that we could be projecting on our present relationships, like my feeling betrayed. Mats and I left Sweden for four months and went to Hawaii with our children to immerse ourselves in studying these profound teachings. ACIM became a passion and a joining force in our lives; we studied it night and day, learning how to apply the teachings in a practical way to our thinking and helping others clear their ego. While based in Hawaii, we traveled back and forth to Sweden every six weeks to teach classes together.

Mats and I wrote together the only training that summarizes the experience of ACIM. The training intended for people to release their pain and suffering and enter their pure freedom of Choice: *Choosing Freedom: The Way Out (of all Pain and Suffering and the Way Back to Who You Really Are)*.

When we all returned to Sweden from Hawaii, we needed a new place to live. So, I bought a good-sized house in the tiny village of Skräddaröd in Skåne county near the quaint town of Simrishamn, the artistic part of Sweden. We moved there so our children could attend the free-thinking Waldorf school with small classes and provincial, healthy living and teaching. The school was set in an apple orchard in a pastoral place with miles of rolling hills. My daughter went there for ten years with mostly the same students in her class and the same teacher; it was a wonderful family experience.

Given our busy training and seminar schedule, I knew we needed more assistance with the family and house. I met Lottie in *The Art of Surrender* training after Mats and I returned from Hawaii, held in Väddö in the Stockholm Archipelago, in a small course center called Fjällbo. She felt called to come and live with Mats and me to study and learn with us in exchange for helping with the children and our home. She became an avid student of *The Power of Clearing* and ACIM, studying with us as her mentors and teachers. She fully embodied the training and aspired to live in Big T Truth and follow God's voice. Lottie had come through a huge mental, emotional, and psychic pain to clear herself of all her emotional conflicts. Mats and I had contributed considerable time to her process of clearing at the deepest level for her to find complete clarity and peace.

After a while, it became clear, through soul searching and clearing with the three of us, that she was divinely destined to be the partner of Mats Stjernqvist. Of course, I went through tremendous turmoil, losing Mats as my life partner while knowing I would always retain him as my holy relationship partner. Then, we were all in a holy relationship at a very committed level to our joined purpose of healing our minds. To make this shift between the three of us, I had to get that she was me and I was her and that the three of us were One. We could never be separate from each other; we would always be one mind and one heart Joined. For many days, Lottie and I went through an intensely deep process that we designed to clear my emotional upset of letting go of Mats as my life partner and supporting them to be life partners forever.

Two months after they came together, they married in a church in 1992. When I attended their wedding, I had to reprocess my pain of feeling abandoned; I went through the emotional pain to Peace. The three of us continued working together in expanding processes in *The Power of Clearing* and ACIM. Eight years later, Mats and Lottie conceived twins. Mats had a favorite joke: "Since the ego never likes to choose, the ego always thinks, can I have two?" I would say that is how they conceived twins. Mats remembers one training when we had a man who had never been with a woman; after clearing and processing his beliefs of not being good enough, we saw the light in his eyes, and he asked, "Can I have two?" A dramatic shift so soon!

Mats and Lottie live and breathe the experience of ACIM, applying it to everything from money dilemmas to work challenges and parenting and relationship evolutions. Lottie was one of the most devoted students out of the thousands I trained; today, she is a teacher and a coach in her own right. Since 1990, Mats, Lottie, and I have shared a strong connection and commitment to healing our minds. Peter and I have a good relationship and have kept in touch since our divorce 30 years ago.

Review of little t truth thoughts

Because I believe I am not good enough, I feel guilty that I have done something wrong and, therefore, need to be punished and atone. I have created a life I don't like based on the core feeling that I do not deserve the life I want. I fear someone will discover my guilt. I have given myself a few crumbs, and I live in the fear that I am not good enough to be cared about or deserve more than these crumbs.

We may be so far from believing we are good enough to be cherished that we embody a limited existence. As a result, we are afraid to step beyond what is familiar and known. This perception could be a repeat of what we witnessed in the lives of our parents living in their limited fear-based reality of generational guilt. We each make up a story in which we are all the characters on the unconscious level of our minds. They are attacking us and acting out fear and guilt from which we need to defend ourselves. This perceived guilt creates in our minds a world where we are imperfect, cannot have a good life, and deserve punishment. For some people, the life of their dreams and living without limits only existed in childhood. As they grew up, they resigned from the life they could have had into a life of survival because of their fears and unconscious guilt. For many people, this perceived story of guilt may come up in ego-minds several times a day in negative self-talk. We need another person to remind us of who we are so we don't believe our ego story. Survival becomes a way of life, rather than thriving, being at peace, and being love. The little t truths replace Big T Truths with the words "should," "must," and "have to." The list can grow longer every day with more strangling directives. This loop always stems back to the original core beliefs of "I am not good enough," "I am guilty," and "I can never have what I want." A core belief keeps us in fear; we doubt we will ever have what we truly want, and we believe our destiny is to always live with a hole in our hearts.

As long as we have a secret that we believe proves we are bad, it will drag us along in life, and we will cover it up at every moment. We are never willing to let it go until the moment we can share it with people we trust. "We don't have a secret; it has us; it controls us at every moment and makes us feel trapped and imprisoned." Each person must create the opportunity in their friendships and relationships to open up to more than one person and feel fully received. We benefit by creating a support system of people who hold us in a light of innocence without blaming us or judging us, who see us for who we are beyond our story, and who reflect the Truth to us in every moment, no matter how compelling the evidence of the story.

The key to release us from this trap is *The Power of Clearing* process: to see the Truth and realize any perceived fear, guilt, pain, or secret is a story we made up that no longer has power over the Truth of Who I Am.

What is *The Clearing Process?*

WHAT IS A *CLEARING?*

A clearing is a process for releasing unconscious guilt, fear, and stuck energy from past traumas. It is a method for letting go of our limiting belief systems and confirming who we really are. Our authentic self and our true worth are complete in who we always are: Love, Peace, and Joy.

WHY DO *CLEARINGS?*

We are clearing each upset, trauma, or contraction we feel in our lives, starting from experiences in the womb and the birth process up to the present day. We remember these negative experiences even at the cellular level, so *The Clearing Process* transforms us through a cellular shift returning us to our true nature. We need to release negative cellular memory to feel complete relief, release, harmony, and oneness. When we heal our minds and beliefs, we can begin healing our hearts and lives, affecting our bodies. When we shift our minds, it can shift our bodies and even our physical appearance. Our minds tell our bodies what to do and how to be regarding conditions and realities; our bodies consciously and unconsciously obey. *The Clearing Process* uncovers unconscious memories of incidents and traumas of the past that a person may not even be aware of before they started *The Clearing Process*. The process goes *very* quickly, like a detective finding the pieces to a puzzle, to the core traumas or memories affecting a person their whole life.

Len Satov, a senior member of our coaching team, says *The Clearing Process*, specifically Step 2 and Step 3 of the process (the forgiveness steps), releases layers of "dark cloths" covering the light of our true nature. As each negative thought, upset, or trauma is released, more light appears within the person who is clearing, thus enabling them to access their true, authentic self and have more access to peace, freedom, energy, and passion in their life. Therefore, they experience more aliveness and joy!

HOW IS *THE CLEARING* DONE?

Before a clearing, I do 2-8 hours with the people or person to see what there is to clear: fears, traumas, relationships. Each *Power of Clearing* coach has a detailed intake form for this in-depth process. Learning how to complete this form with the participant doing the clearing is part of their ten-day course to become a *Power of Clearing* coach. They are trained in ten modules so they can see from a client's whole life what they would want to clear to be limitless and free. This intake includes relationships, money, the body, family history (birth order, siblings), parents, physical well-being, creativity, spiritual beliefs, divorce, separation, or single.

Clearings usually begin by focusing on the most significant figure in the person's immediate family (mother, father, partner, child, brother, sister, aunt, uncle, niece, nephew). This focus gives us the most direct access to a person's true feelings, which are often unconscious. In the clearing, with a coach through a specific format and structure, they talk to the family member by name, as if they were present. While normal conversation can go in circles, *The Clearing Process* structure takes them straight to the main points of misperception about themselves that they need to release.

In most cases, we are clearing the judgments a person has made about themselves in the belief that they have done something wrong in their life and are therefore guilty. We are also clearing conflicts they may have had with anyone in their lives (past significant relationships) that have caused them to become guilt-ridden so that when they think of these people, they can feel peace, freedom, and openness in their heart.

We do the personal clearing of someone's issues in private, one-to-one with a *Power of Clearing* coach who knows how to hold the space for the person so they can fully say anything and feel safe and listened to with love and compassion. So, when learning, couples are clearing about personal issues rather than each other since it would be too triggering for them to hold the space for each other.

They are clearing the false, negative core beliefs they have fabricated about themselves—such as "I am not worthy," "I am guilty," "No one sees me," "I'm not safe," and "I am not good enough." Then they replace these negative beliefs with authentic truths in Step 2 and Step 3 of *The Clearing* in the forgiveness processes with "I am good enough," "I am worthy," "I am safe," "I am free," and "I am love."

We also can use breathwork through the whole process to release stuck energy. Each inhale and exhale can aid in releasing cellular memory through each step of the clearing.

BEFORE *THE CLEARING:* HOW IS THE WAY PREPARED?

Whether you are the clearing guide or the person doing the clearing, it's essential to see that you can let your fears go. It's also important to access your inner knowing (intuition) to discern if you are ready to do the clearing or if you need to read the book a few times to become more familiar with the process, exercises, and philosophy. The benefit of preparing the way is that you will feel more power and confidence to do the clearing, for both the person clearing and the one being the clearing guide.

To prepare the way before doing *The Clearing Process* with your friend or therapist as your clearing guide holding the space for you, sit opposite each other, feet flat on the floor, and look into each other's eyes. Then have them ask you this question at least four or five times: "What would you have to let go of right now with me as your clearing guide in this *Power of Clearing* process to be fully present?" Likewise, you can ask your clearing guide, "What would you have to let go of right now to be my clearing guide and be fully present, holding the space for me in this *Power of Clearing* process?" Answers can include judgments, attachments, or blame on the part of the clearing guide toward their friend who is clearing. For example, "I judged you for being naïve about relationships and that you were making a mistake that you would regret when you decided to divorce your third husband."

Examples of you answering your clearing guide's question:

1. "I feel really scared right now that you don't know enough about the process to support me as my guide because you have only read the instructions once."

The clearing guide will repeat the person's answer: "So, I hear you feel really scared that something might happen in the process, and you don't feel safe with me because I only read the book once and the instructions once. So, you would feel more confident in my ability if I read the instructions two or three times, and I had worked with *The Clearing Process* for years. Is that correct?"

2. "I feel scared of doing the process because I have so much guilt and fear that has come up my whole life, and I'm doubtful any clearing could help me with all of my issues, challenges, and problems."

The clearing guide repeats: "So you feel scared and doubtful because you have too many issues to ever clear or release to come to peace. Is that correct?"

3. "I fear that I would get stuck in one of my traumatic scenes and not be able to let it go and also that I would let it go, and then feel differently about my life. And it would be unfamiliar to me to feel peace."

The guide repeats: "You are scared you might get stuck in one of your traumatic scenes and not be able to let it go, and you are also scared you might let it go and then you won't know who you are because your identity has been your pain. Is that correct?"

Before proceeding with the clearing, repeat what you heard the person say so they can listen to what they said again, which helps them further let go of their fear, thoughts, and resistance to clearing. For the clearing guide to repeat what you said back to you is like walking in your footsteps and getting to know your pace and your reality. Therefore, you can feel confident that your coach understands you, has heard you, and taken in what you said.

STEPS OF *THE CLEARING PROCESS*

SET THE INTENTION

The intention sets the focus for the session and gives the person clearing the momentum to go for Big T Truth as the outcome.

The person clearing will decide upon and then state their intention for the clearing, and the coach will join them in that intention. The intention sets the focus and true desire for the session. For example, **"My intention for this clearing is to uncover and release all conscious or unconscious guilt around ………………… and to remember that I am Innocent and that …………………… is Innocent as well."** All intentions must end with a Big T Truth. The coach will then say, **"I join you in your intention that ………………"**

CREATE AND SAY A PRAYER OR AFFIRMATION

You set the tone of the clearing and ask for support from your guides and your Higher Power (a higher consciousness) by showing you *exactly* what you need to say to release and remember past negative incidents in your life. For example, "Universe, Infinite Guide, Divine Energy, please show me where I need to go in my unconscious mind to find exactly where I am experiencing the blockage or hindrance. Please give me the courage to bring it to my conscious so I might see it, feel it, and experience it, and then let it go from my conscious and unconscious mind."

SUMMARY OF THE 3-STEP *CLEARING PROCESS*

Step 1: Report all negative ego thoughts, feelings, and beliefs on a specific subject (sex, money, power, love, appearance, body, physical condition, self, work, a particular person, or conceptualization of the word God).

Step 2: Ask for forgiveness (correction of misperceptions) for ego thoughts, feelings, and beliefs.

Step 3: Ask for forgiveness for forgetting Big T (Truth). Remember Eternal Truths (reconfirming Big T Truth); reconfirm the truth of our authentic nature, who we truly are.

STEP 1:
REPORT ALL NEGATIVE EGO THOUGHTS, FEELINGS, AND BELIEFS

BASIC CLEARING

The first step in the Basic Clearing provides the person clearing (in this case, me) with the opportunity to feel and express my feelings, thoughts, and beliefs, rather than just acting them out. While I make progress in being able to identify and label my feelings, to integrate them fully, I must be able to speak them without judgment.

I begin *The Clearing Process* by saying *everything* I think, feel, or believe related to the emotionally upsetting incident(s), person, or event that I perceive is responsible for upsetting me, with as much emotional expression as I am feeling.

Following *The Clearing Process* formula allows me to come to know and accept myself while allowing you (the coach) to hear my feelings, thoughts, and beliefs without feeling threatened by them. This first step is an emptying-out process, like detoxifying my body of food poisoning, except it empties all the toxic thoughts, feelings, and beliefs from my mind instead. It clears the field, so the forgiveness steps are the most powerful they can be.

In Step 1, I preface each statement with **"What I want you to know is …"** and keep each sentence as concise as possible with the minimum amount of "storytelling." The story can distract me from where I want to focus, on the main thoughts, feelings, and beliefs, rather than blaming circles or tangents. It is helpful to begin with how I am feeling at the present moment; for example, **"What I want you to know is** right now I feel really anxious to be doing this."

I continue until I have reported *everything* I think, feel, and believe that relates to the emotionally upsetting incident(s) and the person I hold responsible for my upset feelings. I include all those thoughts I have been harboring in the recesses of my mind: "Oh, I can't say that" or "This is too embarrassing."

The person listening responds with "Thank you" after each statement unless they feel they need to give more depth. For example, they might say something like "tell me a little more about that" to help elicit a fuller response before prompting me to do the next **"What I want you to know is …"**

ADVANCED CLEARING (taking it back to the past)

Step 1 for the Advanced Clearing allows me to take ownership of everything I thought, felt, and believed in response to the emotional experience. As *A Course in Miracles* teaches us, *I am never upset for the reason, I think.* (ACIM, W-5 and W-51.5:2) We feel upset because something has triggered unresolved feelings from the past at a deeper memory level than we may be aware of consciously. In recognizing that I am not feeling upset for the reason I believed I was, I begin to make associations between the current experiences and experiences which happened in the past.

I preface each new statement with **"What I want you to know is** that when you did (or said) ………………. **I felt ………………. just like when ……………."** The phrase "just like when" is an invitation for a memory (that evokes the same feeling) to pop into my mind, preferably from my younger childhood. If a memory comes up, I can describe the scene, who was there, where it happened, and my feelings at the time. If no memory readily springs to mind, I continue to the next statement. Again, we are not forcing anything here.

Again, the person listening responds simply with "Thank you" after each statement.

STEP 2:
ASK FOR FORGIVENESS (CORRECTION OF MISPERCEPTIONS) FOR EGO THOUGHTS, FEELINGS, AND BELIEFS

BASIC CLEARING

Step 2 allows me to release my mistaken beliefs about myself and others revealed by the previous step.

This time I preface my statement with **"What I want you to forgive me for, is for thinking/feeling/believing ……………………."** I keep these statements short and precise and keep going until I have corrected all my mistaken beliefs and thoughts.

At this point, the role of the person listening becomes more interactive. They now create the foundation of Truth, where I can see myself reflected in the listener's eyes and know myself to be acceptable in all my vulnerability. The person listening replies, **"Thank you. That is not the Truth. That is a story you made up, and I Love You."** Saying "I Love You" confirms the Truth and the universality of Love.

ADVANCED CLEARING

Step 2 for the Advanced Clearing allows me to take ownership of my thoughts, feelings, and beliefs *that I project onto others.*

The emotional pain elicited by the upsetting experience is intensified by the extent to which I accuse and judge myself for committing the "crime" I am currently accusing the other person of committing against me. The more convinced I am that the other is guilty, the more resistant I am to recognizing that I do what I am accusing him of doing. This step is often the most challenging because it is when I must be willing to confront my beliefs about myself that I may not have been aware of until that moment.

I preface these statements with, **"What I want you to forgive me for,** (name), **is for thinking/feeling/believing.....................** (give specific examples or details), **which means I am...................."** (how I judge myself). I continue until I have claimed all of my projections and corrected my misperceptions. The person listening replies to each statement, "Thank you, that is not the Truth. That is just a story you made up. You are.................... (the opposite of the judgment they made about themselves) and I love You."

There is a place in you waiting all your life to hear the affirmations for who you truly are and your true worth.

These examples of Big T responses match the person's statement with little t beliefs from Step 1. By matching up the statements and responses between Step 1 and 2 the process leads to a reawakening and remembrance of who you are in your divine nature.

Note. In Step 1, we say, "think/feel/believe" and in Step 2, we ask for forgiveness for what we think/feel/believe and add "which means I am..." as a statement of mistaken identity. We correct misperceptions about our identity that we unconsciously took on long ago.

STEP 3:
ASK FOR FORGIVENESS FOR FORGETTING BIG T (TRUTH) REMEMBER ETERNAL TRUTH (RECONFIRMING BIG T TRUTH)

BOTH THE BASIC AND THE ADVANCED CLEARING

This, the final step, allows me the opportunity to remember and affirm the Big T Truth. It is recommended to do Step 3 for the characters in the clearing first and then make the statements for myself. I preface each of these statements with, **"What I want you to forgive me for,** (name of character), **is for forgetting that you are ………………………."** stating one of the Big T Truths about them that, in the pain of this experience, I have temporarily forgotten. The coach responds with "Thank You, that is the Truth. I am ………………(affirming the Big T Truth they just mentioned) and I love You." Just do a few statements for each character, one at a time. When I address myself, I make as many statements as needed to feel complete.

Once I complete Step 3 with the characters in the clearing, I make the statements to myself, which would reflect the answers to the judgments I had about myself in Step 2. An example would be, **"What I want you to forgive me for forgetting**, (my name), **is that I am** Lovable." Holding space as my higher self, the coach would answer, "Thank you, that is the Truth. You are eternally Lovable, and I love You."

IMPORTANT REMINDERS REGARDING *THE CLEARING PROCESS*

You are only clearing yourself. There is nothing else to clear except your ego-mind.

If you commit one hundred percent to the clearing as it is written, you will always experience success. Always remember to set an intention. (Where do you want to be with yourself by the end of the clearing? Not in the future, not tomorrow, but at the end of *The Clearing Process*. For example, "I want to feel peace when I think of my mother.")

Be sure to let go of a specific outcome with a person because this would automatically impose your little t self on the process. Remember, the clearing is only about you releasing your unconscious self-judgments. We allow whatever needs to be cleared at that particular time to bubble up to the surface by itself;

that is the beauty of this work. It will not be successful if you attempt to "steer" the clearing. In any event, it is almost impossible to assess what is "successful" anyway because the actual releasing occurs beyond our conscious perception.

You can only do the clearing when you are fully present in the here and now, committed to being in the space of the clearing. You want to agree on the amount of time you will be in the process, whether it's one, two, or three hours, to allow your full presence with no ego distractions. During the clearing, both parties sit facing each other, straight back with a relaxed posture, and their feet flat on the ground, maintaining easy eye contact. First, you must clear any ego thoughts about your clearing partner (the coach or friend holding the space for you). For example, **"What I want you to know is** that I am feeling apprehensive to clear with you because you remind me of my aunt who was unkind to me." Or **"What I want you to know is** that you remind me of my first-grade teacher who put me down in front of the whole class and made me feel stupid and different from the other children."

State what is going on for you and process it using the three steps of the clearing.

For example, if you are clearing with your mom, your clearing might start with, **"What I want you to know**, Mom, **is** that I feel really nervous about clearing with you."

The person holding the neutral space of compassion, presence, and understanding for the one doing the 3-step *Clearing Process* is either a trained clearing coach, a participant who has taken one of the *On Purpose* trainings, or a trusted friend who has learned *The Clearing Process* from reading this book. This person must be fully present, holding the space for you with no judgment or blame. If any personal interpretation comes up and triggers them from what you are sharing, they will take deep breaths to let it go and acknowledge to themselves they feel triggered. Then, they will say (only to themselves), "I'm letting this trigger go now, and I'm returning to full peace." (See "The Watcher" in the Resources section.)

At the end of the clearing, always express how you are feeling and truly connect with your clearing partner. You can say a prayer of gratitude if this feels appropriate.

Clearing is a forgiveness process. You can go through the motions many times before you genuinely mean it. When you *really* want to clear, you will clear. You only forgive yourself for your misperceptions—your ego thoughts, feelings, and beliefs. It is not about the other person.

You must motivate yourself to give one hundred percent to the clearing at all times and not stop. The ego will sidetrack you to control and stop the process before you complete the clearing. For example, the person clearing may feel fantastic after Step 1 since rarely, if ever, does anyone have the chance to express every negative thought and feeling to the characters they are clearing about and in a safe space. However, completing only Step 1 or Step 2 in *The Clearing Process* will *not* work to fulfill your intention!

It is essential to keep practicing *The Clearing Process* in your everyday life. Be vigilant of your ego thoughts, and if you have a recurring thought about a particular person or issue, that is probably a good starting point for your next clearing. Rather than approaching your clearing with effort and self-recrimination, please remain curious and awake.

WHAT ARE THE LONG-TERM BENEFITS OF *CLEARING?*

As we release the layers of dark cloths through clearing, the light of our True Self comes through increasingly in our daily living. The long-term benefits of clearing are twofold:

- Greater consistency in what we think, feel, say, and do with complete transparency in all our communication without ego strategy; we then know for sure we are truly innocent
- We are able and naturally drawn to turn more of our attention and energy toward fulfilling our life's purpose and accessing our true nature as joyful, loving beings

The benefits of greater consistency in what we think, feel, say, and do:

- Relationships are more joyous, connected, and aligned
- We experience longer times of happiness, peace, and contentment
- Challenges are shorter in duration and easier to put behind us
- We are more loving and present, with more power in our expression
- We experience interconnection with all there is, in complete Presence

The Clearing Process releases everything ready to go at the moment of the clearing, much as ripe fruit from a tree will let go easily without force when merely touched.

So, we are only accessing what we are ready to let go of now in a gentle, flowing way. There is no struggle; only the natural release.

Consistency in what you think, feel, say, and do is the definition of honesty, according to ACIM.

The Manual for Teachers in the third section of *A Course in Miracles* lists ten characteristics of the Teachers of God. There are unusual definitions for these characteristics: Trust, Honesty, Tolerance, Gentleness, Joy, Defenselessness, Generosity, Patience, Faithfulness, and Open-Mindedness.

II. Honesty

1. All other traits of God's teachers rest on trust. ²Once that has been achieved, the others cannot fail to follow. ³Only the trusting can afford honesty, for only they can see its value. ⁴Honesty does not apply only to what you say. ⁵The term actually means consistency. ⁶There is nothing you say that contradicts what you think or do; no thought opposes any other thought; no act belies your word; and no word lacks agreement with another. ⁷Such are the truly honest. ⁸At no level are they in conflict with themselves. ⁹Therefore it is impossible for them to be in conflict with anyone or anything.

2. The peace of mind which the advanced teachers of God experience is largely due to their perfect honesty. ²It is only the wish to deceive that makes for war. ³No one at one with himself can even conceive of conflict. ⁴Conflict is the inevitable result of self-deception, and self-deception is dishonesty. (ACIM, M-4.II.1:1–2:4)

We include these unique definitions of those characteristics in the training of *The Power of Clearing* coaches for them to aspire to in their intention to live in Big T Truth. Trust is the foundation of the ten characteristics that become a core value system in how you view yourself and relate to others.

Only the trusting can afford honesty, for only they can see its value.

(ACIM, M-4.II.1:3)

Big "T" Truth Constant Eternal Truth Real World	little "t" truth impermanent temporary truth unreal world
❖ The World of Knowledge ❖ The Self ❖ Trust ❖ Now (Eternal) ❖ Responsibility	♦ the world of perception ♦ the ego ♦ conditional trust ♦ the past and the future ♦ burden
I am Love *I am Light* *I am Joy* *I am Innocent* *I am Safe* *I am Pure* *I am Peace* *I am Unlimited* *I am Abundant* *I am Whole and Complete* *I am Free* *I am Eternal* *I am Beauty* *I am Grace* *I am Compassion* *I am Present* *You are Everything I Am* *We are the Same* *We are Joined* *I am One with you* *I am as God/Source created me*	Ego thoughts > feelings > beliefs > ego experiences The world of illusions Interpretations & opinions Expectations & disappointments Betrayal & abandonment The body & the physical Addictions Ego games > sex, money, time, power, and control The need to be right The feeling of separation Sin Guilt & shame Fear Regret Attack & defense Pleasure & pain Sickness & suffering Death of the body

© Sandy Levey-Lundén / On Purpose / www.SandyLevey.com. Revised February 2022
tel: (360) 527-2796 email: onpurpose@sandylevey.com

The Advanced Clearing

STEP 1. Report all negative ego thoughts, feelings, and beliefs

Person A: "**What I want you to know,** *(name)*, **is that I think/feel/believe**... *(current ego thought, judgment, attack, accusation, feeling, belief, experience)* ... **which makes me feel**... *(feeling)* ... **just like when**... *(scene from the past)*."

Person B: "**Thank You.**"

("**Thank You**" means "**I heard what you said. I have received your communication.**")

Person A shares the current feelings or experience and relates it to how it is familiar to them from the past.

Person B listens without agreeing with or rejecting what Person A says and helps Person A release.

EXAMPLES OF STEP 1:
Person A: "**What I want you to know**, *Jane*, **is that I think** *that you don't listen to me*, **which makes me feel** *frustrated* **just like when** *I thought my mother didn't listen to me*."

Or "**What I want you to know**, *Dave*, **is that I think** *that I can't trust you*, **which makes me feel** *helpless* **just like when** *I believed I couldn't trust my father not to attack me when he was drinking*."

Person B: "**Thank You.**"

STEP 2. Ask for forgiveness (correction of misperceptions) for ego thoughts, feelings, beliefs

Person A: "**What I want you to forgive me for**, *(name)*, **is for thinking/feeling/believing**... *(little t feeling)* ...**which means I am**... *(little t judgment of oneself)*."

Person B: "**Thank You. That is not the Truth. That's a story you made up. You are**... *(Big T Truth opposite of judgment)*. **I love You.**"

EXAMPLES OF STEP 2:

Person A: "**What I want you to forgive me for**, *Jane*, **is for believing** *that you don't listen to me*, **which means I am** *unimportant*."

Person B: "**Thank You. That is not the truth. You are infinitely important. I love You.**"

Person A: "**What I want you to forgive me for**, *Dave*, **is for feeling** *I can't trust you*, **which means I am** *helpless and not safe*."

Person B: "**Thank You. That is not the truth. You are always powerful and safe. I love You.**"

STEP 3. Remember Eternal Truth (reconfirming Big T Truth)

Person A: "**What I want you to forgive me for**, *(name)*, **is for forgetting that you are…**" (Big T Truth)

Person B: "**Thank You. That is the Truth, I am**… *(confirm Big T Truth)*. **I love You.**"

Person A shares the highest spiritual Truths and at the same time, corrects the misperception of the issues.

Person B confirms each of these Big T Truths.

EXAMPLES OF STEP 3:

Person A: "**What I want you to forgive me for**, *Jane*, **is for forgetting that you are** *Love*."

Person B: "**Thank You. That is the Truth. I am Love. I love You.**"

Person A: "**What I want you to forgive me for**, *Dave*, **is for forgetting that you are** *Innocent*."

Person B: "**Thank You. That is the Truth. I am Innocent. I love You.**"

© Sandy Levey-Lunden, On Purpose SandyLevey.com Revised June 2022.
(360) 527-2796 Pacific. onpurpose@sandylevey.com

The Clearing Process with a Friend

If you decide to clear with a friend who will be holding the space for your *Clearing Process*, here are important guidelines to follow. Please also refer to the next sections on clearing in this chapter.

1. It's essential to *The Clearing Process* to fully understand the chart of Big T (Truth) and little t (ego). Review and discuss the charts with your friend or clearing partner aloud. The downloadable *Power of Clearing* CD in the Resources section clarifies these differences and how to use them in *The Clearing Process.*

2. You have to decide at the outset who will be the one holding the space and who will be the one clearing. These are distinct roles to determine. One person would go through the 3-step process all the way, and then on another day, you would switch roles. The clearing is deep, and you need time and space to have the whole process set in and digest before changing roles.

3. You would do an honest self-assessment that you are able to lovingly hold the space with this friend about the issue you have discussed. You may have a personal bias since you know them very well, and therefore, you might have a pre-formed attitude about their issue that would hamper their clearing. Remember, the only response in Step 1 is "Thank you," which does not mean you agree with what your friend said. It means "I hear you, I'm with you, and continue emptying your ego thoughts." It's essential to follow the format of the 3-step *Clearing Process.*

4. You're not going to clear on an issue between the two of you because that takes advanced training. For example, in Step 1, both of you could be triggered by the issue between you; therefore, one might not be able to hold the space for the other.

5. You must be fully present with each other and awake without anything in your ego-mind going on. Four times, ask each other back and forth, "What do you need to let go of to be fully present now?" and answer in a complete sentence. For example, one replies, "I feel scared, inadequate, and not good enough to hold the space for you, and therefore I might do it wrong, and you won't be able to clear." Then the other repeats what they heard; this exercise is "pacing" in neurolinguistic programming

(NLP). For example, "You feel scared, inadequate, and not good enough to hold the space for me, and therefore you think you might do it wrong, and I won't be able to clear. Is this correct?"

6. Guide the person through Step 1, Step 2, and Step 3 to complete all steps of the process because unless they complete all three steps, they will not have released at a deep cellular level. Have the Big T and little t chart and *The Clearing Process* 3-step description available for reference during the process.

7. Refer to "The Watcher" (in the Resources section) and be in Big T Truth to hold the space in your true nature; if issues that are coming up for your friend trigger you, do not react from the feeling. If necessary, say, "I feel triggered, and I cannot hold the space for you." Then reschedule the clearing if you feel it is appropriate to hold the space for the person.

DISCLAIMER

Sandy Levey-Lunden operates her practice as a Minister and has a Master of Science in Education (M.S.Ed.) from the Bank Street College of Education in New York City as well as a BA in Psychology from the City College of New York City (CCNY). She received her unique, original method of *The Power of Clearing* in 1990 after working on personal development since she was seven years old. Her main aim in life became clearing people of pain and suffering.

Sandy encourages you to consider the benefit of working with a professional therapist or a certified *Power of Clearing* coach. If you are aware that you have significant emotional issues or feel shut down and unable to access your thoughts and beliefs, a therapist or coach can help you identify and clear them. The coaches listed in the Resources section offer a free twenty-minute consultation to answer any questions you may have about *The Clearing Process* and help you decide whether you want to work together. The paid clearing session can be a single session or one of a series of sessions, depending on your needs and your intention. The therapist or coach may ask you several questions to determine your issues. Alternatively, you may wish to focus on a single issue to clear on with the coach. If you book a session, know beforehand the coach's fees and how they prefer to receive payment.

The Clearing Process is a psycho-spiritual method to release negative thoughts, feelings, and beliefs holding you back from living fully. An important component of this process is your awareness that you may have been resisting your healing for years. You may think you want to wake up and live as your authentic self, however your ego may be holding you back. Sandy's trained and skilled coaches will guide you to look deeply within to clear the lies you tell yourself about why you are afraid to heal and are unworthy of having the life you desire.

After you read this book and learn the steps of *The Clearing Process*, please follow your inner guidance in arranging to clear with your therapist who uses *The Power of Clearing* or with one of the available coaches listed in the Resources. Be aware that the ego can be slippery, sneaky, and subtle, giving you seemingly valid reasons to fear looking within. However, once you are committed to living in peace, harmony, love, and innocence, attaining your vision of your best life will be inevitable. So, by fully committing, you will get to that place of innocence by clearing your resistance with your trained coach.

Sandy supports you in practicing *The Clearing Process* material for personal use. However, *the material cannot be utilized for teaching without her official training and express permission. While Sandy is an experienced coach, counselor, and trainer, she is not a medical doctor or a licensed psychotherapist. Therefore, Sandy and the team involved in preparing this book of her life's work are free of liability* regarding how you choose to apply *The Clearing Process* in your life and encourage you to take responsibility for your choices.

My Personal Example of *The Clearing Process*

While receiving what we now call *The Power of Clearing* or *The Clearing Process*, I applied the guidance to my pain and anguish about my husband and Birgitta. When I was in the first stage of *The Clearing Process*, I came up with all of my ego's projected thoughts, feelings, and beliefs negatively impacting me about Peter choosing another woman rather than me. I felt anger and resentment toward them. I felt victimized, betrayed, and abandoned.

It is important to note that while this exchange appears to be between Peter and me, it never took place in reality. The process I describe was a clearing with

Mats holding the space for us as if he was Peter so that I could fully emote all my feelings, thoughts, and beliefs in Step 1 of *The Clearing Process*. We never clear with the person involved unless that person is trained in clearing and holding the space. Listening to the other person's feelings in a situation like I describe would trigger most people who would feel compelled to defend themselves instead of holding the space, listening, and being there for the person clearing.

Because *The Clearing Process* that I received in my prayer has a precise structure and clear steps, I could go beyond the limits of my ego's need to go on and on, making me right that I was a victim. With Mats as my clearing coach holding the space for me to clear in a safe container of Love and Big T Truth, I verbally and emotionally released everything I was going through at a total pain level, being heard and witnessed. I thought the loss of my husband and our marriage would kill me. However, that loss turned out to be a great blessing. My present emotional pain propelled me into my original pain of feeling rejected and betrayed in my childhood. My holy relationship with Mats reminded me of Big T Truth and the purpose of the holy relationship, seeing the other person as innocent in their true authentic nature of love, peace, and joy, and supporting them to release their egoic pain. Through *The Clearing Process*, I found a way to heal my present and past pain and return to my joy. I was excited to see that this process could help others release pain on any subject and return to their joy.

I had felt guilty that this perceived betrayal happened to me and that, in some way, I created or attracted it into my life. Understanding the difference between taking full responsibility for my part and falling into the ego guilt trap is important. We need to embody the idea that we are never guilty of what happens to us in our lives. There is no shame. We are spiritually innocent, no matter what happens, and on a journey of awakening.

An example of Step 3: "**What I want you to forgive me for,** (name), **is for forgetting that I** attracted you into my life and this situation so I could release this betrayal or egoic pattern more deeply and clear myself further. Thank you for being part of my journey to who I am."

Many people need an expressive communication tool to access their emotions, feelings, and unconscious patterns. Through *The Clearing Process*, you identify your held beliefs, immerse yourself in the totality of the experience, and release your pain whenever a person or event triggers you. For example, you are *clearing* a negative thought you may have lived by, and now you are ready to release it.

EXAMPLE OF STEP 1: Expressing ego thoughts on a subject, holding nothing back.

I say: "**What I want you to know,** Peter, **is that I feel** betrayed by you changing from loving me to no longer loving me, **which makes me feel** separate and alone, **just like when** I was little, my brother really loved me and was into playing with me. Then he closed his bedroom door to me and no longer allowed me to enter."

Coach: "Thank you."

Another example of Step 1 of my *clearing*: "**What I want you to know**, Peter, **is that I feel** disappointed and scared about us getting divorced, **which makes me feel** separate and alone with a distance between us, **just like when** I lost my childhood home with so many people around me, and our new home had few familiar faces."

Coach: "Thank you."

I felt more released after identifying and venting these feelings and thoughts for another hour with the coach through completing Step 1 of *The Clearing Process*.

EXAMPLE OF STEP 2: Forgiving yourself or someone else for what they think and what it says about you or them. The end of the sentence is the most important.

Step 2 involves asking for forgiveness and correcting misperceptions regarding the ego's thoughts, feelings, and beliefs. You can only go to Step 2 when you have fully expressed your feelings about the upsetting situation in Step 1.

During Step 2 of my clearing, I said, "**What I want you to forgive me for,** Peter, **is for feeling** abandoned because I think you no longer love me, **which means I am** rejected, alone, and not good enough."

The coach or person holding the space affirms with, "Thank You. That is not the Truth. It's a story you made up when you were very little, and you can let go of that right now. You are Joined, always Loved, and always good enough."

Then I asked for forgiveness from myself. "**What I want you to forgive me for,** Sandy, **is for believing** that your brother rejected you after you gave him all of your love and attention, supporting him however you could, **which means that you are** not good enough to be cared about, loved, and cherished."

I continued Step 2 for about twenty minutes, asking for forgiveness on all of the main issues I identified in Step 1. For example, for beliefs that I held against myself. "**What I want you to forgive me for,** Sandy, **is for believing I am** unlovable because I am separating from my marriage partner, **which means I am** unworthy of receiving love forever."

Answer from the coach, again, "Thank You. That is not the Truth; You are worthy of receiving Love, always. You are perfect Love itself."

EXAMPLE OF STEP 3: Reminding the person they are in Big T Truth.

Sandy: **What I want you to forgive me for forgetting,** Peter, **is that you are** Innocent.

Coach: Thank You. That is the Truth. I am Innocent. I love You.

Sandy: **What I want you to forgive me for forgetting,** Peter, **is that** we are always Joined.

Coach: Thank You. That is the Truth. We are eternally Joined in Love.

Sandy: "**What I want you to forgive me for forgetting,** Sandy, **is that I am** worthy of Love."

Coach: "Thank You. That is the Truth. You are always worthy of Love. I love You."

Sandy: "**What I want you to forgive me for forgetting,** Sandy, **is that you are** Love personified."

Coach: "Thank You. That is the Truth. You are Love itself."

You always confirm Big T Truth in *The Clearing Process* in Steps 2 and 3, the Divine, the eternal Truth of who you are. *The Power of Clearing* process goes to the core issue rather quickly. A person clearing could go straight to the root of their core pain, or it might take several clearings to peel the layers from many months and years of thoughts, feelings, and beliefs about their pain and its origins before the Truth of it is brought to Light. Whether you felt attacked or victimized, it doesn't matter. It's the same thing to your ego. Step 3 is also a process of forgiveness; however, you remember your Eternal Truth and your True Nature this time. You also reflect on the Eternal Truth and True Nature of every person on whom you projected your feelings. Step 3 puts a healing balm over the whole clearing. Steps 1 and 2 hold the container of the Big T Truth that you are now in the present where only Big T Truth is True.

I love to clear because when I do, I feel such a complete sense of Presence and so free, like a plant, fresh and free with its roots firmly rooted in the earth. *The Clearing Process* can free everyone from anything holding them back from anywhere they want to go.

Note: Most people don't consciously remember back to their time in the womb, being born, or infancy unless they have an emotive feeling therapy like Primal Therapy. The only way I have that original memory from six months old is from doing two years of Primal Therapy in my thirties working on this specific incident, one of my life's most traumatic experiences so far. Going back to the original trauma is unnecessary to clear something from your past. Sometimes it is just emotion that comes out during Step 1, and you can get back to the origin of the pain from when you were little when you were pre-verbal, so there are no words to express your experience. You allow yourself to review these thoughts, feelings, and beliefs (from Step 1) and correct your ego's perception of them. All ego thoughts are little t truth (temporary truth) when we feel them and while going through them. Since the little t truths seem accurate and true to us feeling them, we are convinced of and committed to these perceptions, so we act them out in our lives. They can quickly shift once we feel them and speak them. The purpose of Step 1 is an emptying out of all the grievances and upsets you have with the character, declaring all of your little t truths.

I have seen people who access an original memory during *The Clearing Process* where the subconscious mind will suddenly reveal the memory in Step 1 when we do the part "just like when." (We're allowing a space in this part of the clearing for a memory to come forth.) This memory will appear when the subconscious mind is like ripe fruit falling from the tree, landing in your hand with no effort. In other words, you have reached the time in your life when you are ready to immerse yourself in that memory and release it at the core.

For example, the clearing coach, holding the space for Step 1 from a Big T Truth place, would say "Thank you" and be present without judging, agreeing, or putting me in a box with a label. Instead, they merely offer compassionate support. I would continue revealing everything in the little t truth of what I think, feel, and believe in my ego-mind about my pain and suffering about this betrayal. In other words, we stick to a subject that has upset us and go as deeply as we can into that feeling about a person or subject.

If you do not know what to clear about or what you are upset about, have a colleague, friend, or therapist you trust to ask you the following questions. What do you constantly obsess about in your mind? What stories do you repeatedly review in your self-talk that support your feelings of being neglected, unimportant, unseen, uncared about, victimized, and what painful parts of your life do you relive in conversation with close friends? Or to anyone who will listen? Do you include one of these stories when you meet a new person? These stories or vignettes are what you need to clear. You can ask one of your closest allies what they think you repeatedly talk about as an upset from your life. The best person to ask these questions of you is someone you are willing to be fully transparent with and who you trust to share your deepest responses. It is ideal if the person who asks you these questions is holding the space for you in the clearing, like a clearing coach, another person trained in the clearing, or someone who has read *I Just Want Peace*. In the Resources section at the end of this book is a list of trained *Power of Clearing* coaches who are available to answer questions and go deeper into *The Power of Clearing* process with you. You can arrange for private sessions and private clearings with one of them.

You can do much on behalf of your own healing and that of others if,
in a situation calling for help, you think of it this way:

I am here only to be truly helpful.
I am here to represent Him Who sent me.
I do not have to worry about what to say or what to do,
because He Who sent me will direct me.
I am content to be wherever He wishes,
knowing He goes there with me.
I will be healed as I let Him teach me to heal.

(ACIM, T- 2.V.A.18(8):1-6)

It's What You Are

Waves of light landing on the shore that is your heart
It's what you are, it's what you are.
Open arms that welcome you in spite of what you thought
It's what you are, it's what you are.

Could it be that it was always only you keeping love away, thinking it would never stay?
What if you could see that love is always here, living right inside, would you change your mind?

Angel wings are holding you in such a gentle peace
It's what you are, it's what you are.
Merging into everyone as far as you can see
It's what you are, it's what you are.

Could it be that it was always only you keeping love away, thinking it would never stay?
What if you could see that love is always here, living right inside, would you change your mind?

Why do people love you?
Do you think it's the things you do?
No, it's what you are. It's what we are, it's what we are, it's what we are, it's what we are, it's what we are, it's what we are, it's what we are, it's what we are, it's what we are, it's what we are, it's what we are….

Song and lyrics by Charley Thweatt
Wave after Wave - Inspired Acoustic Music - musicangel.com

CHAPTER 7

IMPORTANT CLEARINGS

God Clearing and Family Clearing

Some religions talk about a specific doctrine that, if not followed to the letter, can suggest you have made mistakes, are guilty or sinful, and may be subject to imminent punishment. This sense of God's wrath is ever foreboding for someone living in fear that God will see they are guilty of doing something bad or wrong, something no one knows. Even though everyone says God forgives us for our sins, we make up that God will never forgive us for what we have done and will withdraw unconditional love and support at any moment. All these negative beliefs and thoughts can cause us to live in lack and ultimately prevent us from being reunited in divine connection because we believe we don't deserve it.

The Power of Clearing says all "mistakes" can be forgiven, by you, for you. In truth, only you can forgive yourself. When *you* forgive *yourself*, you will live in Peace. Therefore, our primary goal or intention in every spiritual process is to forgive ourselves for what we think, feel, or believe we did wrong and for how we judged ourselves.

Many clients who have done *The Clearing Process* with me arrived feeling strongly about not being at One with their God or themselves because they had done something they were hiding deep within that they needed to clear and forgive. It was so deeply engrained that they had trouble drawing it from their unconscious. I've noticed how *The Clearing Process* can bring forth a buried memory in a split second and make sense of a person's pain. They may not have thought about it consciously for dozens of years. In many cases, we are *clearing* the doctrines of religious practices they learned in childhood. Feeling they have failed to live according to these doctrines, they believe they deserve punishment and feel various degrees of guilt and shame. As a result, they make up an interpretation about themselves that they are guilty. So, they punish themselves because of their perceived guilt with, for example, a lack of money, a problematic relationship, a disease, a meaningless job, and a constant pursuit of a comfortable, secure home. They may also not know their purpose and constantly feel lost, including fear and distrust of everyone, blaming others for their plight, including God. They may also be skeptical about connecting with anything that looks like religion. Still, at the same time, they are wary of spiritual practices that don't encompass rules and boundaries like a religious doctrine. Once they clear the fear of having been indoctrinated *by* religion and the associated guilt deeply rooted within them, they are again able to embrace Oneness and connection with All.

This clearing of religious beliefs can take an intense form of releasing for the mind to let go of its programming. Afterward, they may be able to create an alternative philosophy of universal consciousness that works for them. For example, feeling connected with nature and like-minded people. The main objective of feeling safe and secure is to experience connection with "all there is."

> *You are one Self, in perfect harmony with all there is,*
> *and all that there will be.* (ACIM, W-95.13:1)

One of the most significant clearings a person does in any of the *On Purpose* trainings or my counseling is the specific clearing called the "God Clearing." It is an all-encompassing *clearing*. *The Clearing Process* works very well to release anything from one's consciousness they no longer want to embody about God, sin, guilt, and punishment. The person will then be able to feel and know the peace within their true, divine self and their connection to source in a whole new way once they have done the God clearing.

In this clearing, we speak our thoughts to God directly, out loud and forcefully, almost screaming, so we hear ourselves declaring the power of this thought process that has taken up so much room in our minds.

"What I want you to know, God, **is that I believe** I am bad, wrong, and a sinner, **which makes me feel** guilty and punished, **just like when** my father was always looking for things to blame on me." This perception is especially true for people who have had a strict Christian upbringing with the belief that we are born sinners and will always be guilty, with the wrath of God being ever-present. Therefore, God clearing involves releasing the belief that I am bad, wrong, and guilty, and that God is punishing me with everything that's going wrong in my life. The ego's range goes from suspiciousness to viciousness. The ego is always talking from a fear point of view and is constantly looking for guilt in yourself and someone else: the fear that you or someone is always guilty of something. Some of us have, as our greatest fear, that we are bad, wrong, or guilty, and God will punish us somehow. This perceived fear draws our own insatiable punishment to our lives. Forgiving these negative thoughts toward God and ourselves is another great awakening in *The Power of Clearing* process.

We can then see ourselves as forever innocent and forgiven when we finally forgive ourselves for every negative thing we have made up in our story about ourselves. Then we confirm we are love, light, and true innocent children in our true nature. In our awakening, we see that we only forgive ourselves for anything we thought we did because judgment is an ego construct. Anyone with religion in their life, or no faith, can do *The Clearing Process* and succeed in coming to Peace, Joy, and Love. The only reasons they wouldn't be successful in *The Clearing Process* is if they want to believe they are guilty and so are unwilling to surrender that perception and if they get up and leave the clearing before it is complete.

Alanna, client, workshop participant, with her Advanced *Clearing Process*

I have worked intensely with Sandy for several years with great success. Intermittently, I've had long periods of time in between sessions where I have felt no need to clear anything. I have worked through my biggest childhood traumas, and I was able to work my job without difficulty. However, I never fully believed or embodied the Big T Truths for very long. I never felt the "peace of God that passes all understanding" and had resigned myself to listless, boring, and safe living. I just worked lots of overtime to avoid human relationships and still experienced episodes of severe depression, anxiety, chronic fatigue, and loneliness.

Then several months back, I experienced a bee sting and started going into anaphylactic shock, and had to use my emergency EpiPen for the first time in my life. I called an ambulance, but there was no need to take me to the hospital as the EpiPen did its job and stopped the reaction.

Sandy and I did a session where we discovered that I still wanted to die and needed an "outside force" to do it for me since I had promised my sister that I would not attempt suicide again. So, we cleared this, and I thought we were okay.

Sandy has been urging me to move on in my life and create relationships and good experiences. I always got angry, resistant, and annoyed at her because that felt like a futile exercise for me to attempt. I felt I had no ambition, consistency, or energy to pursue anything that would bring joy. What was the point? I felt the same thing I had always felt since I was a child, namely that death is preferable to life, and I would just bum around until I died and figured things would be better in the afterlife. Why bother getting into a relationship with someone, building a family, or switching careers if this was my outlook on life? I wouldn't want to be with someone who had this worldview.

Shortly after that bee sting, I began experiencing panic attacks for the first time. Even on my deepest, darkest, most suicidal days, I never experienced panic attacks, so I was terrified. My blood pressure skyrocketed to 200/110, and my heart rate was over 120 with flushing, dizziness, and palpitations. I couldn't drive for long periods. I felt "thin" and "trembling" inside, and I no longer felt resilient. I went to the doctor for blood work and an EKG to check it wasn't my hormones or my heart. The levels came back within normal ranges. It was all anxiety related.

I did clearings with Sandy and Valerie, and they helped, but then I experienced "the big one," where I believe I went into a hypertensive crisis for two hours, and I thought I might die of a heart attack or stroke. I took aspirin, called a friend to help talk me through to get home, and I canceled two shifts off work, and stayed home. I almost went to the hospital, but because my blood pressure was fluctuating directly with my anxiety, I knew they could not help me except give me a Xanax and tell me to chill out.

Once I calmed down, I immediately started a 7-day water fast and cut out wheat, dairy, sugar, and caffeine. I began doing TRE (trauma release exercise) therapy, where you shake your body as if you were having a seizure to release emotions and energy. I also did hours of EFT (emotional freedom technique), where you tap your hands and parts of your body to release and program emotions and beliefs. I did all of these changes for two weeks straight with great success and was able to return to work and drive within a few days afterward. However, the hours and hours of stuff coming out while shaking the trauma loose exhausted me. My body and mind were not tolerating *any* anxiety or ego thoughts that would come up. If something hit me, I needed to clear it *right then,* or I felt like I would die. It really did feel like my death was imminent.

I had been keeping in contact with Sandy, and she gave me directions that I would work on for a few days at a time. I finally called her and asked for her opinion because I could not figure out why I was still dealing with all this stuff, and it was getting worse after all the years of successful clearing. I was in a living hell of my own making, and it wasn't going away no matter how much EFT or TRE I did.

She asked me a simple question: "Why do you still believe that something is wrong with you and that you need to be different to be accepted and loved? Fear and worry have to do with punishment. Why are you still punishing yourself?"

I spent a day thinking about these questions, and the answer came. "Why? Because I *am bad*, worthy of death and punishment, and unworthy of love." I realized I had internalized this message from birth, school, and the church being passed unconsciously through the family line. I had never questioned this core belief. It was absolute and rooted like iron in mind, body, and soul. I was a bad seed and knew it. No loving experiences to the contrary from parents, siblings, life events, or Big T Truths from clearings had ever shaken this belief. So, I called Sandy and we did the clearing. She has asked me to summarize *The Clearing Process* we did, which I have outlined.

Intention: "To release and let go of the thought, feeling, and belief that I am bad, wrong, guilty, and unworthy of being loved, and that I need to be punished. To know that I am whole, complete, perfect, and innocent as I am."

Prayer: "Dear Jesus, God, and the Holy Spirit. Please be with me and Sandy during this clearing and bring to my mind the true core beliefs needing to be cleared so I may finally have peace." *(Note: Alanna is praying in the traditionally religious sense of prayer.)*

Step 1 of *The Clearing Process*:
Report all negative ego thoughts, feelings, and beliefs

Here, the coach is holding space for all of Alanna's distressed, fearful, self-deprecating ego thoughts, feelings, and beliefs. The coach always replies, "Thank you," as in, "I'm here, I'm present, I'm listening," and "thank you for sharing your feelings so vulnerably and truthfully."

Alanna: **"What I want you to know,** Alanna, **is that I feel** I am BAD and wrong, **which makes me feel** I am guilty **just like when** the children at school didn't want to play with me, so it must be my fault."

Coach: "Thank you."

Alanna: **"What I want you to know,** Alanna, **is I feel** like I have to be different than who I am, **which makes me feel** unsafe **just like when** the Sunday School teacher said I would be punished if I told anyone what her son did to me."

Coach: "Thank you."

Alanna: **"What I want you to know,** Alanna, **is I believe** I am evil and bad, **which makes me feel** afraid that God is going to punish me, **just like when** He didn't stop the boy from raping me."

Coach: "Thank you."

Alanna: **"What I want you to know,** Alanna, **is that I believe** I am so bad, **which makes me feel** unworthy of anyone loving me, and alone and separate, **just like when** I was in school and all the other children were chosen to be part of a team and I was the only one left unchosen."

Coach: "Thank you."

Alanna: **"What I want you to know,** Mom and Dad, **is that I believe** I am a bad seed, unworthy of being born, **which makes me feel** hopeless and unlovable, **just like when** I felt bad that my teacher humiliated me in front of the whole class by telling me to be quiet and not to share my creative drawing with anyone that I was so excited about."

Coach: "Thank you."

Alanna: **"What I want you to know,** Alanna, **is that I believe** the core of me is bad, can't be fixed, and needs to be destroyed, **which makes me feel** unworthy of being alive, **just like when** the children were bullying me and I felt rejected, alone, and separate."

Coach: "Thank you."

Alanna: **"What I want you to know,** Alanna, **is that I believe** I am a mistake and deserved to die, **which makes me feel** hopeless, alone, and guilty, **just like when** Mom had high blood pressure and preeclampsia and I should have died in her womb instead of being born."

Coach: "Thank you."

Alanna: **"What I want you to know,** Mom, **is that I believe** you tried to kill me when I was born with the umbilical cord wrapped around my neck, **which makes me feel** unworthy of life, **just like when** I could barely breathe and felt choked, like I had no space to live many times in my life."

Coach: "Thank you."

Alanna: **"What I want you to know,** Mom **is that I believe** I was supposed to die and that you kept me alive against my will, **which makes me feel** powerless and weak **just like when** I was a little girl and you pressured me to always say that I was happy when I felt so sad and alone."

Coach: "Thank you."

Alanna: **"What I want you to know,** Mom and Dad, **is that I believe** you are to blame for keeping me alive when I was born, and that I should have died, **which makes me feel** hopeless and guilty, **just like when** I feel guilty for being alive now, so I am creating high blood pressure to have a heart attack and die."

Coach: "Thank you."

Alanna: **"What I want you to know,** Mom, **is that I believe** you should be punished and that you deserve to take care of me now while I'm incapacitated, **which makes me feel** angry and guilty, **just like when** I was born and I was in an incubator."

Coach: "Thank you."

Alanna: **"What I want you to know,** Alanna, **is that I believe** that a life of pain, suffering, and isolation is what I deserve, **which makes me feel** alone and separate, **just like when** I was in grade school and no one wanted be my friend."

Coach: "Thank you."

Alanna: **"What I want you to know,** Alanna, **is that I believe** I was supposed to have died at birth, **which makes me feel** guilty and worthy of punishment, **just like when** that boy took me to his bedroom."

Coach: "Thank you."

Alanna: **"What I want you to know,** Alanna, **is that I believe** I attracted the situation of being raped at 6 years old by a boy, **which makes me feel** guilty, **just like when** I felt frozen in fear that he was liking me so I had to give him what he wanted."

Coach: "Thank you."

Alanna: **"What I want you to know,** Alanna, **is that I feel** that part of me did die in that rape but my stupid body kept living, **which makes me feel** unworthy, terrified, panicked, and anxious with high blood pressure, **just like when** I was almost strangled by the umbilical cord."

Coach: "Thank you."

Alanna: **"What I want you to know,** sister, **is that I believe** you made me promise not to commit suicide, **that makes me feel** stuck, trapped, and powerless with no choice **just like when** that boy was raping me and I felt I had no choice but to go along with it."

Coach: "Thank you."

Alanna: **"What I want you to know,** God, **is that I believe** You are not who You say You are, a loving God, **which makes me** feel guilty for the belief that You are not bigger than my fear, anxiety, and panic, **just like when** I was a child sitting alone in my bed, wondering where are You, God, and am I so bad that You have deserted me?"

Coach: "Thank you."

Alanna: **"What I want you to know,** God, **is that I feel** there is no point for You and that You don't care about my suffering, **which makes me feel** hopeless and unworthy of You saving or caring about me, **just like when** you let me be raped by that boy."

Coach: "Thank you."

Step 2: Ask for forgiveness (correction of misperceptions) for ego thoughts, feelings, and beliefs

Alanna: **"What I want You to forgive me for,** God, **is for thinking** You do not exist, **which means I am** alone, unsafe, and unprotected."

Coach: "Thank you, that is not the Truth. You are always safe, protected, and never alone. And I love you."

Alanna: **"What I want you to forgive me for,** Alanna, **is for believing** that I am a guilty sinner, always deserving of pain, suffering, isolation, and being separate from everyone, **which means I am** fundamentally flawed."

Coach: "Thank you, that is not the Truth. You are whole, perfect, complete and innocent in who you truly are, and nothing will ever change that."

Alanna: **"What I want you to forgive me for,** Alanna, **is for believing** that I should be dead, should never have lived, should have died in the womb, and should never have been conceived, **which means I am** a bad seed that should never have existed."

Coach: "Thank you, that is not the Truth. That is a story you made up when you were very small. As a child of God, your existence is purposeful and you are here to be your authentic self, in pure love, peace, and joy."

Alanna: **"What I want you to forgive me for,** Alanna, **is for believing** that I am totally unworthy of love, peace, joy, and happiness, and destined to a life of suffering, **which means I am** unworthy of living."

Coach: "Thank you, that is not the Truth. It's just a story you made up and was never true, so you can let that story go now. As a perfect, infinitely worthy child of God, you deserve to live with perfect peace and happiness."

Alanna: **"What I want you to forgive me for,** Alanna, **is for believing** that the rape was punishment for my sin of being born and existing, **which means I am** worthless and should have never existed."

Coach: "Thank you, that is not the Truth. That is also a story you made up for very good reason when you were little. The Truth is that you are innocent and will always be innocent, and nothing can change that. It is part of your true nature and I love you."

Remember Eternal Truth (reconfirming Big T Truth)

I completed all three clearing steps with Sandy over the phone. Then she told me to go over the third step ("forgive me for forgetting") whenever the ego is drawing me again into believing that I am wrong, bad, and guilty, and to reinforce it by saying it aloud in the mirror. I bought a compact purse mirror just for this purpose. Sandy told me to repeat each affirmation of truth one at a time. Over the following hours, days, and weeks, this additional advice was valuable since this core re-programming requires reinforcement because of the ego's tricks. I would feel good and relieved after the clearing until later, when the ego would draw me back into anxiety, flushing, and panic. The fear would prick my neck, and I could feel it trying to overwhelm me and my body. So, I would repeat variations of these words of affirmation, such as:

Alanna: **"What I want you to forgive me for forgetting,** Alanna, **is that I am** Love."

Then I would answer, aloud to myself or in the mirror: "Thank you, that is the Truth; you are Love, and will always be Love, no matter what, and I love you."

"What I want you to forgive me for forgetting, Alanna, **is that I am** Innocent."

Answer: "Thank you, that is the Truth, you are Innocent, and will always be Innocent, no matter what, and I love you."

"What I want you to forgive me for forgetting, Alanna, **is that I am** Perfect, Whole, and Complete."

Answer: "Thank you, that is the Truth: you are Perfect, Whole, and Complete, and will always be Perfect, Whole, and Complete, no matter what. And I love you."

"What I want you to forgive me for forgetting, God, **is that You and I are** Love, and that perfect love lives inside of me. That is my true nature and there is nothing else. Nothing, no one, or any event can change this Truth."

Answer: "Thank you, that is the Truth. I am Love itself. You are a loving person at your core."

"What I want you to forgive me for forgetting, God, **is that I am** Innocent and that You know that I am Innocent." (I experienced a great deal of grief after expressing this affirmation.)

Answer: "Thank you, that is the Truth. You are Innocent, and will always be Innocent, and I love you."

"What I want you to forgive me for forgetting, Alanna, **is that I am** in the likeness of God's true nature: Perfect, Whole, and Complete, in every way."

Answer: "Thank you, that is the Truth. You are the essence of God's true nature: Perfect, Whole, and Complete in every way."

"What I want you to forgive me for forgetting, Alanna, **is that I was** born to live. God lives inside me as life itself and life abundant."

Answer: "Thank you, that is the Truth. You and God are one. One Will, One Mind, One Truth, One Heart."

"What I want you to forgive me for forgetting, Alanna, **is that I am** wanted and loved and have always been wanted and loved."

Answer: "Thank you, that is the Truth. From the moment you were conceived, your essence has always been valued and loved by God and the true self of everyone."

"What I want you to forgive me for forgetting, Alanna, **is that I am** Whole and Healed. I am Perfect in God's Eyes."

Answer: "Thank you, that is the Truth. You are Perfect, Whole, and Healed in God's eyes."

"What I want you to forgive me for forgetting, Alanna, **is that I am** Perfect, Love, Peace, and Joy, and that is my true nature."

Answer: "Thank you, that is the Truth. You are Perfect, Love, Peace, and Joy, and that is your true nature."

Alanna's account after completion of the clearing, days later

"When the ego throws something up that causes me fear or anxiety, I say to myself: 'The story I'm telling myself is that I will always have panic attacks and I will never get rid of them. Clearings are stupid and I'll likely die of a stroke or heart attack and there is nothing I can do to stop this.' I'll follow this with: 'self, that is just a bullshit story from my ego that I'm telling myself, a story that isn't serving me anymore, and I choose to let it go right now completely.' Lastly, I would follow this by repeating the Step 3 'forgiveness for forgetting' part of the clearing to reconfirm and reprogram the Truth."

Some new thoughts from Alanna in 2022

When I met Sandy, I was 28, and for 12 years, I had been stuck in the scene with the young man who raped me when I was six years of age. It was not until I was 16 when I was first interested in a boy and imagined kissing him, that the whole memory returned. Then, the dimension of the effect of this event on my entire growing-up life was more evident to me. My schooling, friends, and self-expression were affected by feeling overpowered by others and rejected, abandoned, and afraid of being fooled by them. I remembered that the young man (around 20, who I knew and trusted) and his mother threatened me that if I told my parents or anyone else, they would hurt me. She was my Sabbath School teacher, and I needed to be in her class every Saturday and pretend everything was okay. My father had entrusted me to their care while my parents went out of town overnight for business. It was the first time they had left me with someone overnight. When they returned to get me, they could tell something was different about me, but they didn't put together what had occurred. I had been a vibrant, excited, passionately alive child filled with curiosity and wonder. That boy and his mother victimized me and robbed me of my passion for life.

At 35, I have yet to have a love affair or boyfriend. I have never considered that I am worthy of a relationship for life with a man I can trust and count on for full support and who would authentically see me as I am rather than a body. I thought I was damaged, pessimistic, and powerless. I couldn't conceive of something so simple as a better life (that emotionally felt different or better) than my experience so far.

Sandy told me I needed to "WANT life, WANT love, and WANT peace" in order to change and attain it. Unfortunately, my worldview was so skewed that those words felt hollow, strange, and impossible to imagine. My concept of "Life" has been something hard, serious, exhausting, and hopeless. Who would WANT more of that? Why would I WANT more life?? That's why death was so much preferable to me. To me, death was a concept of literal release from the cares of this life, and I was so miserable that I wanted death to end the misery.

For someone living in this turmoil like me, unable to conceive of a way out of the bare minimum of survival, they need to question and trust there is another way to live beyond struggle, pain, and heartache. I thought I would live in that old paradigm forever until I met you, Sandy, and *The Power of Clearing* process. Life beyond the pain IS better and is totally worth getting to because now I have a sense of hope, optimism, and Big T trust that I was missing in my early life experience. I still need to keep confirming my authentic self and Big T truth when the little t from my past triggers me. Then I do Steps 1, 2, and 3 of *The Clearing Process* with myself in a mirror. I am in this process of awakening and remembering who I am every moment of my life. I am experiencing more joy, fun, and a sense of possibilities now in Big T than when I lived in little t. I am not defined by fear, guilt, and defensiveness anymore.

Today in 2022, is my 35th birthday. I am hopeful and trusting that I can experience a true celebration of my life and existence at this moment on this day.

THE GUEST HOUSE

by Jalaluddin Rumi, translation by Shahram Shiva

This being human is a guest house.
Every morning a new arrival.

A joy, a depression, a meanness,
some momentary awareness comes
as an unexpected visitor.

Welcome and entertain them all!
Even if they are a crowd of sorrows,
who violently sweep your house
empty of its furniture,
still, treat each guest honorably.
He may be clearing you out
for some new delight!

The dark thought, the shame, the malice,
meet them at the door laughing
and invite them in.

Be grateful for whatever comes,
because each has been sent
as a guide from beyond.

Rumi poem from the book *Rumi: The Beloved Is You: My Favorite Collection of Deeply Passionate, Whimsical, Spiritual and Profound Poems and Quotes,* by Shahram Shiva.

PART III

DIVING DEEPER

CHAPTER 8

HEALING ACCOMPLISHED

Surrender

Most people think they have to be in control and can't let go or everything will fall apart. They use considerable energy to avoid letting go of control and believing they know everything. Their belief in being right is pervasive and accepting that they might be wrong feels like a stretch. It's a common belief that without controlling the outcome, it may become destructive. This predicament results in a lack of trust in everything.

Definitions of surrender from the Oxford Canadian Dictionary are shocking examples of how "surrender" is shifting into "submission," such as: "Give up possession or control of (something) to another, especially on compulsion or demand; relinquish, yield. Abandon (hope, etc.), offer or give oneself up as a prisoner to an enemy or the police; submit. Submit or abandon oneself entirely to some influence, emotion, course of action." Our general understanding of surrender is that it is a scary action of submission.

Metaphysical thinking and *The Power of Clearing* process understand surrender as letting go and allowing the force for good—a Higher Power or Holy Spirit—to guide us and trust that everything is for our highest benefit.

When I lived in Sweden, people asked me to write a training course to demonstrate surrender. So, I created *The Art of Surrender*. While there are many words in

Swedish that could mean "surrender," they didn't have a clear meaning according to my definition. I like the way I demonstrated surrender so much in that training that I still use the same content thirty years later.

> To surrender is to let go, to trust life, to walk the path of Love, to trust the process, to be the one you really are, to dare to do the unknown even when you doubt, releasing to a Higher Power, accepting ANY situation, what is IS, to say YES! To share and dare to show yourself, to let go of control, to open, to release to Love, to give up wanting to be right, to stop struggling, to know what you really want. The freedom to give and receive fully. To let go of all belief systems, to let go of blame. To dare, dare, and dare some more. To be open to whatever, even though it is threatening. To make a passionate commitment to who you truly are. To join with others to experience oneness. To join God. To give up defiance. To have complete presence knowing You Are; nothing else matters.

From our Big T Self (in Peace, Love, and Unity), we can still, as ever, trust that everything is working out for our best interests despite any onslaught of little t truth experiences. By living and trusting in joy, we manifest our world to expand in that joy.

Everything is for your own best interests. (ACIM, W-25.1:5)

How Is Healing Accomplished?

The third section of *A Course in Miracles* is the Manual for Teachers. Chapter 5 is entitled, "How Is Healing Accomplished?" and the answer follows: *Healing involves an understanding of what the illusion of sickness is for. Healing is impossible without this.* (ACIM, M-5.1)

The first section of Chapter 5, "The Perceived Purpose of Sickness," (ACIM, M-5.I) also answers the question: *Healing is accomplished the instant the sufferer no longer sees any value in pain.* (ACIM, M-5.I.1:1) The next question forms the basis for the exploration in this chapter. *Who would choose suffering unless he thought it brought him something, and something of value to him?* (ACIM, M-5.I.1:2)

I find this first section, "The Perceived Purpose of Sickness," to be a compelling description of how to heal any existing condition you no longer want. I have found little written about this section, and I've always been surprised that more ACIM teachers don't focus on this vital material in the Manual for Teachers. I think it's one of the most significant parts of the book because it supports healing on all levels: mental, physical, emotional, and spiritual, and describes how to heal and release anything that you no longer wish to have in your body, mind, or spirit. Since, according to ACIM philosophy, the body is not real, some ACIM students may perceive that the book does not support physical healing. However, I find that when the person I'm working with clears the mental and emotional aspects, most of the time, the physical condition disappears. Perhaps it disappears because, as a participant, witnessing and coaching the person, I believe it will disappear; the student and I join in the purpose of fully releasing the meaning that the condition held for the person.

For a person using this inquiry process, I strongly recommend reading pages 17-18 in the Manual for Teachers three or more times. (See Appendix E for the full ACIM text of these pages.) I have read them at least one hundred times, and in every reading, I see another aspect to focus on in someone's healing. These two pages were the catalyst for me to write eight questions for a person to ask themselves when they want to heal from any condition. When working with students, I ask them to go deeply through the questions to see how their thoughts, feelings, and beliefs impacted the condition in their bodies. I ask them to do this exercise to free themselves from their perceived guilt. For most of the people I have worked with, in the trainings and my therapy practice, the student's emotional or physical condition disappeared when we did the entire process in *Choosing Freedom: The Way Out of All Pain and Suffering.*

Having a trained coach working with you helps clear your ego-mind of your emotional pain, fear, guilt, and separation feelings. When the person is familiar with the history of your life and the stories you repeatedly tell, it is easier for them to see the main points of your ego story self-talk or discussion and what you need to clear. However, they can only be a neutral guide if they don't collude (agree) with you about your ego stories, such as "my mother never loved me," "I was never a wanted child," or "I am all alone."

Since the ego is circular, it's most beneficial for a *Power of Clearing* coach or a trusted friend who has read this book to ask you these eight questions rather than simply asking yourself. You will go deeper with your inquiry and search for the real answers in your subconscious when someone asks you these questions out loud.

Here are the eight essential questions to answer for any emotional or physical condition to be released.

1. When did this sickness begin? (What was happening in your life, and what were your prevailing feelings in the months or years preceding the condition?)

2. What is the condition's value, payoff, or benefit? (What does it help you do or not do? Why do you want to maintain the condition and keep it in your life? Make a list of the reasons and payoffs.)

3. How does this choice for weakness give you strength? (How does it give you a sense of control or make you feel more powerful? How does it make you think you are better than God? What does the condition prove to you?)

4. What (with this insane conviction) does "healing" stand for? (What is the benefit of not letting go of the condition and not recovering?)

5. How would you like to be your own physician and heal yourself through your mind releasing the condition?

6. Who would you blame if you died? Who would you want to be sorry if you died or never healed? When you die, what would be happening at your funeral? How many people would you like to attend your memorial service? Who would be leading it as the MC? Which friends or family would you want to be speaking about you, and what would you want them to say? In other words, what do you want people to acknowledge you for after you die?

7. What do you feel guilty about in relation to your condition? (What have you felt guilty about in the past several years, and with whom? Additionally, look at any conflicts, disagreements, and upsets in your relationship life—mother, father, siblings, friends, romances, life partnerships.)

8. What do guilt and sickness, pain, disaster, and all suffering mean to you now?

If the sickness has no purpose now, it can leave. Answering these questions in conjunction with the 3-step *Clearing Process*, will welcome the real answers to why you are in resistance to Love. Expect to do more than one clearing because the puzzle of the ego-mind is complex, with many aspects to be revealed to you.

Further inquiry

If your condition will possibly lead to your death, please become aware and speak about: Why would you want to die at this time in your life? For example, ACIM says, *"No one can die unless he chooses death."* (ACIM, T-19.IV.C.1:4) You are the creator of your life and death by your choice.

Subsequently, ask yourself, and express: Why would you want to live? What would be your purpose for living right now? Why would you not want to heal right now? Are you attached to being right about anything?

In choosing to release the condition, you need to know your purpose in continuing to live. Having a clear intention and purpose for living creates great movement forward in your healing process. When you choose to live and recover from the condition, there will be a significant expansion in your life and available time and energy. This inquiry process in conjunction with steps such as specific foods, practitioner visits, and healing practices are necessary to regain your healthy life. What will you choose to do with your newly-emerged self, clean, clear, and innocent?

Questions Answered about the Condition

For a condition to disappear through the mind is a fully-committed, thorough process of clearing about aspects of the condition and answering these eight questions I have adapted from "The Perceived Purpose of Sickness." Here are examples of answers for you to consider and utilize in your healing. This ACIM student was releasing the condition of endometriosis in a series of personal counseling sessions with me.

> 1. *When did this sickness begin?* What was happening in your life? What were your prevailing feelings in the months or years preceding the condition?
>
>   This condition of adenomyosis sickness began in approximately 2004. However, I didn't know it at the time. I was noticing heavier than usual

bleeding in my periods. And more cramps lasting for a few days. I treated it with Tylenol, acupuncture, and herbs. I sought out other alternatives as well.

Late in 2008, at age 36, I noticed a bit of hardness below my belly button in the uterine area. My periods were becoming more difficult, heavier in bleeding and pain. That was when I started dating a man who would be my husband. I went to see the OB/GYN for a routine exam and mentioned it to her. She palpated it externally and said it was a fibroid and, although small, would grow. She noted that if I wanted to have children, I had better hurry up and be careful because the fibroid may interfere with the healthy development of a baby. I was fearful and dove further into many healing modalities to "fix" it.

At this time, I was nurturing my relationship with my future husband, dealing with a busy, demanding practice, and caretaking for my father, who was very ill, and my mother. She had difficulty taking care of both of them. In addition, I lived an hour away in a neighboring state, so I was quite stressed, worried, and worn out then.

My feelings about my period and having children in the months and years that preceded the sickness were that I always seemed to have reproductive stuff and uncertainty about my past abortions and motherhood in general.

After getting married in 2009, I saw another ob/gyn, and she said that although my fibroids had grown, I could get pregnant and carry to full term. I got pregnant, and my ob/gyn saw the fibroids and confirmed that everything was all right. However, I miscarried early, and she told me to try again. I got pregnant the second time and miscarried in week seven. Again, the ob/gyn said it happens and to try one more time. I got pregnant a third time and miscarried early. This ob/gyn then sent me to an IVF clinic. I went to the IVF clinic and went through the paperwork and examinations but got pregnant before we could even start IVF. I miscarried early again. I did not go back to the IVF clinic. In 2013, I went to fertility support, Julia Indichova. My husband and I went to her workshops and did a lot of inner work. I got pregnant for the fifth time and then miscarried early. In 2014, my father passed, and many months later, I got pregnant for the sixth time.

My dear friend recommended another ob/gyn, who again told me that although the fibroids were larger, it was still okay, and the pregnancy looked great. At five months, I miscarried. The ob/gyn suggested that I have an MRI of the uterus, and that's when he saw that it wasn't fibroids but rather a condition called adenomyosis. He told me there is no cure and that the only remedy he knew of was a hysterectomy.

I was deeply afraid that I must have harmed my uterus because of the number of sex partners, sexual activity, and abortions. Therefore, I had extreme guilt to clear from myself.

2. *What is the value, pay-off, or benefit of your sickness?*

The value, pay-off, or benefit of my sickness, condition of adenomyosis, and everything that goes with it, is to be right about how bad of a girl I am, how guilty I am, and how much I deserve punishment.

The value, pay-off, or benefit of my sickness is that I get to be a victim and blame others, especially my parents.

The value, pay-off, or benefit of my sickness is that it serves as proof of control or power.

The value, pay-off, or benefit of my sickness is that it is sort of an FU to God.

3. *How does this choice for weakness give you strength? (How does it give you a sense of control or make you feel more powerful? How does it make you think you are better than God?)*

This choice for weakness gives me strength in a sense like I'm taking control here and I am in charge of the judge and jury. I'll be the one determining whether I'm guilty or not and what punishment that I am meting out. It makes me think that I am better and more powerful than God because I am right. It makes me think that God has no say in this and if he has no say, he has no power.

4. *What (with this insane conviction) does "healing" stand for?*

Healing stands for forgiveness. Healing stands for being unconditionally loved. Healing stands for God Loves me. Healing stands for that I am the extension and reflection of God, aka Love. Healing stands for being created as God created me, not how I created me. Healing stands for real Power.

5. *Would you like to be your own physician and heal yourself, with your mind releasing the condition? What would be your purpose for living, or healing? Why would you want to die, or not heal?*

Yes, I would like to be my own physician and heal myself, with my mind releasing adenomyosis and ALL guilt!

My purpose for living or healing would be to help others remember God and remember who we really are in Truth.

Why I would want to die or not heal (this is in the past) is because I am and was ego identified and fearful of Love.

6. *Who would you blame, or want to be sorry, if you died or stayed sick?*

I would blame or want to be sorry, God and my parents, if I died or stayed sick.

7. *What do you feel guilty about?*

At this point, a lot has cleared, but I did feel guilty and blamed myself for: abortions, miscarriages, being a burden, being born, being sick, and not having children or a family of my own.

8. *What do guilt, sickness, pain, disaster, and suffering mean now?*

Guilt, sickness, pain, and disaster mean nothing; I see them now as ego thoughts and beliefs that lead to guilt and punishment.

If the sickness has no purpose now, it can leave. I declare that I have no need for adenomyosis in any shape or form or effect in my mind, body, and spirit! I declare that I do not need or want adenomyosis and all its forms anymore! I declare that all guilt, resentment, and punishment are released from my mind!

No Order of Difficulty in Miracles

In Chapter 1 of the ACIM book, the first of 50 "Principles of Miracles" says: *There is no order of difficulty in miracles. One is not "harder" or "bigger" than another. They are all the same. All expressions of love are maximal.* (ACIM, T-1.I.1:1-4) I have found this truth to be so when I practice clearing physical or emotional conditions with the knowledge of "The Perceived Purpose of Sickness" (ACIM, M-5.I) and "The Shift of Perception" (ACIM, M-5.II) sections. The miracle will not happen if you are in pain, fear, or guilt. You must be in a total love state in order to allow the condition to depart.

In my counseling and courses, I have had people who were extremely sick with conditions that had existed for years. When I work with a student, I ask them to go deeply through eight to ten questions about the condition. They are able to clear the condition and are amazed it can happen so quickly and easily by clearing the mind. These conditions have included prostate cancer, allergies, colon problems, urinary tract infections, environmental illness, breast cancer, and the inability to conceive. While we have witnessed these healings, we make no claims that these healings will happen for everyone.

Here are some actual experiences of course participants in the healing process:

The first story is about a woman in Ontario, Canada, who couldn't conceive because of endometriosis, a fibrous tumor filling her womb. Her doctor said for $50,000, he could remove the tumor, and she would have a fifty percent chance of conceiving. She was one of my students, and I said, "If we fully commit to clearing during the ten-day *Power of Clearing Coaching Certification Program,* we may be able to clear the tumor through emotional processing so you can conceive." Months later, the doctor confirmed there was no longer any trace of the tumor, and she has since given birth to two lovely boys.

This second story is about a woman who attended one of my courses in Halifax, Nova Scotia, Canada, with a gas mask and a special lounge chair because of her pain. I held courses in that location because of environmental chemicals and their significant effect on people in the community. This woman had been in bed for two years because of environmental sensitivities, including smoke and gas fumes. By the end of the weekend workshop, her clearing work had alleviated the symptoms enough that she called her husband and said, "I have completed three days at the workshop, and now I want to go to a restaurant with you because we can have a normal life again!" He replied, "You haven't been able to leave the house for two years until this weekend; how can you go to a restaurant?" She told him, "I cleared my issues causing all my symptoms and anxieties about smoke, chemicals, and toxic fumes, so now I can go outside and be normal. I am no longer under attack from the outside because I have cleared my inner attack." Now, she can pump the gas at the gas station, after she couldn't entertain the idea of even going to a gas station; it would have been completely debilitating.

Two other women in Halifax had not left their homes for between three to five years. After the first training, they could go outside again and live normal lives. Within a year, they each had a job and no longer needed to collect disability from the insurance company. As a result, the insurance company was thinking of hiring me to help people heal from their disabilities so they would no longer need disability insurance payments. If someone feared no longer receiving the insurance money, they needed to clear about that. *The Clearing Process* wouldn't work for someone who didn't want to release their condition due to the financial benefit.

Whenever I went on location, I would hold three courses in a row, for example, *The Art of Surrender, True Women's Power,* and *Choosing Freedom: The Way Out of All Pain and Suffering.* By the time I left, people's conditions had gone or largely disappeared. They kept the healing philosophy of *The Power of Clearing* process alive through local support teams of people who had participated in the workshops. Watching their thoughts, feelings, and beliefs and clearing the dissonant ones as they arose became a way of life.

I had a friend who had a growing cancer tumor that was late-stage when she showed it to a doctor. She felt so guilty for having this breast cancer because she knew it represented her non-forgiveness toward her father. After she died, her father held a huge memorial service in the community where she lived for all her friends with a banquet to celebrate her life. He built a fountain in her honor so everyone would remember her nature as flowing water. When alive, she would say all the time, "He doesn't care." And I would say, "That is not true. He does care. He just doesn't know how to demonstrate his caring." Same with her mother.

The ego-mind of a person may depend on taking prescription pills to eradicate the symptoms for immediate relief. The exploration to discern the meaning and cause of the symptom at its root requires a willingness by the person to review their entire life drama demonstrated by the pain or condition because that is not the truth of who they are. Of course, this process would take time, energy, and effort, and most people's egos convince them that they don't have the time or are not worth the effort, so it's simplest to take pills or even have an operation. So, the person can choose to take medication for temporary relief while they investigate, clear, and release the actual cause of the condition in their mind, heart, and life. Naturally, everyone is free to choose not to investigate and only take the pills or opt for surgery. However, if they choose to work with the mind-body connection, the following questions play an integral part in their process: What is the purpose of the condition? What value does the condition represent in their life? By investigating these questions, the person cannot bypass lessons the condition shows them about what they need to clear. Any symptoms are a wake-up call to pay attention to the root cause. To completely heal the condition will require them to work deeply with their minds and release guilt, fear, and separation thoughts.

Sometimes the pills or the operation are the "special agents" to help release the whole process and bring it to a conclusion, and this happens after the forgiveness in the person's mind has occurred. These special agents can be anything we give power to, like a certain kind of doctor, a prescription pill, a vitamin, a special medical device. We can consciously say we are giving power to this person, drug, or device and name it as having the ability to heal me. For example, "I give this chemotherapy the power to fully clear all tumors from my body."

Prescription pills can offer an escape from dealing with the condition in the mind. For example, thinking, "I just want to obliterate my responsibility for this problem." But, as a result, new symptoms could manifest in another place in the body.

It takes great courage, fortitude, and persistence to heal something in your body through your mind, and your commitment must be one hundred percent to your process within yourself. We can especially do this healing when we have a holy relationship partner who understands this process for healing the body through the mind and supports the understanding that the illusionary condition is not True. In this crucial moment in releasing the condition, we need someone who does not believe in it and so will not collude in making it appear real, serious, and unmovable. When two people confirm an egoic idea through collusion, it becomes real to them. A significant way that we support each other is by confirming who we are when we forget. And this process, remembering who we are as authentic, spiritual beings rather than a body, is essential to healing.

ACIM says that we can't be sick unless we think, feel, or believe we are separate from others and God, our Source. The belief in separation is a necessary condition of sickness. We must forgive the person, persons, or the incident we are blaming, or we will project this blame onto someone else. A person's wish to separate from someone could involve their feeling of guilt about something in the past. They may reject themselves for what they think they did. So, when we work together (or you are with your coach or guide) with One mind and One intention to heal, the process would involve answering a series of questions to recognize and release the benefit or payoff of having this physical condition.

When I coach a person with *The Clearing Process*, the condition often disappears because they were ready and ripe to let these conditions go when the illness no longer served a purpose in their mind. They were amazed at how quickly and easily a clearing could be done.

About forgiveness: I am only ever forgiving myself for what I think, feel, or believe, and what it says about me, and that I keep to myself like a "secret," such as, "I am worthless," "I am not good enough," "no one loves me," "no one sees me," "no one wants me." This secret will only be released when I am willing to go through all aspects of what I believe the sickness represents. At the moment we forgive, we release the sickness entirely. It is important to remember that forgiveness is a gift to myself because as I release the other person or myself, whatever I give comes back to me like a boomerang. Forgiveness will not work until we truly mean what we say when we forgive. It can sometimes take many motions of forgiving until we can truly forgive and release it completely.

Well-known healer and guide Byron Katie has a four-step inquiry process called The Work. The first step is asking the question, "Is it true?" For example, she asked a man, "Is it true that you really want to heal this cancer?" He says, "Of course." Then she asks him the second question, "Can you absolutely know it's true that you want to heal this cancer?" He comes up with so many reasons and payoffs for having cancer that he is amazed.

Dr. Gary Holz and Robbie Holz perfectly describe Gary's healing journey in their book, *Journey to the Heart: Secrets of Aboriginal Healing*. Gary experienced multiple sclerosis (MS) and healed himself in a process with Aborigines in Australia.

He reviewed every benefit and reason he chose to be numb in his life and feel nothing, thereby creating MS. He discovered that when you deeply feel and taste your reasons for creating the condition and experience the emotion that the state reveals in you, then you are on your way to releasing it. Once you realize you no longer want to have the sickness for any reason, it will slip away. After he had mastered the process in himself, he did the process with Aborigines, which is very similar to "The Perceived Purpose of Sickness."

The first section of "How Is Healing Accomplished?" (ACIM, M-5) teaches that it is essential to understand why we created the illusion of sickness at this time in our lives. When we have hidden a thought, a feeling, or belief in our body, it becomes a sickness. We store it in our body as a secret; guilt stops us from admitting these hidden thoughts and thus releasing them. It is important to note what was going on in our lives a year to a year or more before the illness manifested, paying special attention to negative self-talk and thoughts. We also need to consider the influence of traumatic childhood experiences that could be the root of the condition, even though the traumas may have occurred many years earlier. For example, I have heard that it can take fifteen years to develop a serious cancer condition. In that case, the person would review what was happening fifteen years earlier and clear on those events. Then the person can choose to find a way to clear the condition's root cause. Otherwise, a bankruptcy, divorce, an accident, or even another illness, for example, may manifest, prompting them to look more deeply into their process and life lessons.

Many years ago, one of my students was an orthopedic surgeon, married with four children. After taking the *Taking your Place as Leader in the World* three-week course in Hawaii, he concluded, "Why did I even become an orthopedic surgeon? All I need to do is work with the cause in the person's mind of what they created in their body or structure." This doctor was the head of the orthopedic department of a big hospital in a prominent city in Sweden. He put the whole *Clearing Process* on his office wall, including the little t and Big T chart. He then told his patients that if they wanted to clear their physical condition through their minds using the questions and *The Clearing Process,* he would work with them to see if they still needed an operation. He would give the patient's body time to release the condition after *clearing* before the operation or procedure. He did several sessions with each person. It was more time-consuming than an operation, yet it cost the taxpayers much less. Of course, the person often was able to avoid having the dangerous operation. He then would say to the patient, "If you don't want to go through *The Clearing Process* and work with your mind-body connection, then you can go to my colleague, and he will just operate." About half of his patients would work with him in the inquiry process to resolve their issues. Weekly, he would share *The Clearing Process* with his fellow doctors, attendants, and aids on how to release conditions through clearing.

In "The Shift in Perception," it says: *One need but say, "There is no gain at all to me in this" and he is healed.* (ACIM, M-5.II.1:2) The meaning is that I have gone through all the benefits in my mind that this sickness or condition has given me, forgiving myself for making up and believing in these thoughts and forgiving anyone I feel the sickness involves. It also means that I am reminding myself of spiritual truths and feeding them to myself, that none of these beliefs I made up are true, and that I do not need to live in this fantasy, which is at the core of the physical condition. Generally, this is a secret to the person; when they divulge it to themselves or others, it no longer has a hold over them.

The Power of Clearing process brings clarity to the puzzle of your life. Before doing the advanced "The Perceived Purpose of Sickness" eight-question exercise, it is best to do several clearings of different people and subjects (mother, father, money, or sexual guilt). You will benefit from this exercise once you have cleared your traumas and understand your life lessons to see how your issues fit together like pieces of a puzzle.

If the Sickness Has No Purpose Now, It Can Leave

After you have completed the whole process of answering the eight questions one-to-one with me as your clearing coach, another member of my team, or your clearing guide, you can stand up in front of your coach with all conviction and power, with your head held high. Then, with arms outstretched like Superman or a bird ready to fly, declare, "I release the condition of… (exactly), and I no longer need this condition (named) for any further benefit or pay off. I am free, whole, and complete as I am."

You might say this declaration a few times, letting yourself feel the words as Truth, because by thoroughly feeling the words with your mind, body, and spirit, you will know if you are congruent and clear with releasing the condition. "There is no more gain at all for me in this condition. I choose to release it now." Note that it can also be a psychological condition of depression or anxiety that you have released through this process. This fulfilling process is exciting for me to go through and witness, and I am always delighted for the person as they see and know the Truth of their condition.

> *The acceptance of sickness as a decision of the mind,*
> *for a purpose for which it would use the body, is the basis of healing.*
> (ACIM, M-5.II.2:1)

Remember that the condition becomes like a familiar friend; in many cases, people have an attachment to the condition and symptoms, like a habit. In essence, we will discover the purpose of the condition for you and what it represents in your mind and in your life. When you have cleared all the payoffs and benefits of having the condition and forgiven the meaning that you had in your mind and heart of what the condition was for, you will no longer have any purpose for the condition. At that point of clarity, upon completing your healing process, you have truly forgiven yourself, and anyone else you believe was involved in its cause when you agree, *There is no gain at all to me in this.* (ACIM, M-5.II.1:2) By acknowledging that you have made up these thoughts (your interpretation of the condition's purpose), you are taking responsibility for its creation and you are healed.

Then, you can recognize your true essence as in "I am love, I am peace, I am joy, I am Oneness," which can never be altered or changed for any reason. "The illusionary belief of the physical condition that I take responsibility for and no longer need to live allows me to release the purpose of this condition in my mind and body." The person asks, "How quickly would I like to see it gone?"

As a longtime student and teacher of ACIM, whenever I have a negative feeling in my body ("sickness" or "disease") or emotions ("anxiety" or "depression") dominating my life and disturbing my peace of mind, I constantly refer to this section, "The Perceived Purpose of Sickness."

> *For forgiveness literally transforms vision,*
> *and lets you see the real world*
> *reaching quietly and gently across chaos,*
> *removing all illusions that had*
> *twisted your perception and fixed it on the past.*

(ACIM, T-17.II.6:2)

Love, Serve and Remember
Song and lyrics by John Astin

Why have you come to earth?

Do you remember?

Why have you taken birth?

Why have you come?

To Love, to Serve and Remember

To Love, to Serve and Remember

Remembrance

johnastin.com

CHAPTER 9

TRUE WOMAN'S POWER

Women's Core Beliefs

I have been working with women extensively since 1979, beginning as the Marketing Director of Women's Success Teams in San Francisco, California. Every weekend, we had a course for the Women's Success Teams in the Ashbury Heights building with about 15 women, many of whom wanted a divorce or had recently been divorced and consequently had large sums of money they didn't know how to manage. It was scary hearing how little they knew about the personal management of their lives since their husbands had taken on that role for them; now, these women were divorced and alone without support.

Every weekend, I hardly slept, with so much to learn and thirsty to gather any information to help them improve their lives. Synchronistically, Laura Boxer, owner of the Women's Success Teams, knew a lot about working with money, investments, and how to track money, being a stockbroker for twenty years. Laura had purchased the west coast franchise of Women's Success Teams from her best friend, Barbara Sher, who had authored *Wishcraft*, a ground-breaking book in the late 1970s. She wrote about finding your wishes, desires, talents, and gifts to create your career and the vision for your life. (Please see "Daring to Risk" in the Resources section.)

In 1980, I initiated the *Women's Sex and Power Course*, later renamed *The Women's Training* with Justin Sterling and his institute. Then, in 1996, I wrote my course *True Woman's Power*. I was impressed by the power of having only women sharing and breaking through issues they had always accepted as the story of their life. A woman can find it challenging to communicate because it's so heartfelt for her, and revealing her true essence is like allowing her soul to be naked and vulnerable. Finally able to release, let go, and move to new levels of full expression, a woman's power comes from her heart, feelings, and integrity, with a strong sense of what she feels is right and true.

In therapy or a group, it is powerful to tell a secret to someone you can trust and who holds you blameless. You don't have a secret; a secret has you, controlling you in what you share and divulge in every moment. In *True Woman's Power*, most women reveal their secrets to their coaches or a woman they feel a rapport with during one of the exercises. The space in the training is extraordinarily safe for women to share profound and hidden incidents, traumas, thoughts, feelings, and beliefs. Thousands of women who have experienced this training have learned what they need to let go of to achieve their full potential. To be truly powerful and successful, each woman needs to clear their mistaken beliefs and limiting emotional blocks to attain their goals and dreams. It is essential to develop the self-confidence to step up and speak out in the world. My three-day course specifically looks at these issues and empowers women to permanently overcome whatever is standing in their way to their *True Woman's Power*.

A core belief comes in early, maybe in the womb, during the birth process, or early childhood, and becomes "a ground of being" from which the woman lives her life. Here are some common negative core beliefs that women can release and clear into empowerment.

- I am weak
- I am not good enough
- I am powerless
- I am unworthy
- I am unlovable
- I am not wanted
- I am bad
- I am guilty

- I am flawed
- there's something wrong with me
- life is too hard for me
- I need to struggle for everything to get all my needs met

Additionally, limiting beliefs may hinder a woman from living to her full capacity. Repetitive ego thoughts become a system that attracts negative experiences to prove these limitations.

- I don't have enough knowledge
- I didn't go to school long enough
- I failed at school
- I don't have enough learning to succeed
- I don't have enough money to succeed
- I don't have enough education to succeed
- I am not assertive or outgoing enough to succeed
- I am afraid to communicate what I want fully
- I have always been rejected
- I don't deserve what I want
- I will never get what I need

By women clearing these beliefs, they are stepping into their inherent power and are now coming forward to speak up and take their place as natural leaders.

The Comparison Game

Many women naturally compare themselves with other women and rarely admit to it because they are embarrassed and ashamed; they have a core belief that something is wrong with them, or somehow, they are not enough.

- I am ugly
- I am too fat
- I am too weak
- I am too much

One of the more challenging and empowering exercises in *True Woman's Power* was The Comparison Game. The women in the circle each opt out or in of the game. If they stay in, they agree to be honest and say aloud ego comparisons with other women in the group. Many women opted out because they were scared of exposing their egos. Then they could choose to stay in the room holding the space for the others, although no one would include them in the ego comparisons. Therefore, they felt protected and safe from comparison, judgment, and criticism. They could also opt to leave the room during the exercise and clear with a coach on what it brought up for them—why they opted out, their fear of exposure to what they would hear (whether positive or negative), and the meaning they made up about themselves.

The more courageous women entered the arena with their demonstrations of a "better than" role, such as,

- "I feel I am better than you because I am better educated with two university degrees."
- "I believe I am a better mother and spend more time with my children because I focus on them, not my career."
- "I am a savvy businesswoman because I think in a more business-like way and make more money than you."
- "I believe I have a more attractive and richer husband."
- "I think I am a better teacher, entrepreneur, athlete, wife, and mother than you."
- "I feel I am better-looking, richer, thinner, and prettier with a sexier body and generally more dynamic and exciting personality that you could only dream of."

We also heard the opposite beliefs in "less than" statements, such as,

- "I think you're better than me because you have a more caring partner."
- "I think you are slimmer and more attractive than me."
- "I feel I am not as good as you because you have a better education than me."
- "I believe I am not as good as you because I earn less money."
- "I think I am not as good as you because I couldn't conceive children."

- "I feel not as smart as you, which is dumb."
- "I feel less intuitive you appear to be."
- "I feel less spiritual than you."
- "I don't have as many friends as you because I spend more time alone and with my children and husband."
- "I don't have as big a house as you and I am not as well-traveled as you are."

We can only do these exercises in The Comparison Game because these women in the course are trained to recognize when they are triggered and have the tools to clear their upsets. The only reason any of the comparisons would trigger a woman would be if she already judged or considered herself "less than" or "better than" already, for example, of being too heavy, not smart enough, or not stylish enough. Then, they can go out of the room with a *Power of Clearing* coach and clear what they have projected onto themselves based on what someone said about them. The exercises are about being daring and willing to expose ego thoughts and judgments that we usually keep to ourselves like secrets in a safe container. Letting go of the fear of being judged or blamed for these thoughts, they recognize that they have something to clear if they feel hurt by what is said.

"You cannot give me any pain, only bring up the pain I already have."

By fully disclosing our ego thoughts, we find that others can hear us without being upset and hurt by our words that we previously assumed would cause them pain so that we would feel guilty. The exercises are about freeing ourselves from the fear of hurting someone's feelings, which is one of a woman's greatest fears, to say something incorrectly. The women were always surprised that they had been scrutinized so carefully by the other women in the room.

After the women confronted their fear of doing the exercise, they had lots of fun and laughed about it. The ego can be pretty humorous. For instance, "I have better-looking feet, especially my right big toe."

My Body Judgment

Another exercise to release little t thoughts was for the women to stand naked in front of the whole class one at a time with everyone's focus on them and describe everything they don't like about their bodies. The group holds space for each of them while they go through this cathartic and highly emotional exercise. Each woman confronts her fear that other women will judge and criticize her in the same way she judges herself. So, each woman is greatly relieved that the whole exercise shows her that she can accept her body as perfect the way it is and let go of the ideal picture as they imagine it should be. Others have seen her body now; they feel accepted as a unique personality, being, and body—no longer a secret that they hide with shame or disgust or compare to a picture.

Some women had mastectomies and didn't have reconstructions, and it was the first time they showed their altered bodies to anyone. Then they can let go of the fear that they are not good enough or the need to hide their perceived flaws like a secret. Sometimes they will experience enormous relief from not being rejected for some physical characteristic of their body.

In all their beauty, bumps, and brawn, the women become more self-accepting and self-loving of what is. Of course, all of the exercises in the workshops are voluntary, so participants can choose what they do and even witness. As noted, when the exercise triggers a woman, she can go to another room to clear her perceived fear or judgment and discern why she chose to opt-out.

We didn't always do this exercise with the women naked or the naked man exercise in *True Woman's Power* (TWP). I always go with my inner voice; I channel the entire training, so each time, it's unique and dependent on the energy of the group dynamics. We asked participants to preserve the anonymity of these more intimate exercises because potential enrollees might be intimidated and miss potential growth opportunities by attending the workshop.

Two Men Having Breakthroughs

Nothing better illustrates the ego games of a woman and man than what emerges in the training called *True Woman's Power*.

Since we started teaching *True Woman's Power* in 1996, men have often asked me half-jokingly if they could be a participant in the course, and I always said no. From an egoic level, they may have felt that they wanted to participate to meet women. However, I thought they wanted to participate to truly understand women and learn how they think and feel differently from men. Certainly, this TWP course is about the deepest a man could see into the psyche, fears, anxieties, hopes, dreams, and the true mind of women in essence.

Finally, however, there were four men in 25 years who I intuitively knew would have breakthroughs in the *True Woman's Power* training. I knew they would gift the women in the room an in-depth understanding of men, and the women would get value out of the way these particular men were able to share themselves, being vulnerable and transparent.

The Programmer

The first man who attended *True Woman's Power* had participated in two of my other trainings, and I understood all the places inside of him that he wanted to break free. He was an attractive forty-five-year-old virgin with a deep-seated fear of women. He had never kissed a woman passionately or touched a woman sensually or sexually, rarely dated, and didn't believe any woman would want to be with him. He was like most people would call a computer nerd, with his mind strictly on computers. He was also interested in a woman who it turned out wanted to be friends with him, not involved romantically, so he was very disappointed.

When the women (a total of 45, including 15 in the support team) realized that he was in the course, considerable upset arose among them in the room. One woman stood up and said, "If he stays, I go because I can't be myself, and I will feel completely disempowered. I would not be able to be spontaneous and freely share about my feminine cycle and sexual feelings if he stays." Another one agreed with her. Then I said, "That means that the minute you leave this property, you'll see men everywhere who may disempower you, so you would not be able to be yourself there either. So, let's keep him as a token male. Then, you'll learn how to go beyond your self-imposed limitation in a man's presence of what you need to share and demonstrate." By the end of that *True Woman's Power* course, the group of women was completely open and at ease with the "token male" and his man-ness; they felt fully joined with him as a being.

The women perform solo ceremonial rituals in the final hour or two of the TWP training course. Each woman's demonstration confirms that she has taken a movement forward to a new level in her life. Preparing for the completion segment, the women in the training room bustle with excitement as each one spontaneously creates from her authentic self in the present moment—unplanned. It is an act of mysterious creation.

Sometimes, women play a part as family members in another's ritual. The whole support team is involved in the process since some may also ask them to collaborate in their ritual or play a part. We gather costumes and props from the whole environment of the retreat, home, or center where we hold the course to add a creative dimension to the rituals; musical instruments, scarves, sketch pads, crystals, hats, gloves, and beautiful gowns. In addition, there are original poetry, songs, and a whole joyous atmosphere, often transforming a negative scene from the past into a positive portrayal during this ritual.

The man began his ceremony dressed in a white Japanese outfit. All of the women were spell-bound as he acted out in pantomime how he would treat his new life partner in sacred union. He had a round white rug with a white kimono symbolizing his beloved's energy that he placed in the middle of the rug in the space where she would be. For the fifteen minutes of his ritual, the room was silent as everyone followed his every move, mesmerized by his reverential and welcoming movements, bringing forth his beloved into his heart, mind, and the core of his being. Every woman imagined herself being sanctified and revered in the symbol of the kimono holding space of his beloved on the rug. Of the many ceremonial rituals I have seen at the end of TWP courses, his creative and poignant process is the most memorable in my heart I have ever taken part in and witnessed.

Following everyone's completion ritual, the man asked if he could demonstrate one more of his movements forward. No one had any idea what he was going to do. He then removed his white outfit, draped it beautifully on a chair, and danced naked around the circle, pausing in front of each woman, looking into her eyes to connect with her, and saying, "I am not attached to what you think of my body." If he had stopped to overthink it, his ego would have given him a reason to say no to his impulse to be naked in front of a group of women, something he had never done before. And even though no one was prepared for his vulnerable display, each woman's face expressed complete awe, understanding the significance of his action since he had never even been naked in private with a woman in his life. At the end of his dance, he put on regular clothes, and everyone danced together in the final moments of the training.

The Cross-Dresser

The second man who took TWP was a cross-dresser compelled to dress like a woman in the finest outfits with full makeup, bouffant, jewelry, nails, frills, nylons, and heels. He was the prettiest, most decked-out woman in the room.

Everyone gazed at him when he appeared in each new outfit. When he left the USA to cross the border into Canada, the border guards went into his van and were shocked when he told them, "Those are my clothes." They thought he was bringing the clothes across the border into Canada to sell; if so, he would have to pay duty on all of them. What could they say when he told them he was a cross-dresser?

At the TWP, the women were sleeping in a dorm room together, and he wondered if he could sleep in the same dorm room so he could be part of the women's discussion that took place at bedtime and early morning. And they said yes. So, he slept in the dorm with them for the whole weekend training. He did all the exercises as a woman, from his point of view of a woman's perspective, dressed in full makeup, heels, jewelry, and dresses. He was a heterosexual and interested in dating women. He was interested in marrying a woman as his life partner. In TWP, he did the training from a woman's point of view and got his woman essence acknowledged. After that training and beyond, he no longer dressed as a woman as frequently after fully experiencing it in *True Woman's Power*, so he could let it go from his psyche.

Women Saying "No" to Men

One of the most powerful and revealing processes in my workshops, included in some of the *True Woman's Power* intensives, is when I invite a man into the space to play a pivotal role in the women's healing journey. Generally, it's on the evening of the second day, once we create a safe container and establish trust amongst the women, that we discuss the process. I carefully choose this man for his ability to hold a strong masculine presence and be fearless and compassionate for a woman's evolution.

I have only sanctioned three men (in thirty years) to lead this exercise after I professionally trained them for years as members of the regular *Power of Clearing* program assistant team and had them do several trainings with me. We only held this sacred ritual with the man in about twenty percent of the *True Woman's Power* trainings where I intuitively felt these particular women would have value and breakthroughs in the process.

In his role, the man instinctively follows each woman's process to encourage her to go deeper; by smiling, moving away from her to give her space, or moving closer. There was no touching of any kind. It was a type of psychodrama skill. One of these men had been a psychodrama student training for years to be a master psychodrama teacher. For almost fifteen years, he was the one who customarily held this space for the women in the "saying no to a man" exercise. He had taken most of my trainings and been an assistant in the trainings many times. He is one of the most enlightened men I have ever met. Looking at the naked man, the woman is looking at every man who has ever stopped her, controlled her, abused or overpowered her, held her back from the full expression of what she thought or believed, and what she wanted to be or do. Boss, father, brother, another relative, friend, all power and authority figures, doctor, or even people she's never met who have triggered her and, in her mind, threatened power and control over her.

The women would then practice saying "No" to this man in their full power to hear and to know what it sounds like to say "No" since most women have not heard themselves say or scream powerfully "No!" at this loud and clear level and have an effect. Only when you can say "No!" and mean it can you choose to say "Yes," and align it with what you feel.

For more details on this process, please see Appendix D.

The Programmer continues exploring his sexuality

After the *True Woman's Course* that the programmer attended, I invited him to go to the next level by attending the Tantra course I was organizing in Sweden. He was excited about the opportunity to practice holy relationship skills in action and explore his sexuality and fears in a safe container. So, we flew together to Fjällbo, a small course center owned by Lena Kristina Tuulse in the small town of Väddö in the Stockholm Archipelago. I matched him with this woman from Sweden who owned and lived on a farm in complete naturalness; even the sheep came into the living room. My daughter Charisma thought it was one of the most far-out, outrageous ideas I'd had in my life to make this match of two people so directly opposites. She thought they would never get along or like each other. Computer-like in every way, he was organized, methodical, and detail-oriented; in contrast, she was free, like a goddess living off the grid in nature without chemicals and outside influences. The goddess and the computer-like man met in the tantra room on the first evening for four hours. We never saw them again in the official class during all our sessions. I saw them a few times outside the training room, and I discovered they were doing an intimate tantric class on their own in many rooms of the course center buildings. When I saw them, they looked like they were on cloud 9, almost in a drug-like state, euphoria and bliss; he had never found himself before in oneness and joy.

The "opposite" they saw in each other had produced a significant attraction and created the most divine connection. The computer-like man told me of deciding to return to his Canadian home, get his things, return to Sweden to marry her, take on the joy of being her husband, actively take on the responsibility of her four daughters, and help to operate the farm. He intended to support them as "what a man should do." He had come into "a huge purpose, motivation, and direction for living, for being alive," he told me. "Far greater than anything I had imagined before."

The next step was for the goddess to call her ex-partner, the children's father, the Frenchman living in France. Her plan was for her and then the computer-like man to tell him and get his sanction and blessing—in full communication and transparency. During the call, the Frenchman said to the man who proposed to marry the mother of his children, "I want you to teach me what you learned in the clearing course and the tantra course and for you to be my guide. I'm coming back to Sweden to be with my children. I want you to be my teacher and mentor and share what you've learned. I don't want you to take my place with my goddess wife. I want to show up in my rightful place." So, he did that! He taught him on the telephone, which cost a fortune, from Sweden to France and then from Canada to France when he returned home. Then he withdrew and continued his original life as a single non-virgin, and the goddess reunited with her previous partner, the Frenchman, in Sweden.

Then, the programmer became involved with another of my students. Their relationship went to a certain point where the relationship may have been stopped or blocked by each of their ego issues. He never seemed to move beyond that point, and he got cancer; however, the standard Western healing methods cured him, and he is continuing with his routine life in the field of computers.

All relationships are essential to our growth. If we choose to remain isolated from others, we may never find the opportunity to go to the next level of development by releasing fear, guilt, and limited belief systems. It takes great courage and dedication to want to continue clearing your issues to the point where you face your barriers and go to your maximum in your capacity to give and receive love. We are always doing the best we can in the moment we are in it. There is always another opportunity in the next moment if you can see it and want to re-engage in that moment with another person. Our lifelong lessons come up in the area of relationships with others.

> "Everything will be all right in the end...
> if it's not all right then it's not yet the end."

Final quote in the movie, *The Best Exotic Marigold Hotel*

> "I've known Sandy a long time
> and attended several of her trainings.
>
> One of the women who came to the *True Woman's Power* course was like the walking dead when she arrived. Her face was gray, she looked down, and she would not participate.
>
> However, by the end of the training, this woman was bright and lively, wearing a tutu. Sandy never pushed her; she was gracious, loving, patient, and kind and kept opening the door until the woman walked through.
>
> This transformation work is so important.
> And it's not a one-shot deal;
> it's a daily practice that takes courage,
> time, and the willingness to be present."
>
> **—Jennifer Simms,** organizer of Live Peace Concert

True Woman's Power Testimonials
Embracing the Truth of Who I Truly Am

True Woman's Power and Me—Irene Williams
Certified *Power of Clearing* coach

I first met Sandy Levey-Lunden, creator of *The Power of Clearing*, at a mutual friend's home in Vancouver, British Columbia. Before meeting Sandy, I attended one or two meetings of an ACIM study group, my initial introduction to ACIM *(A Course in Miracles)*.

Raised in a very conservative Protestant church, I developed a deep trust in God through my early exposure to Christianity and by the example of my mother's unwavering faith despite many personal losses. I accepted early on without question that all of the experiences in my life were essential for my learning. However, as I listened to the many Biblical stories and readings, I could not accept that I was inherently flawed and bad. I could not make sense of the mean, angry, vengeful God that I heard about over and over. I felt deeply at one with my Creator but in complete discord with what they were teaching me about Him.

At my first meeting with the ACIM study group, the message I heard matched my vision about God. Finally, at last, I was hearing words that truly represented my connection with my God.

Shortly after my introduction to ACIM, I attended the *True Woman's Power* weekend at Sandy Levey-Lunden's home. I had no idea what to expect and knew very little of Sandy and her *Power of Clearing* work. I had recently experienced the most heartbreaking profound grief I could imagine, and when I met Sandy, a great deal of unresolved sadness and grief was still burdening me. I had come to realize that I had no idea what love was, and I felt alone and separate from everyone. I was very judgmental of everything and everyone, myself included.

As I prepared to attend the *True Woman's Power* workshop at Sandy's home in Bellingham, I experienced every possible emotion. At the time, I visualized it as a rainbow of emotions.

I had no idea what might happen that weekend, and to me, it felt like the equivalent of jumping off a cliff and having virtually no information about what to expect.

My goal for the weekend was to get to the bottom of why I was unable to accept love. I wanted to be freed from whatever was holding me back from living my life to the fullest and from the grief that continued to grip me.

As the women attending the weekend workshop assembled for the group's first meeting, I immediately became aware of my judgment of several of the other women. I felt irritated by some of them and very impatient with the pace of the meeting. I felt a sense of superiority that I grasped concepts much more quickly than most other participants. Additionally, I felt irritated by their preoccupation with their ills, pains, and traumas. I felt a particular impatience and intolerance with one of the participants and, compared to the emotional grace of another woman, I felt like an emotional bull. I felt detached and separate from the group.

As the weekend progressed, I came to realize that I had become so accustomed to intellectualizing my emotions—in other words, moving them away from me—that recognizing, let alone naming them, had become very foreign to me. Initially, I viewed other group members' clear recollection of the multitude of hurts and tragedies inflicted upon them as their "wallowing" in the negativity of their life and their "weakness" in not being able to "get over it" and get on with real life.

Looking back, I can see how imprisoned and joyless my life had become with my judgment of everyone and how my projection onto others was merely a reflection of the depth of self-judgment I carried. So, it's not surprising that the true beauty and love of all of the participants and coaches, especially myself, was invisible to me. However, as the weekend progressed, I began to see the complex journeys that each of us was on. In addition, I began to appreciate the depth of pain each of us carried due to events in our earliest childhood, some seemingly very benign and insignificant.

Through Sandy's inspired direction, and with the assistance of her equally inspired team, I was at long last able to bring to my awareness the early experiences that had so profoundly impacted the way I would experience my life. Through *The Clearing Process,* which is based entirely on the teaching principles of ACIM, I was able to see how the beliefs I held about myself were only illusions and interpretations that I had unconsciously accepted and that I could also choose to correct those illusions.

The Clearing Process of forgiveness lays bare the patterns in our lives for us to witness. In it, we can choose to forgive what no longer serves us and let it go.

We can apply this process to any situation in life. It is a simple yet profound process for speaking our total truth, acknowledging without judgment, and releasing any negative conditioning from our past from the subconscious mind. As these negative feelings and beliefs are released, we can realize and then embrace the truth of who we really are.

Then, as the weekend progressed, I became aware that I was a "trigger" to some women in the group. The ugly head of separation continued to raise its head! I saw this as "their issue"; I didn't feel triggered!

Again, as the weekend progressed, I realized that my ongoing sense of superiority was judging them as flawed and stuck in their self-absorption. Through *The Clearing Process*, I was at long last able to see how I had kept myself separate and distant from others as a way of insulating and protecting myself. I was able to release my need to control my life and embrace and trust the flow of every life. I came to see that love does not exclude. Only fear stands in the way of all-inclusive love.

Finally, I was able to see myself as I had always believed truly was possible—that I was unlimited love, gentleness, joy, and light. I felt unconditional, unbridled love—toward myself and my entire world. At the conclusion of the *True Woman's Power* workshop, we celebrated our journey of the weekend. Each woman reflected her individual growth. For myself, I felt I was at long last taking the steps in experiencing and extending all-encompassing love. I saw each participant and myself with new eyes.

Following the *True Woman's Power* weekend, I knew without a doubt that I needed to learn more about *The Clearing Process* since I had experienced deep and total release of paralyzing, self-sabotaging negative self-beliefs. I needed to know more!

I enrolled in Sandy's ten-day *Power of Clearing* Coaching Certification Program. During this intense and transformational training, I unpacked and brought to awareness every area of my life where pain, grief, doubt, control, fear, and guilt still resided. Through the profound simplicity and deep effectiveness of *The Clearing Process*, I released the "stories" of my life, one by one. Then, with relief, I let go of my belief in my "smallness," and in its place, I came to see the true unlimited magnificence of myself and every single person I encounter.

To this day, the stillness of my mind fills me with deep, deep peace. I continue to study ACIM and gain a richer sense of oneness and connectedness with the entire Universe. I continue to practice clearing in my life whenever I sense a shadow fall over my inner peace. My desire to extend love and peace has led me to establish my practice as a coach, teaching and sharing *The Clearing Process*.

In every situation, my guide is always *Teach only love, for that is what you are.* (ACIM, T-6.I.13:2) Gratitude and love fill me to overflowing.

> *When you meet anyone, remember it is a holy encounter.*
> *As you see him you will see yourself.*
> *As you treat him you will treat yourself.*
> *As you think of him you will think of yourself.*
> *Never forget this,*
> *For in him you will either lose yourself or find yourself.*
>
> (ACIM, T-8.III.4:1-5)

Introduction from Sandy Levey-Lunden to the next article by Christina.

The purpose of including Christina's article in this book is to portray how we can spontaneously work through conflict and upset to peace, joining, and conscious awareness. The situation turned out to be a fantastic live demonstration that we can work through something upsetting in our lives when we are willing to take responsibility and be completely transparent with our thoughts, feelings, beliefs, and actions and correct our misperceptions through forgiveness. We also need effective communication tools, such as *The Power of Clearing* process.

Three into One—Healing the Triangle

The Encounter between Amber and Christina in *True Woman's Power* (TWP)—Christina's story

Once upon a time, in the late 1990s, a *True Woman's Power* course was being held at a beautiful retreat center on the outskirts of Vancouver, BC, in Canada.

My work partner and good friend, Sue Wilde, and I decided to volunteer as assistants at our favorite workshop. We had inspired Sandy to create TWP only a few years prior. *True Woman's Power* was a transformational three-day workshop for women to share, heal, release, and integrate their egoic issues within a safe, sacred container. It was a rare opportunity for women to clear what is in the way of experiencing and living in their authentic, intuitive, and loving feminine power, which is innate, internal, and eternal.

Sue and I both cleared our calendars so we were able to attend and assist in the workshop. Since it was a last-minute decision, we would be arriving a few hours late on day one. We called ahead and then again enroute to let the organizer know we were on our way, with an approximate eta. However, it turned out that Sandy didn't know about us coming because she was already in the workshop teaching the training.

Therefore, Sandy never got the memo that Sue and I wanted to be on the assisting team and arrive late. If she had known, she would have said "no," because she was aware of my potentially volatile situation with one of the women in this particular course. I was having an intimate affair with this woman's husband for two seasons, which the woman discovered only a few weeks prior. I knew she was attending this particular TWP workshop. I imagine that the reader's eyes may roll with judgmental filters and hair-raising fibers at this point. I may have had some shame about the extent of my relationship with her husband. It was minor and well-shadowed, as I justified my sense of guilt by telling myself that he and I did love each other with a deep connection, aside from the integrity issue of him still being legally married.

Let's call them Amber and Jonathan to protect the innocent. My understanding was that Amber had an agreement with her husband that if he was having an affair with another woman, she didn't want to know about it. It wasn't exactly an agreed-upon open marriage, but it was not entirely monogamous either. They had a unique relationship with unspoken ego contracts, sacred secrets, and agreements. Amber and Jonathan had been married for twelve years, had known each other for sixteen years, and shared a successful, lucrative business of several years. They were in the middle of making significant changes in their lives, and selling their house. They had already decided to relocate for mutually beneficial reasons. They were still married and moving to another country.

When Jonathan and I met through a mutual friend, we were immediately drawn to each other like magnets. We shared a passion for adventure, holistic health, and personal growth with a soul connection beyond the physical. I had met Amber once before and knew they were married, yet in my mind and awareness from Jonathan, they were in an open relationship. However, he preferred to maintain our sacred secret. As our relationship progressed and our connection deepened, I did have this underlying nagging feeling that it was still a covert act of betrayal toward his wife, and womanhood itself to be involved with this man without clear consent from her.

Jonathan and I were on a business-pleasure trip in my hometown of Toronto when Amber inadvertently found out that we were together. I had left a sexy voice message for him on his home phone line. Unfortunately, she picked up his messages that day, which was unusual, as they were in the process of selling their house and juggling many balls simultaneously. Busted! When Jonathan called Amber to check in, she replayed my message for him, and he was so shocked, he dropped the phone on the sidewalk. In her anger, Amber immediately canceled her planned trip to Toronto to meet up with him. A few weeks after she found out about our love affair, they agreed to do Sandy's workshop called *Choosing Freedom: The Way Out* since they were both working on individual and relationship issues. Thus, Amber was already aware and familiar with the 3-step *Clearing Process*, which they had practiced with each other. And now, in full awareness, I was about to walk into the *True Woman's Power* training room that Amber was attending and *face the music*.

I had hoped Amber and I could have had an honest discussion and agree that we were sharing her husband; however, it never happened. I knew it took guts and real nerve to show up to this workshop. My primary intention was to clarify the potential of this holy triad with Amber and Jonathan. I knew it was a key and a pathway to my own liberation. My desire for this joining was more important than my fear of shame, blame, and feelings of insecurity. I was confident that the combination of Sandy in her infinite wisdom, with the workshop itself, the clearing methodology, and the grace of spirit would support me in this vision of resolution. People may think I would enter the training room with shame, guilt, trepidation, and fear. However, I felt in my body that the only thing that was real was the love and the only missing piece for me was that I didn't have Amber's permission to be with her husband. Because of the ambiguity, my women friends were always saying that I wasn't in full disclosure and integrity with Amber or myself. I still felt there was an abundance of love in this triad of me, Amber, and Jonathan with enough love to go around for each of us. Little did I know or consider how much it would impact all the women who witnessed this process. Naturally my showing up would have the most impact on Amber.

In retrospect, it was an outrageously bold, daring, and audacious last-minute decision that I acted on to assist at this course. I was always comfortable and confident in the assistant role; however, this occasion had a significantly unique twist. I could feel some anxiety coming up from an underlying fear of being attacked, judged, and crucified as "the other woman" by Amber, the support team, the participants, and Sandy at this workshop.

When we arrived, Sue and I waited in the kitchen off the main workshop space for the right moment to join the group of twenty-five women. As we were original promoters and organizers of past TWP workshops, we both knew some of the attendees and all the assistants participating in this divinely orchestrated course.

Finally, one of the assistants invited Sue and me to enter the room. Including the assistants, there were over thirty-five women. When Amber saw me, she instantly leaped out of her chair, screaming, "Who let that bitch in here? Sandy, I trusted you, and I'm leaving—how dare you allow this woman in here who stole my husband? Who do you think you are?" She went ballistic, intensely enraged that this betrayal was happening, wanting to either run for the hills or annihilate both me and Sandy.

With an explosion underway, in Sandy's innate intuition, she managed her surprise at my appearance by giving us options. I, the assistant, would leave, rather than Amber, the participant. "Or," Sandy said, "we can take this opportunity to reveal, heal, and clear this current situation in front of us, using *The Clearing Process* to get to the root of the pain, projections, blame, anger, and guilt, and ultimately release it NOW."

Amber was still on fire, spewing rage, with a few assistants stepping in to support her and calm her down. I sat quietly, witnessing and wondering what would come next, confident that we could get through this stand-off alive and in one piece.

Sandy continued speaking to the whole group. "There is no accident this situation is showing up here and now. This can be an opportunity to let go of something that is really bothering us by demonstrating *The Clearing Process* in a live and volatile situation. Issues related to this clearing could include feeling rage toward Christina for being involved with this woman's husband and perhaps feelings of betrayal, rejection, fear, righteousness, separation, abandonment, or changes in your life that are unknown and scary. So, Christina can leave the training, or, if Amber agrees, we can clear this upset and let it go, returning to peace, love, and innocence."

Naturally, the group's focus immediately turned to Amber, wondering what she would choose. Amber was terrified that her life had fallen apart. She and her husband were selling their house, changing their business focus, and moving to another country; everything was in transition. In her ego-mind, in that moment, she felt betrayed, and all she wanted was revenge. Finally, after calming down and some consideration, Amber agreed to allow me to stay in the training and do the first part of the basic clearing with her in front of the whole group.

Now the real work in the training began. Using the structured format and container of *The Clearing Process* of Step 1 (stating all negative ego thoughts), Amber ripped up one side of me and down the other. We stood facing each other as there was such a dynamic heated energy. Generally, clearings are carried out from a seated position, for comfort's sake, never knowing how long it may take unless there is a structured time boundary or limitation. I could feel the tension and trepidation in the room, as this was a real, live, up close, and personal demonstration of an ancient and deep betrayal with a lot of commotion, devotion, and upset.

There was one *"what I want you to know"* after another, non-stop. I said, *"Thank you,"* after each one when there was space to do so. Amber was fully activated and charged up, with no holds barred. She was triggered for real and went full out with every thought, belief, and feeling she could muster until she was spent. Finally, the lengthy and assertive session exhausted Amber, and I felt inspired to spur everyone on to continue after a well-needed break.

None of us had ever experienced such an explosive public confrontation in a workshop that brought up so much fear, anger, and guilt with most of the participants, giving rise to a unique and rare opportunity to heal deeper core wounds.

> *The first step toward freedom involves*
> *a sorting out of the false from the true.*
> (ACIM, T-2.VIII.4:1)

On the break, when we went into the kitchen for tea, Amber held my hand and called Jonathan in excitement, announcing to him on speakerphone that "Christina and I are now friends!" I was blown away by this 180-degree turnaround. I wondered how this might threaten Jonathan now.

After completing only Step 1 so far of *The Clearing Process* with me, Amber's shift of perspective showed that she was capable of a huge letting go. Miraculously, for Amber, I was no longer the other woman, the enemy, the bitch from hell. I was her best friend, her savior, a co-creator to help recognize lost parts of self and help heal a core wound, ultimately for both of us. In this clearing, we were each going through feelings of separation (isolation and exclusion), fear of abandonment, deep-rooted sexual guilt, and other ego strategies to protect our unresolved pain. In some ways, we were mirrors for each other.

Nevertheless, Amber was not ready for the final step of forgiveness until day three. It took all of day two to get through Step 2 (asking for forgiveness for thinking, feeling, and believing egoic thoughts) and the last day for Step 3 (asking for forgiveness for forgetting Big T Truth, that we are loved, one, joined). She was brave, bold, and strong in her willingness to play full out, and I, of course, had my piece for learning and growth.

The deeper mirror reflection for me included the fear of loss, separation, rejection, abandonment—the works, all in one. I was cautious of joining with any man, fully and completely. Therefore, I wouldn't have anything to lose if it didn't work out. Being a mistress had its benefits and advantages, which outweighed the consequences on all levels. I didn't want the whole enchilada. I loved the lightness of being, the fun and adventure, the sacredness of the sweet true love without the dynamics and complexities of merging all the other ego stuff, like domestics, money, and family. That seemed like the dream life back in the 90s. I had already gone through a divorce, so I was a single mother of one young son and enough security and financial independence. I had always considered myself either "not enough" or "too much" for one great man to handle. My only discomfort with Jonathan was our deception and withholding from Amber, his life partner.

Now, in the TWP training, everything was out on the table. Not surprisingly, many participants were facing challenges in their relationships. A few suspected their husbands of having affairs, some were in the midst of separating from their partners, and most were in some form of personal transition. Much was cleared and healed in that workshop over those three days, some of it just the tip of the iceberg, opening up Pandora's box. It was uncanny how the universe had magically created this epic opportunity for all parties involved. Like a pebble dropping into the ocean, there was the possibility of a huge ripple effect of this healing and joining.

Amber appeared to go from projections of betrayal to hatred to anger and came through to the other side with self-responsibility and a greater awareness of her role. I went through a wee bit of guilt, from shamelessness to shame, from moral indignation, feeling righteous, to acceptance and innocence.

The holiest of all the spots on earth is
where an ancient hatred has become a present love.
(ACIM, T-26.IX.6:1)

I remain friends with both Amber and Jonathan to this day, grateful for the incident that feels like lifetimes ago, a catalyst to deepen my awareness of deep-rooted patterns, experience many holy instants, and move through suppressed pain from the past.

Amber and Jonathan were then facing lifestyle changes and more authentic relating opportunities, which led to quite the adventures with a somewhat unconventional return to innocence, especially for Amber. A few years of working with a transformational Tantric coach inspired her to write a book about her profound healing journey and living out her authentic truth.

The process in that *True Woman's Power* course demonstrated living *A Course in Miracles.* Sandy Levey-Lunden's incredible mastery and direct clarity supported me, along with unconditional love from my dear sister Sue Wilde and the wisdom of the collective and higher consciousness to divinely align the pieces, the people, and the process. Love, compassion, and forgiveness are three of the most powerful healing forces in the world, and through a commitment to these desired states, we eventually got there. Rather than a romantic tragedy, it was a transcendent love story. Rather than a heart-wrenching breakdown, it was a profound breakthrough. We each rose to a higher place, a higher awareness of self through the other, activating valuable lessons and learnings. We gained a new recognition that there is plenty of love to go around by healing past abandonment issues while sharing our truths, fears, and defenses. Although it may piss us off at first, the truth will always set us free.

With Love and Gratitude,
Christina Ireland

Questions for self-reflection:

What came up for you while reading this article by Christina?

What were your assumptions, thoughts, feelings, beliefs, and judgments?

Did you find yourself taking sides? With whom, and why?

Can you see your own past negative history portrayed in this entire scenario?

Your answers to these questions could point you to what you may need to clear from your own past and mind.

Sandy's reflections

Even though Christina communicated with the workshop organizer that she wanted to be on the assistant team, I was already doing the training, unaware that she was coming, and had that intention to assist. For consistency and follow-through with the participants, my rule for the trainings is that assistants need to be present for the entire process. Therefore, they are not permitted to be on the team if they are going to arrive late. Also, if I had known Christina was intending to be at that particular class, I would have told her in advance that she could not assist because she was intimately involved with a participant's husband. I felt that it would not have made a safe space for this woman in the workshop and could have hijacked the focus in the workshop from all the participants to only those two women. However, when Christina appeared in the training room, the woman saw her before I did and was immediately upset. So, I had no chance to remove her from the training room because Christina was already integral in the process. I made a once-only spontaneous decision and gave the participant the choice of whether Christina would stay or leave since my code of ethics for this kind of situation to be acceptable in the first place would be for the participant to make that decision. Another essential factor I considered was the participant had already experienced *The Clearing Process* from recently attending another of my trainings; otherwise, she would not have had the tools of *The Clearing Process* and "The Watcher" (watching the ego-mind and judgments). See Chapter 6 for the precise words and wording of the 3-step *Clearing Process*.

At the human ego level, Christina's action could be seen as stupid, thoughtless, inconsiderate, and intensely provocative. However, at the spirit level, this demonstration that Christina initiated, and I permitted based on Amber's agreement, was a beautifully orchestrated process of healing beyond what we could have arranged consciously. The right women were present to do this necessary healing for themselves. Whatever we are healing for ourselves, spreads out into the universe for everyone who has the same energetic to clear.

Everything that happens in my life or in the workshop, I use as a teaching moment, to teach myself or others the essence of the lesson. The situation with Christina and Amber was a real example of what is possible for anyone with a life situation of issues and upsets. We can let go of the fear that we have had, as women, that "if I lose this relationship with this particular man, I will be losing love forever, losing love that I will never get back. No one may ever choose me again and I may be alone for the rest of my life." Amber was willing to face her fear and set the intention for healing in her relationship to love. As she demonstrated for us, everything in our negative ego-mind that isn't the truth is possible to release if we're willing to let go of our pay-off or negative benefit in choosing to live in a contracted state. In the workshop, we had a trained team of skilled coaches dedicated and committed to assisting Amber and every woman in truly moving forward in their lives, from fear (little t truth) to love (Big T Truth). It is essential that each of us has a committed support team of a few people who confirm in their own lives their choice to live in love and remind us to live in Big T Truth when we forget and return to our ego, believing in little t and fear.

Almost twenty-five years have passed since that workshop, and these two women and the man in the middle are still in transparent relationships with deep and meaningful friendships and bonds.

Amber's reflections

My memory is not crystal clear about all that happened at that workshop because I was so deeply shocked and traumatized by Christina appearing in the training room. I barely remember what she describes as my initial reaction.

I was so completely and massively triggered, and in fear and shock that I was literally, "Out of My Mind and Body"! I remember Christina standing there, in her genuine, authentic self, but in my rage and fury, I couldn't hear what we were saying. What I remember most of all about my interaction with Christina was feeling my RAGE! So, I am always and ever grateful for the "space" in Christina's spirit that provided for me a safe place to scream and rage at her the way I did. She was full of grace, Presence, love, and patience.

I feel Jonathan is a unique man who just flits about in his life like a little Butterfly, "pollinating" all his flowers. Somewhere in my mind I truly believe I was in total denial about his actual way of being. Revisiting that time in my life reminds me once again that, "I am always in the perfect place, at the perfect time, doing and being exactly what I am doing and being in that moment." This has been my mantra for many years. My oh my, when I look back at how wounded I was and never even knew it.

I will tell you that the *True Woman's Power* workshop gave me the realization that I am able to forgive and move on, which is more than I can say for the vast majority of the population. I cannot understand why couples, who are estranged, separated, or divorced, bear such hatred and ill will toward their partners. In this respect, I have had the grace to forgive and to continue in love because, as Dominic, my Teacher, always reminded me, "All we as Beings ever truly want is to love and be loved." I believe we always attract the perfect people into our lives to embrace change and show us new ways of being.

Of course, at this point in my life, I have "done enough work on myself" to realize that my reactions are always about me and not about the other person or event. However, that being said, every step we take toward "Conscious Awareness" is yet another obvious indication that deep within all of us is that search for wholeness and love and to come out of fear.

Christina and I worked our issues out by the end of that *True Woman's Power* workshop, and I forgave and moved on. I have always considered myself to be a total friend with Christina and she, in her grace, still loves me deeply.

Jonathan's reflections:

I clearly remember Christina's playfulness (that continues today) when we first met, joining with my childlike spirit. I felt immediately endeared to her.

What I wanted to share with people that is significant about what happened in Sandy Levey-Lunden's *True Woman's Power* (TWP) workshop is that it's not just the incident of Christina's arrival that upset Amber so much, with anger and rage dominating her reaction. It was more about situations in her past that triggered her—a significant woundedness of feeling abandonment, low self-esteem, and betrayal.

What was critical to me was that I was not in my integrity with a half-truth shared with Christina about the status and agreements in my marriage with Amber. I had a strong realization that I messed up. I needed to own it right away with no more deflection and justification. Finally, I did—so much so that I surrendered by phone during the workshop, listening to Amber's ego truth and holding space for her. I recognized how much my indiscretion had impacted her, and how important communication is for her, so my full support was the potent piece that kept the energy moving forward for her. She was able to rise above her anger and get more in touch with her story and move through it.

Also, my willingness to be vulnerable and ask for forgiveness played a critical role in bringing our hearts back to center.

This miracle happened because my beloved did not waver and was ready to confront Christina while at the same time confronting her own demons, shadows, and triggers.

Christina was like a time bomb for my marriage, but thankfully it didn't explode us to fall apart and separate. With her awareness and consciousness, by holding her ground, what Christina did was monumental and moved everything forward to completion and expansion. Christina didn't detract from my relationship with Amber; as a catalyst, she gave us the opportunity to deepen our connection.

Amber and I have learned so much through our experiences in Sandy's trainings and *The Power of Clearing* process. Since then, we have helped many people, just sharing our experiences, and we are very excited that Sandy's book will help so many more people learn what is possible.

In the years since the late 90s, I am saddened to witness many couples splitting up, and see how often they are projecting onto their partner what they blame their parent or sibling for from the past. Therefore, they are experiencing the unhealed past rather than the Presence of their partner. So, being open and having a willing heart when listening to what someone else is going through helps them feel heard and eventually let go of their limiting beliefs. I am grateful for Sandy's *Power of Clearing* process providing the tools for further investigation, forgiveness, and surrender. People can feel more open to explore and release their past and then connect more deeply in relationships through their willingness to communicate with their partner and dissolve barriers to union.

For us, when we set up the table of communication properly, I am grateful for all that happened, for our growth. As a couple, Amber and I were always questioning everything and one another, being willing to be vulnerable, even in front of friends, allowing them to witness our process. Clearing and sharing was always more important than food. Sometimes they had to wait for dinner! Amber always said, "Handle what's in front of you."

I want to add something about my experience when Amber and I attended Sandy's workshop, *Choosing Freedom: The Way Out,* soon after Amber learned I was involved with Christina.

I remember when I was in the course, it was almost like all these women were ready to attack me and jump on me, this bad guy, this inconsiderate, uncompassionate guy. I was fortunate not to let it go deep into my inner world because I knew from my heart there was nothing that I was doing that would belittle this remarkable woman, my wife, or in any way demonstrate that she was less than amazing. I recognize in life that we're all such judgment machines, so when we look at a particular situation, this guy had an affair; therefore, he is bad, naughty, and such an awful man. It's so far from the truth. Yet, it's how we've been taught through TV programming and indoctrination to look at how relationships are to be. It's like, "they make me happy," or "she will make me happy." So, even though I felt all this attack, I was fortunate not to let it pierce through me because I know who I am. I know my intention, and I'm not a bad guy. I've always loved this lady, Amber, no matter what. Other people don't know, but they think they know based on their interpretation of their experience.

Several years ago, Amber and I had a conscious uncoupling and today we remain close friends. We've all learned and grown though grace. For almost forty years, Amber has helped me be the man who I always wanted to be and knew I could be. I believe I have done the same for her in being the woman she always knew she could be. We are so blessed by continuing to confirm with each other the living of our lives only in Big T Truth whenever we forget.

Zoom reunion in mid-March, 2022.

Almost twenty-five years after that *True Woman's Power* course, we get Amber, Jonathan, and Christina together with Sandy. The triad live in three locations in two countries with mostly only phone contact between them for many years.

Amber – "Every life is a destination unknown: a journey of tragedies and triumphs that ultimately allows us to discover, not only our world, but more importantly ourselves." (Outer Limits)

That *is* what life is truly about and what is so wonderfully amazing is to watch Jonathan discover his true self. When I read what he had written, I was deeply moved beyond the beyond because I had never heard him ever speak or write with such clarity and I thought to myself that he really is in the process of "discovering not only the world around him but ultimately himself."

Jonathan – Amber, it's so wonderful to see you here on Zoom and share and know that what we have experienced together will impact a lot of people from Sandy's book. I think it's so powerful and daring that you would go where few women would, with your guts and vulnerability. In all the courses we've done, you were the first one to start and go naked emotionally and spiritually. You made it all happen for people to feel comfortable; they could also be in their authentic selves and be vulnerable and emotional. So that's what made it impressive is through the emotion and pain, you didn't let it get stuck like cement. You didn't dig in and say, "No, no, no, no!" And of course, when I shared the story with people, "Here's my very dear friend, Christina, who is part of the TWP course, and do you think Amber would have her in the room, or do you think she'd have her leave?" Almost everyone said, "Amber would want to have Christina in the room," and that was brilliant.

Christina – Maybe not at first...

Jonathan – And then a few hours later, I get this call from Amber at Sandy's workshop, and I think, what an amazing process, so fast! That takes huge courage.

Christina – Amber, why did you make the decision to let me stay in the workshop? Do you remember?

Amber – Well, since I was so out of my body after seeing you appear in the room, one must wonder. I guess the truth is that inside, it's like what my teacher Dominic said to me since then, "All we as beings ever really want is to love and be loved." Not knowing that at the time, believe me, because being so wounded in my life,

I guess a part of me wanted to be loved. Also, something in me knew that this woman who was a crazy butterfly, like my husband, Jonathan, had that capacity within her, to love me. So, my first perception of you, Christina, even though I looked at you and judged you, thinking, "Oh, my God, she's just like Jonathan, oh, help me, please," I thought, there's a lightness of being in a butterfly. Right?

Christina – You're saying that at some level, you recognized that opportunity to heal and find your way to love even though you were so upset?

Amber – Willing to go where no man has gone before!

Jonathan – She loves challenges and opportunities. So, perhaps to see if she could get the upper hand, maybe get this person to recognize the inappropriate behavior, so Amber wins, and Christina loses. It's my sense, initially, that Amber felt, "No one's going to put me in a place of apprehension and fear and close the door." So, Amber chose to keep the door open, thinking, "Wow, keep her in here because I want to get at her! I want to really lay it on her!"

Christina – You took the opportunity, which was absolutely brilliant. And you were given that opportunity too, because Sandy said, "If anyone's going to leave, it's Christina, not the participant."

Jonathan – All of this coming together now, after all these years, is magical synchronicity when we remain open and daring. Sadly, though, from what I have observed, a vast majority of people live very contracted and constricted lives. As a result, they lose opportunities such as we are experiencing. That is why I am so grateful for Amber, Christina, and all of us here today in this Zoom call reunion with Sandy.

Prayer Dance

A prayer of forgiveness
For the illusions of sin we've accepted
Releasing the Demon King that often rules our Sacred Kingdom
And awakening to the truth of innocence
The truth of our Birthright to be free
And living a life of Support, Abundance, and Joy!
This prison is one we've created
Not by fault of our own
But through lifetimes of being taught
And buying into illusions
A prayer dance of Peace
A prayer dance of Release
And complete acceptance of ourselves and our creations
We are not wrong
We were ignorant once
not skilled in listening
To (our inner guidance) Wisdom
But we are opening now
And thankful for the gifts of pain and struggle
For this was our training tool
Used to carve out a new future
Of Love
A time of learning and sharing ourselves with the world
Letting go of beliefs that no longer serve
Once the veil is lifted
We are brought back
Into the Light

Katya Kudrov, Russian Power of Clearing coach

PART IV

TESTIMONIALS

CHAPTER 10

CHANGING LIVES THROUGH
THE POWER OF CLEARING

The *Fri Sikt* Project

From the 1998 documentary movie, *The Difference: Fri Sikt*—translated from Swedish to English by the moderator.

In 1996, forty youth, mostly high-risk with serious problems, from Stockholm and Malmö in Sweden, enrolled themselves in the first *Fri Sikt* (*Open View*) ten-day youth program camp. They didn't know what the program was about when they enrolled. They also didn't know that the program would continue for one-and-a-half years and that they would have a chance to be part of the whole program. In total, 120 youths participated in numerous programs flexibly, according to their circumstance. About half of that total ended up going through the whole year and a half program.

I was inspired to organize this youth project after a participant in one of my adult trainings in Malmö read a newspaper article aloud to me in English from the Swedish. It was about a father who was suing his son because he wouldn't get out of bed or find a job or enter a vocational training program. His son had no idea what to do since graduating from high school. The father was suing the son for all the money, time, and energy he had invested, because he perceived that his son was wasting his life and his youth. The father wanted to recover his investment, and motivate his son who had been in bed for weeks and told his father he was not going to get up. He said there was no reason to get out of bed because there was nothing worth doing of any importance or value. There were no jobs he could get because no job openings were posted in newspapers. He could think of nowhere to go to find help in finding a job. He was inert and could see no future for himself.

Inspired by the newspaper article and my response to it, seven people in that training decided to mobilize and commit to join me in creating this youth project and sourcing funds. We named the project then and there, *Fri Sikt,* "*Open View.*" With this dedicated, enthusiastic, synergistic group of passionate adults joined in a common purpose, the project came together easily and joyously for us. I knew that for a benefactor to be motivated to fund the project, they would need to have experienced and know the benefit of my counseling and training on themselves and their family. While the others researched government funding for the project, I asked only one person to financially support the project.

A few months earlier, this businessman, who was a family man, agreed to a divorce from his wife. They were separated for a while and then he really wanted to get back together with her. However, their relationship was not improving right away. When they started to meet again as a couple, they did several courses and sessions with me until they were both ready to rebuild their marriage with passion and purpose. The reason I was so committed to help them reunite was because he told me if he was not with her, he would stay alone for the rest of his life. Then, when they became more joined with their children again, this couple decided that the whole family should do a course with me. This course was called *The Art of Joining a Family,* and four generations of their family came together to work out their issues and differences with each other.

At the beginning of that course, this businessman's father (who was about eighty years old and a self-made businessman, from being a waiter to building a massive company), stood up and addressed his whole family. He said that he had never learned to communicate with his wife, even after more than forty years of marriage. This weekend course was a possibility for each of them in the room to learn to communicate at one hundred percent levels and set their lives on a new course. Each one now had an opportunity to fully let go of all blame and judgment they were holding against each other in the family. He wanted each of them to play full out about what was upsetting them and go for releasing these judgments with one hundred percent commitment. He especially wanted his other son who was in the wheelchair with MS to fully engage with everyone in the room to see if it would make a difference to improve his condition. "And get out of this wheelchair!"

The weekend was a huge success and everyone in the family was very clear with every other member of the family, letting go of blame and judgment on deep levels. They had each done the personal process clearings with each person they blamed. Everyone could witness (seeing and hearing) each *Clearing Process* if they chose. Each pod of two had a coach guiding them through the exact 3-step structure of *The Clearing Process* to end up in full forgiveness.

Since the businessman's entire family had received such great benefit from the training, I knew they would be perfect to support this youth program. Every time I saw him over the following six months or so, I asked him the question about being the benefactor. After asking him many times, there was something in his eye that told me he was ready to commit to funding the program. Once he committed, we could take action. Within three months, I had mobilized the staff and refined the program. We went all out on it. I consider it the most profound project of my career. It was the first of twelve similar programs that followed, mostly in Canada.

When the couple discussed my funding proposal, they agreed it was such a successful experience for their family that they wanted to gift it to other families who had communication challenges and relationship problems. In the end, his wife had got what she wanted, her husband to be more expressive of his feelings. Now she could emotionally connect with him. So, they thought surely the whole process would work for other families because it had worked to reunite them all at deeper levels than ever before.

Because I had a private benefactor for the program, I could choose any young person I wanted because they didn't have to meet outside criteria for normal government funding. They had to meet my criteria of being open to changing their lives in a purposeful way. Therefore, each youth had to volunteer to go through the program; no one was forced to participate because it was a high level of involvement, thinking, introspection, self-awareness, and learning how to fully communicate.

We told everyone in our networks that we had openings for this ten-day program in the summer at a camp that would take place in the Stockholm Archipelago called Life University. The follow-up year-long program would include support groups and trainings for the youth and their families. We would have two office locations, in Stockholm and in Malmö. We had a project organizer for each of these locations and they went out on the street and began talking with youth. They were looking for youths who were ready to make changes in their lives and also youth who, even though they were apathetic, were open to the possibility of change or evolvement.

Many of the youth enrolled themselves, certain parents recommended others, police directed members of gangs to us, and also gave us other ideas of who to enroll and how to enroll them. Some middle-class youth or young people in the program were involved in drugs, violence, prostitution, and criminal activity, as well as suffering from confusion, anorexia, depression, and alienation from family. These circumstances created feelings of hopelessness in their lives. Many had difficulty in relationships with their parents, friends, siblings, and school authorities. They were young and feeling that their lives were going nowhere. Living seemed hopeless, futile, and like they would never find the answers they desperately sought.

Most of the youths in the *Fri Sikt* program had been living in extreme stress in their daily lives with their families. They were numb and turned-off, unable to be touched or connect with deep-seated emotions. Life on the streets taught the youths to be tough and not to feel anything or cry, so during the course, they found it difficult to access any feelings of sadness, happiness, guilt, love, peace, or fear. With support staff and clearing coaches who were listening, paying attention, and caring deeply about what each youth communicated, they experienced a novel world unlike anything they had ever known. A few people, who were part of a gang, left the program early because they thought it was so weird to have people listening and caring. They originally came for free food and free camp. The rest of the youth stayed and participated in the program, and enjoyed the live, healthy, organic food. They also bonded like a community with each other and the support staff. Every day they always looked forward to the deep, emotional rebirthing process—both individual and group sessions—which was very freeing for them. Rebirthing is a technique to free up energy from the body and clear the way to the embodiment of who you are. (Please see books in the Resources section.)

We had youths from all social classes and backgrounds, from poor sections of Swedish society to wealthy families. Hierarchy was released among the youths and the staff, creating a oneness, and we became equals in the training program, applying *The Clearing Process,* the philosophy of the clearing, and the psycho-spiritual therapeutic process to all aspects of our lives. The youths and their families learned how to communicate with each other, even though there was great fear, resistance, and distrust in the beginning prior to *The Art of Joining a Family* training.

Our benefactor was the controller of their family business, and paid all of the expenses (I never handled any of the money) for one-and-a-half years' worth of training, courses, and programs with these youths in the *Fri Sikt* project and their families. The programs took place in two locations, Malmö and Stockholm. We had support and group sessions twice a week for several hours with all the youths, and their area leader during the weekdays, with many trainings on the weekends. It was an intensive immersion program. Everyone had at least one private session a week with their youth project counselor in the form of a clearing, a life coaching session, or a re-birthing. There was total continuity in the program for the one and a half years. We went on location to different youth camps for three ten-day intensive courses with the entire staff of coaches, assistants, and program leaders in a beautiful country setting where we all lived together and bonded as a healthier family-like group.

Three-quarters of the year after beginning the project, we invited the parents to join us with their children for *The Art of Joining a Family* weekend course. At that point the youths were highly-skilled with *The Clearing Process* and the philosophy of the teaching, so we were concerned that the parents were novices. The benefactor required the parents to pay the cost for the three days food and lodging at the castle to demonstrate their participation, interest, and commitment to the program. It was the only money that the parents of the youths were asked to pay in the one and a half years of the program. Some of the parents thought that if they said they couldn't afford the nominal cost, that they could get out of participating. I worked with each parent to assess whether that was true and to go through any resistance and fear they had about attending the family training. All of them were able to overcome their anxiety about attending the weekend course with their family. At the end of the course the parents thanked me, especially the resistant ones. One of the challenging jobs of my life was to enroll every single parent (who was alive and available) to participate in *The Art of Joining of a Family*. They had fear of being attacked, being judged by other parents.

The Art of Joining a Family weekend course was one of the highlights of the entire *Fri Sikt* program at a castle (Rinkesta Slott) where the original youth project participants joined with their mothers and fathers, even if they were divorced. This family program is depicted in the youth project movie with very emotional scenes of projected anger by the youth onto their parents and at the end full forgiveness and joining. Each family had their own personal coach to help the youths to fully communicate everything they wanted to say to their parents with nothing left out. This 36-hour weekend, lasting three full days, was one of the most poignant and dramatic parts of the whole program. I felt that the youths entirely changed their dynamics with their mothers and fathers as a result of this program. Also, the parents cleared their judgments of the youths and what they blamed on them. So, in the end, we had a huge reunion with the parents and the youths. This weekend was one of the highlights of my life, seeing such dramatic shifts in the youths and in the perspectives of the mothers and fathers. They each went through their deep feelings to express themselves and release what they had been holding back and suppressing for many years. In the movie you can see this expression in a lot of screaming that went on, which I call projection. After each youth had a chance to fully emote, they did the full clearing with their parents and took their feelings of blame, anger, and rejection to full forgiveness.

There was only one youth, the oldest at 28, who didn't bring either of his parents to the course. I worried about him, wondering if he would not clear enough about his feelings with his family and thereby, end up in a life of crime. Even though he was older than the age range, the reason I took him into the program was because the person who owned the treatment center he was attending really wanted him to be in the program. He was the only youth I had doubt about, that he would attain the goal of full clearing and forgiveness. Many years later, he attacked someone and was attacked, and he died.

With the exception of this 28-year-old participant, *The Art of Joining a Family* training had one hundred percent forgiveness with the youths and their parents. Therefore, each person achieved one hundred percent understanding. Understanding follows forgiveness.

In the end, after one-and-a-half years, the total program cost added up to a million-and-a-half dollars (in 1997). The follow-up program included the parents, siblings, and partners of these youths. In the initial process of negotiating the funding with the primary benefactor, I committed to him that the high-risk youth would be transformed by my program and would never end up (or be back) in jail. He said it would have cost two million dollars over thirty years for even one of these youths if they had gone to prison, so he perceived it as a small comparative amount.

The filmmaker who made the *Fri Sikt* film, Peter Mayer, was the most outrageous person I'd ever met! For example, when people in Sweden asked him to take a TV series (that he created, produced, and directed) off the air that was "over the edge" for normal Swedish thinking, he refused. When they threatened his life, rather than discuss the situation, he built bullet-proof windows and doors to ensure his free speech. We named the film *The Difference*, the difference being one of love.

Peter died after the film was complete. He always said that next to his wives and mother, I was his favorite person; therefore, he made four films about my life and work. I always wanted to help him clear all of the blame and guilt he felt. In my perception, Peter was extremely stubborn and judgmental. So, his refusal to do this deep inner work on himself may have resulted in the manifestation of the pancreatic cancer, which was more fatal in 1999 than it is today, and difficult for anyone to release. In my estimation, he was as talented and unique a film producer as Fellini. He followed the *Fri Sikt* process for one-and-a-half years with his Oscar-nominated cameramen. He loved the project and was completely inspired by filming it and participating in it as a witness because the program was so heartfelt, heart-opening, and inspiring. He thought it was fantastic to film this project. Peter felt that a film needed controversy because that would make it interesting to the public. So, he added "new age" words about me to create that controversy in a traditional society like Sweden. The film was shot and created throughout the project and afterward, for an additional cost of $100,000. If you would like to see this four-part 45-minute film yourself, the link to it is in the Resources section.

Here is an excerpt of something I said during the movie when Peter asked me to tell him about the youth project and what it means to me. I said, "This work is very deep. It's about guilt, mostly—most of us have felt guilty, that something is wrong with us, that we fear we will make a mistake, and that we are not good enough, and that we have some kind of problem and sometimes we don't even know what that problem is. Many people grow up into functioning adults with this very deep feeling inside that something is wrong with them and they are never really going to be happy. No one will see them for who they are and no one will love them for who they really are. At the core of this feeling is what I have come to clear in my work. They feel separate from everyone else because either they do not feel as good or they feel better than everyone else." These deep-seated core beliefs are some of what the youth released in the *Fri Sikt* process by the end of the year-and-a-half-long program. By the time most of the youth completed the program they felt free from the deep-seated blocks that had been hindering the joy in their lives. They were eager to enjoy their lives at a passionate and purposeful level. Some were immediately hired by schools to be aides and mentors for high-risk youth, incorporating the learning they had from the *Fri Sikt* project; the students had now become teachers. I had trained them for close to 1,000 hours including ten-day courses, 15 weekend trainings, and weekly personal sessions during the project. They could recite my trainings and philosophy verbatim! It became part of them, each one individualizing their learning according to their life experiences and their personalized, expanded thinking.

The narrator for the *Fri Sikt* movie said, as part of creating controversy, "People are afraid of this type of deep feeling and dramatic portrayal, like one student who let out a huge scream in the rebirthing, a process that brings up many emotions." Everyone was affected, letting out huge sighs in response, as if they had a chance to scream with her.

I would say that "people are afraid of what they do not understand and have never deeply thought about."

In part of the movie, we see Martin, one of the youth project participants, who projected his entire emotional fear and problems into the symbol of a spider. Martin loved heroin, and it scared him how much he loved it. He loved heroin because it took away all fear and guilt and created a numb, vacant feeling space. He had every single emotion tied up in the fear of a spider.

I spent hundreds of hours in the *Fri Sikt* project. I didn't expect to get so deep so quickly with all of the youths. The whole staff and I were amazed at what they were saying about their lives and what they thought, felt, and believed. The narrator of the film said, "Most criminals are young men with very difficult relationships with their fathers." They developed negative life patterns passed on from their fathers that they also chose, thinking that was their only option of lifestyle and these feelings became habits. It was the only pattern they knew and it was familiar to them. Familiarity brings comfort. We continuously heard stories from the youth who had experienced, seen, and heard about men who raped and beat their wives. The male youths were afraid of becoming like these men, uncaring, unkind, agitated, angry, and violent. The female youths were afraid of being passive and becoming victims to these types of men. Most of the youths were looking for role models and they found it very difficult to find a good male role model. Therefore, many of our professional coaches, assistants, and mentors were men. The youths formed very deep bonds with these young men who were part of the *Fri Sikt* staff. When the youths worked with their fathers in the *Fri Sikt* training, the staff noticed that the youths were very scared and felt unsafe while fully communicating with their fathers. They feared the anger and rage of their fathers because they had witnessed this type of attack, both on television and in their lives.

Everything that happened in the lives of the participants and staff during the whole one and a half years of the project, in the trainings, personal sessions, and their lives outside the *Fri Sikt* program, was used as clearing items. For example, in the first ten-day course at Life University, after the staff had been paid from their normal jobs outside of the program, they put a lot of cash in their suitcases and wallets that they left in a room with everyone else's baggage. We soon discovered that a total of $4,000 had been stolen from the staff's suitcases, likely by one of the youths. The question was, by whom? And for what reason? I meditated for about 24 hours and determined whose bag we should look into for the money. I said that two people from the staff had to go together to verify the contents of the youth's suitcase. They found a lot of the missing cash and also a huge amount of candy that she had purchased with some of the money. We took back the cash and returned it to the staff members. The youth, who had anorexia, learned how to do the clearing and cleared about stealing this money and having the compulsion to eat an extraordinary amount of candy. In the training, everything that happens is an issue to clear, for the staff as well, who cleared on being angry and feeling betrayed.

It was an equal opportunity for everyone to expand and grow, both staff (a total of 20 adults) and participants, as an extended, bonded family. We, the coaches, support staff, and youths, created a safe place for each other to fully share ourselves with one another. We had complete confidentiality of the personal stories told in the training rooms, in the sharing chair, in the clearing sessions, with the coaches, and among the youths themselves.

In several of these ten-day trainings we had our psycho-drama training coach, Jack Barnard from Los Angeles working with youths in dramatic skits that portrayed breakthrough parts of their lives. At the end of the *Fri Sikt* program, we had a final event and party (called "High on Life" rather than "High on Drugs") in a hundred-year-old big barn at in Väddö at Life University where the youth project began. All of the youths invited their families, friends, and relatives. This event, including a banquet, is portrayed in the movie, *The Difference*.

From the narrator of the movie: "These children who live on the streets are in a desperate situation, in urgent need of healing. Sandy has found a beautiful way to take kids who are despondent to a very deep place within themselves so they feel empowered and confident to take responsibility for their lives. Children get in touch with the true meaning of Love and how people can join together in love and purpose."

Then I say in the movie the following comments: "There is a lot within each youth that has never come out or been expressed from the deepest part of themselves. They are learning how to express their feelings, taking responsibility for what they have done, and releasing blame. As the *Fri Sikt* program continues, with personal sessions and trainings for the youths, the support staff help them see their present life and envision the future they really want to create from their truest desires. We all have something negative to clear from our past so that we can be ourselves and create the life we want."

In 2000, two years after the completion of the *Fri Sikt* program, and at the request of the program's benefactor, we gathered feedback from the youth involved in the program. We reviewed their progress in terms of success in their present and potential careers. With a series of structured questions, we interviewed 85 of the youth participants, and through analyzing the results, we found that 82 percent of them either had a job or were in an educational program to further their skills and create desired employment. We felt these were high statistics of success. The benefactor and I along with the project leaders, support staff, and coaches of the program, were very pleased with the results.

Twenty years after the project (in 2016) in Väddö, we had a reunion at Life University where the project began. Twenty-five years later, in 2022, we are still speaking with some of these youths about their lives through the *Fri Sikt* Facebook group or by email. Many of them have attained supervisory positions or started entrepreneurial businesses, and now have their own families. We (staff and youths) all continue to be moved by remembering the breakthroughs for these youths from pain, anguish, and suffering into love, peace, joy, hope, purpose, and productivity.

Testimonials about *The Power of Clearing* process
Preface by Sandy

When coaching a session of *The Power of Clearing*, we are able to identify the core beliefs that have been held, often for a lifetime, by the participant. Some are unexpected, many are shocking, yet simultaneously, a revelation. By uncovering the truth of what is driving the mind—and then by association, the body of the participant—we are able to help them see, understand, accept, and release old patterns of thoughts, feelings, and beliefs about themselves and their world. In turn, this release creates space and allows the focus to move toward more life-enhancing and sustaining thoughts, feelings, and beliefs. Through this process a sense of freedom and joy is created that leads to perfect peace.

The process of putting together all the puzzle pieces in someone's mind about an issue and releasing it through forgiveness can be very fast because of the structure of *The Clearing Process*. The process quickly points to the source of why a person thinks a certain way. This effectiveness is a major reason for the growing popularity of *The Power of Clearing* in all countries and across all cultures. In clearing, there is no one and nothing that is seen or believed to be separate in any way.

(The following are accounts of client clearings that highlight common core themes, while the circumstances and stories are of individual experiences.) This is what course participants have said about the value of this work and the difference it has made in their lives.

1) DG

"I first met Sandy in Lansing, Michigan, in mid-October in a two-and-a-half-day course. I was so impressed with the changes I experienced that I moved heaven and Earth to take her ten-day *Power of Clearing Coaching Certification Program* in Stowmarket, England. When I left for England, I was financially challenged and mate-less.

(In fact, it had been years since I was in an intimate relationship.) I came to the training partly to heal a block in forming a lasting, loving relationship that I had carried for perhaps 30 years since I experienced the first of two rapes. I had never thought that I could be authentically honest with a man on every level and be received. I thought I was too much for any one person and that I had to bite down on my truth and hold back, rather than reveal myself, lest I be rejected.

"During the training, I worked through lifetimes of grief, disappointment, and despair, freeing myself to what *A Course in Miracles* would call the real me. When the training concluded, I felt light as a feather. In essence, I am my true self now and live from who I truly am.

"Four days after the training, my financial situation began to improve. A week later, a man contacted me about exploring the possibility of a relationship. Six days later, we met and it was the most magical, soulful meeting of my life. Within two hours, we knew that this was something different, something so exquisite we could not have orchestrated it by ourselves. We are partners who share a common purpose; even our dreams echo one another's. It's not that we are in love, although that is true. It's that we are remembering together the Love we have always been, appearing now, in time and space, as two mouths sipping from the cup of Eternal Fullness."

DG went on to take the ten-day *Power of Clearing* Coaching Certification Program and became a certified *Power of Clearing* coach.

2) Gillian Hibbs, B.Ed. (Hons.) in the U.K., certified *Power of Clearing* Coach

"I have known Sandy Levey-Lunden since 2005. After enrolling in several of her courses, I undertook her *Power of Clearing Coaching Certification Program,* and since then, I have coached and travelled with her extensively. As a result, I constantly appreciate Sandy's deep knowledge and sincere integrity. I see her as an authentically gifted and intuitive healer, full of energy, life, and committed to her work.

"Sandy provides a warm, safe, and non-judgmental atmosphere where her course participants may release past traumas that prevent them from living life fully and realizing peace. She connects with people by employing deep listening and insights in achieving these results. She is also extremely funny. I have had profound results in my own life with my family, friends, and myself, shifting me in many extraordinary ways by living this process.

"I have been on the staff as a coach in many of her courses—the *Art of Surrender, True Woman's Power, Choosing Freedom,* and the *Power of Clearing Coaching Certification Program*. I've enjoyed being part of the journey and the process with participants as they've released the old patterns of who they are not and value the truth of who they are. As a coach, I have found tremendous fulfillment from participating in these courses and appreciate the value of each one.

"Since completing the courses, I'm constantly using *The Clearing Process* in response to triggers from the ego. Whilst I can't control the triggers, I've learned to deal with them differently. For example, with a fellow coach "holding the space," I can go back to the source of my emotional disturbance where I can examine the pattern of emotions and ego thinking that followed. I can then safely release the ego thoughts when I see that holding them has no purpose or value in my present life. I find that Sandy's *Clearing Process* enables release so that love, peace, and joy can flow. I find it quick, gentle, effective, and very wonderful. I have such gratitude for the teachings of dear Sandy Levey-Lunden.

"If asked how clearing has changed my relationship with my children, I would say that at one time, I felt that I was constantly walking on eggshells. I felt they were judging me for how I had handled things in the past, and now, in the present. I believed that if I didn't get something right, they would judge me unfavorably and that the judgment would not be a fair one.

"When I first started to put Sandy's teachings into practice, I saw that the first thing I needed to clear for myself was my constant judging of the people I encountered in my life. Thoughts like 'they had no empathy,' 'they only considered themselves,' and 'they just couldn't be bothered' always seem to mar the quality of my connection with them. I needed to 'clear.' I was guided back to the source, where I judged the treatment that I received from a constant unloving adult in my life as unfair, and I had continued to employ this belief when meeting adults who could influence my life. Having seen this perception in me, I corrected and released it in a very fluid way. In the process of clearing it, I was also releasing my perception that my children were always judging me. I then needed to clear my guilt and troubled belief that I had been too absent in my children's teenage years. This clearing touched a profound level in me. With the release of judgments and guilt, I've experienced a lightness and flow in my connection with them. It has happened gradually. It is warm, loving, and completely wonderful, and it has happened with others in my life too.

"I am also asked how it feels when I hold a sacred space as a coach for a participant during *The Clearing Process*. I feel it is a privilege to be trusted in this role. I completely dedicate myself to the person I'm coaching in the clearing, and I resolve to give one hundred percent to the process, assuring the clearer that I safely hold all that transpires in that space. I've found that some releases in *The Clearing Process* can be very gentle or extremely powerful and tumultuous. Long-held beliefs force their way out in separate points during the clearing, maybe in anger, coming together and creating a whole body of truth that can overwhelm the person. But the space is very safe. Both coach and clearer can feel the release in their bodies; such is its power. Our inner guide will always be there with us. Then our clearing Step 3 of Affirmation fluidly takes us to the truth, and we reach that beautiful state of Peace when I can ask, 'Are you complete?' and with this assurance, we are held together."

3) Gizella Nagy in Vancouver, Canada, certified *Power of Clearing* Coach at bodymindcocoon.com

"On my journey to seeking for higher meaning and my true purpose in life, I was introduced to Sandy's *Power of Clearing* process in 2018. Shortly after my first session with her, I started my deep inner transformation. She was able to retrieve and help me release my most hidden memories and safely and gently guide me back to peace and oneness. I loved her longer workshops because she incorporated complementary therapeutic interventions such as Holotropic Breathwork, Rebirthing, Tension & Trauma Releasing Exercises, and Advance Hand Analysis. These modalities complemented the POC clearings seamlessly, and the ratio of one facilitator per student was extremely generous. These experiential modalities were in perfect harmony to gradually unfold, embrace, and integrate my painful beliefs and life experiences. My work with Sandy and her team of *Power of Clearing* coaches has profoundly changed how I relate to myself and others, and the results are evident, both in my personal and professional life. With Sandy's inspiration, continual support, and under her guidance, I became a *Power of Clearing* Coach in 2020. Now my clients can experience therapeutic sessions of Spiritual Bodywork, a fusion of *The Power of Clearing* process combined with my 20 years of experience in providing Holistic Massage Therapy. I am forever grateful for her influence in my life and can't wait to celebrate the publishing of her book."

4) Claire Melling – Homemaker and part-time administrator

Date and course attended: March 2015 Dunblane Scotland POCCP Training

What exactly did you get out of this course?

Sandy, you are an awesome teacher. You allowed me to grow before your and my own eyes. It's not just a spiritual growth, but a deep knowledge and assurance that I am good enough and really, the person who was doing me the most harm was in fact I.

It was an amazing thing to experience the so many clearings in such quick succession – on reflection; it feels like I was joining the dots in my own life – recognizing the patterns that have been repeating themselves and my own responsibility for projecting these patterns of behavior back toward me. The subject of 'triggers' was fascinating and the knowledge that I am never upset for the reason I think I'm upset is still resonating with me.

Ultimately, I feel a deep sense of peace and joy which has stayed with me even after Ewen came in and threw all the abuse he could think of in my direction. For the first time ever, I was able to stand up for myself, hold my head high, and NOT cry in the face of his verbal abuse. Additionally, it only took an hour or so for me to regain my equilibrium after he left.

Would you recommend anyone to the course? Why?

Absolutely; it's helped me to discover who I am—and I find I rather like the me that has been hidden for so long. I am filled with a joy and deep sense of contentment that I didn't think possible in my current circumstances. I also realize that the fear of the future which was my constant companion has faded into the background.

Sandy, you did this work together with a tremendous team and guided me gently with the right balance of firmness, love and encouragement on stepping stones of self-discovery. Your voice competes with the ego in my head which has reduced mental self-harm by providing me with a set of tools and a framework for my thought process. I remember now that there is only love or fear; and I choose love.

December 2021—Thank you for reaching out and checking with me if you could use my testimonial from what seems a lifetime ago. When I re-read it, I was filled with gratitude to the universe for bringing you and Len (and Iona plus others) into my life at that most pivotal point. I have used the teachings in my life on such a regular basis since then and I do believe that it's not just me who has benefited, but everyone that I have strong relationships with are better and stronger relationships than they were before.

5) Valerie Shahan – Re-birther and *Power of Clearing* Coach in Washington State, USA

By attending both workshops, *The Art of Surrender* and *The Holy Relationship*, I am glad to know that insight and clear answers to these questions can truly be found.

Do you know who you truly are?

Can you be free of guilt, attack, and fear?

Can you see "a new you" emerge in this world?

Do you realize that you are not alone?

Can you be in a relationship with a joint purpose?

Extraordinarily, the light is within each of us, as is the tunnel, and the answers.

It starts with a story; my story, your story, our story.

Like you, I have searched for many years for answers to the pains of the past I have experienced. Like you, I have read books, from philosophy to psychology to self-help to religions, had therapy, counseling, met gurus, shamans, done workshops, and practiced meditation and yoga.

All of these processes have helped me to become attuned to a better version of me. Something was missing—*an experience and simple tools* which I found to be unique in *The Art of Surrender* and *The Holy Relationship*, and the *Power of Clearing Coaching Certification Program*.

An experience and simple tools: An adventure unlike any other. For each workshop, we meet as a group in the welcoming home of a past or present student of transformation.

Immediately, I feel safe and surrounded by a nurturing energy coming from Sandy and Len (one of *The Power of Clearing* coaches).

From a place of great pain, we, as a group, are able to experience and witness from each other, transformative moments of peace, universal love, and joy. It is done with the understanding of key words and, through processes, the sharing of our broken life stories.

We come to understand the *Art of Surrender*. During the training, we are guided by the coaches, often in pairs, to release the pain that we create from subconscious stories we believe, feel, and think about ourselves repeatedly in our ego. We surrender beliefs such as judgment, self-loathing, unworthiness, guilt, separation, isolation, undeserving of love, and let go of the fear to love ourselves.

We let go by a Clearing Process. It is Sandy's gift, given to her in a moment of trauma in her own life. Its effect is truly magical by its simplicity. Our stories are deactivated in the 3-step Clearing Process, creating awareness, surrender, and forgiveness. Once experienced, The Clearing Process, a tool for life, can be applied to open our heart every time necessary whenever we fall out of love and into ego thoughts and ego fears.

Our stories are then released by **forgiveness** in *The Clearing Process*. Moving from a state of false belief from our broken life stories, we learn to cancel the blocks in the mind that stop the flow of life or love energy that connects us all. That energy has many words with God-like terms, like universal love, universal consciousness, divinity, and nature. It may sometimes feel loaded, sometimes exclusive, but in truth it has no simpler definition than that we are all the same, spiritually. Forgiveness and remembering who we truly are as divine beings is a beautiful completion step of *The Clearing Process*.

And so, we make a *true connection* with ourselves and everyone else. This connection is explained through the holy relationship. From an early age, we are mistaken to believe that we are special, independent, and disconnected, and that we need to defend ourselves from anyone who might want to hurt us. This belief is no longer important or real once we understand *The Clearing Process*. Understanding comes after forgiveness. Our newly-discovered intention is to understand the common goals that we have in any relationship. We learn to definitely commit to a position of togetherness, twoness, to communicate openly, transparently, without blame, and then connect into love. In *The Holy Relationship* training, we learn to clear the triggers of separation in our relationship, to receive together and give as we received.

At the end of the two workshops, we all have the light to start walking the path in unison, with innocence, freedom, and love that had never left us, that of the child within. We all are shifted through the workshop experience; we can now join in a holy relationship joint purpose. We no longer need to be independent to be safe, and we are no longer chained by fear so that we can now risk being who we truly are in our holy relationship. Once we have attained this state of safety and newness as we are reborn into our true authentic self in the holy relationship, we can then bring that safety, innocence, and support into any of our chosen relationships.

The experience of *The Art of Surrender* and *The Holy Relationship* workshops is unique. Each member of the assisting team of the workshops is truly committed to giving, with one purpose, universal love and compassionate support. The workshops are organized in small groups with beautiful meals provided. These dinners and mealtimes are moments of true bonding and can be used as a reference point to never feel alone again. These two workshops come with follow-up calls, a buddy system, new friends for life, laughter, and a newly-found freedom.

> *"There is light at the end of the tunnel."*

Valerie went on to take the ten-day *Power of Clearing Coaching Certification Program* and became a certified *Power of Clearing* coach.

6) Elaine Clark – Langley BC, Canada, Registered Counselor

"Hi Sandy,

This note is a great big thank you! Doug and I got married in December to celebrate 23 years of working on having a great relationship. That work would never have started if not for you. I am so grateful that you cared enough about me never to give up, even when I wanted to. Of course, our relationship is not perfect; however, it is fulfilling and peaceful as it has never been before. Love has won again! I intend to teach other couples how to transform a relationship from painful to peaceful. So, I became a registered counselor and have worked with your method for many years. I experienced great peace, joy, and love, and as I extend it to others, I receive it back ten-fold."

7) Susan Culverwell – London – 2018, psychotherapist

The Workshop: *The Holy Relationship* training

"I attended two of your holy relationship courses when I was single. The process helped me understand the Truth of relationships, what they are for and how we can heal through relationship. My own healing paved the way for an intimate Relationship with a new partner. Plus, my relationships in general. And yes, Loving is an Art and the finest gift from God to heal."

8) SB – Real Estate Agent, Vancouver, Canada

To Sandy, SB appeared to be seeming relaxed and full of life.

"I can't believe it was just two short months ago that I was in so much pain with a broken heart. I was reeling from breaking off an engagement, coupled with having the belief that I had already failed at two marriages. I was trying to escape from my pain and thinking of where I could run to when I began listening to a CD for the second time. *The Power of Clearing* CD led me to Sandy Levey-Lunden and her programs where I found the answers I so desperately needed, and to release the idea that I was a failure and that I had failed in my marriages."

9) LB – 61-year-old female artist, art and meditation teacher, Canada

LB worked through the ten-day intensive *Power of Clearing Coaching Certification Program* (**POCCCP**). Her one goal was to reduce or preferably eliminate her frequent (up to twelve days in a row, up to twenty a month) migraines, and release whatever is in the way of her creative energy so she could express more of it.

"Since I have been home, I have had ten days headache-free. That is a record in my lifetime. I have also worked on several new paintings and thought about where I could hang more art, in the library, or doctor's clinic, or other offices.

"I had wanted a better conscious connection with a Higher Power for a long time, and feel that I made a major breakthrough there while doing the clearings. I actually felt and experienced the Presence of and At-Onement with God, and that we are all one, the same, and joined. Best of all, I have a way to clear the constant negative thinking, complaining, judging default of my ego, which led me to being in a depressed, hopeless, angry, and at times, suicidal state. I observe my ego-mind and thinking and catch myself much sooner now than I did before. The payoff of feeling that I am right and justified is way less attractive a feeling or belief than before the POCCCP, so I'm practicing letting go of this wanting to be right, and best of all, I am able to let go of it! I had trouble letting my thoughts go before. I feel more empowered now to do change more than ever. Mostly on my own, I do mini-clearings during the day, even while in the car on errands. I am living *The Power of Clearing* process that I was taught in the ten-day course.

"Another important thing is that before coming to the POCCCP, I had blamed my parents relentlessly for my failure at life, and since then, I am understanding and loving my parents in a more tender and forgiving way. While I was already in a forgiveness process, before I started the training, in ACIM for six months plus using a 12-Step program, *The Power of Clearing* course has supercharged this forgiveness process to an even deeper level. My parents passed away a few years ago, and the healing process between us continues. This is very significant and is an ongoing process because as I notice my ego thoughts and become vigilant in what I am thinking, feeling, and believing, I can identify the thoughts for applying the 3-step mini-clearing process in my mind.

"I have felt calmer, stronger, and clearer, and I am sleeping better than before the POCCCP. In general, I feel like I have less guilt weighing me down. I did tons of one-on-one clearings with my coaches for hours during the POCCCP. I learned so many details that I had never realized were bothering me while looking at my past fearlessly with new eyes and in a safe, supportive environment. People say I look younger, seem lighter, and sound clearer."

The Coach asks LB: "How will you use what you learned from the course to change your life?"

LB answers: "I am painting more, and I will eventually have the courage to charge more for my paintings. I intend to approach a new art gallery. I am mainly using everything I learned in the POCCCP to be a better sponsor in AA, a better friend, and meditation instructor. I am also kinder to myself, after being very mean, self-recriminating, judgmental, and impatient with myself for a very long time. I can more easily let my complaining stories go today and replace these horrific beliefs with forgiveness statements."

The Coach asks LB: "Would you recommend the *Power of Clearing Coaching Certification Program* to anyone? Why?"

LB answers: "Yes, I would, because of all the benefits it has already brought to my life. It was definitely worth the investment of time and money."

Case Studies – POCCCP *(Power of Clearing Coaching Certification Program)*

As part of the certified training required to become a *Power of Clearing* coach, each person takes the ten-day course, and then after returning home, conducts eight case studies with eight people. We are including six examples of case studies to illustrate how *The Clearing Process* works. You will see in these case studies how each person broke through to their true self during the clearing session.

Note: Each participant begins the session with a clear intention that is repeated by the coach, confirming that they join the participant in that clear intention.

Case Study #1

Issue: The client reported that she did not feel safe in her life performing, striving, and achieving in order to be acknowledged. She felt that important people in her life were not listening to her, so she stopped speaking up and expressing herself. She acted as if she were invisible.

Clear intention by the client for *The Clearing Process*: "To know I am safe to be visible in my life as who I really am, including being intelligent."

The client describes her life experience: "My goal was to be invisible and mediocre in my life. This fear came about because of my parents testing me and finding out I had genius level IQ. I felt that I was always on the edge of the group, walking a tightrope of being rejected or falling into things and not knowing what the game was: How to fit in? I believed I didn't know how to fit in and if I did fit in, I would spoil it, hurting peoples' lives, feelings, and making mistakes. Therefore, I didn't risk anything and stayed on the edge, not being involved, being an observer in life.

"At the age of seven, my peers chose me to be the Fairy Queen in my school play. I wanted to be a mushroom so I could be in the background because I didn't want to be in the public eye, speak, or perform. Since I believed I couldn't say the lines, they took out the lines so I sat there as the Queen of the Fairies. They made me a beautiful dress out of someone's silk and lace wedding dress to wear.

"I believed I couldn't expect anything from anyone, such as consideration, respect, compassion, understanding, or love, because my mother didn't treat me that way. There must have been something wrong with me that spoiled everything; like I was a black hole, an empty hole, so that my mother couldn't love me. So, instead, she tried to make me into something that she could be proud of, like a genius.

"As an adult, I broke my marriage vow, that I believed I had made before God, by getting a divorce. I believed that it put distance between me and God, so He would no longer support me and therefore, I needed to support myself and do everything by myself, for myself. So, now I was on my own, on the outside of the group, the edge of my family, and now, the edge of my marriage. I am all alone on the edge of everything, including my children."

Outcome of *The Clearing Process*: Until recent years, I was resisting the idea that I could thrive, or imagine thriving. The switch from surviving to thriving happened when I met someone who was a Power of Clearing coach who actually listened to me, heard me, and cared about me. It was a complete revelation. I did The Power of Clearing process with her as my coach for multiple clearings. Until then, I was treading water, trying not to drown, and grasping at things floating by. The coach asked the me if I got my intention met in the clearing. I said, "Yes. I now feel safe to communicate what I really want to say. I feel I have let go of the need to pretend to be invisible. I realize that only I can fill the imaginary hole that I made up that I am. Because I'm not a black hole, and because I made that story up, only I can fill it since my imagination knows what it looks like and feels like."

Case Study #2

A married woman in her mid-sixties claims to struggle with her weight (although her weight is quite normal), and within the last ten years has remembered an incident of molestation by a neighbor man when she was six and seven years old.

Issue for clearing: I began with a *Clearing Process* for clearing with my father. The coach held the space as my father's true self. In my ego-thoughts, I perceived my father as grouchy and unavailable.

Clear intention by the client for *The Clearing Process*: "To release my shame about sex and heal my addictive relationship with food, and to remember that I am lovable and I am safe."

The client describes her life experience: "I remember that it was my father who encouraged me to visit the neighbor down the street who molested me. During *The Clearing Process*, I felt my anger at my father for not protecting me or keeping me safe. When I was learning to ride my bike down the alley, I would always fall into the flower bed of that male neighbor and everyone would laugh at me. That confirmed my belief that I was not safe, not lovable, and that no one would come to my defense. I was also allowed to walk to the corner store by myself at age six and was once bitten by a dog. I perceived this incident as evidence of a belief that I was not protected and therefore not lovable or valued. In my second marriage, my husband soon turned to masturbation instead of sex with me, which confirmed my perception of being unlovable. I saw it played out, that by keeping the molestation a secret in my marriage, I created our non-sexual relationship because I was still afraid of sex and penetration. When I heard my husband make sexual jokes at a party, portraying himself as a sexual stud, I would feel guilty, knowing the truth about the situation, that we didn't have sex and felt like it was my fault because I had rejected him."

The client was able to connect many threads that came together after the clearing to make sense in her current life: weight gain as a child after the molestation and fear of gaining weight now; fear of dogs, and blaming her parents for not watching out for her; being uncomfortable with sex due to not feeling safe, and feeling unlovable.

Outcome of *The Clearing Process*: "I feel much better after the clearing, and I am amazed at *The Clearing Process* and how quickly it worked for me emotionally. Even though I had tried so hard on my own to make everything right in an intellectual way, I now feel like I am awakened and that for the first time, I have passionate energy and hope in my life. Instead of existing, now I have a life worth living."

Case Study #3

A single gay male in his thirties who is a state worker and the youngest of six children.

Issue for clearing: After quite a bit of discussion, the client decided to clear on groups of people in his life whom he believes judge him because he is gay.

Clear intention by the client for *The Clearing Process*: "To let go of past judgments about myself, so that I am no longer being embarrassed and that I can openly be myself. (I had a fear of even going into public bathrooms.) To know that I am safe, and that I am Whole and Complete and Love."

The client describes his life experience: "I began Step 1 of the clearing with an incident from when I was six years old on the playground, playing a game called 'smear the queer.' I had asked the other kids, 'What is a queer?' When I was told it is a boy who likes other boys, I recognized that energy in myself and felt quite embarrassed and humiliated, and felt my face turning red. Then, when I saw the anger and negativity directed to the queer, I reeled and almost blacked out, pleading with God, 'This can't be true of me, that I am a queer.' My upset translated into my perception that the first reaction of people about me would be judgment. I have carried this sense of shame that I am different, bad, and wrong throughout my whole life since then. I found out after the clearing that people did not judge me, however that didn't matter because it is how I perceive the world due to that childhood game that kept replaying unconsciously through my whole being. I cleared on the boys on the playground, the boys in the bathroom, the kids in my elementary classrooms, my co-workers, my bosses, and the audience at Toastmasters. The place where I really touched into my emotion in the clearing is when I realized I had labeled myself as 'irredeemable.' My coach encouraged me to let all the emotion come up that I had held in for so long, to let it totally go through my whole being and then release it."

Outcome of *The Clearing Process*: "I recognize that I am hardest on myself, and from *The Clearing Process*, I have been able to soften around my strict self-judgment. I no longer saw myself as different and separate from everyone. I realize that I have felt unrecognized for my true self because I thought people were judging me for being gay rather than caring about how I expressed myself and who I really am. I feel better about myself in general after the clearing about the boys in the elementary school class. I have forgiven myself for making this interpretation through their game that there is something wrong with me."

Case Study #4

A single adult male came to his coach with a clear fear of safely expressing himself. He felt inferior to everyone, especially men.

Issue for *The Clearing Process*: Feeling afraid of all people, especially speaking to large groups in his position with his company.

Clear intention by the client for *The Clearing Process*: "To let go of my fear of being judged and not good enough and to see myself and all people in the world as innocent."

The client describes his life experience so far: "I remember that my mother and father were so cruel to me in the home setting and then would put on a different face around their friends and act nice to me in front of them. So, I created a belief that people are phony and you can never trust their intentions, especially men. I had teachers who did not support me and instead failed me, so I blamed them for my feelings of inferiority. My fear of men carried through to the men at church and in study groups. I felt inferior and less knowledgeable while they appeared to be more confident in themselves and what they had to say. So, I was not able to express myself clearly and with conviction. Therefore, I believed I needed to keep a wall around myself as a defense because I feared they would attack or judge me, or put me down."

Experience of *The Clearing Process* by the client: The client began *The Clearing Process* by addressing his fear directly as, **"What I want you to know,** fear, is that you have ruled me all my life and stopped me from saying what I really feel and mean. **What I want you to know,** fear, is because of you, I feel isolated being with people, **which makes me feel** alone and separate **just like when ..."** (He came up with a specific incident from the past.)

After a couple of statements of ego thoughts in Step 1, the client focused on specific men with their names in his life who had attacked him directly as well as feeling the fear that he will be attacked by them again. The other groups of people that the client focused on in the clearing who he felt had attacked him were "guys in the Navy," "kids in grade school," "teachers," and "men at church and at the study groups." Women were seen as being the group where he could feel safe. The client went on to do Step 2 forgiveness for thinking, believing, or feeling on everything he said in Step 1. And then the client went to Step 3 forgiveness for forgetting Big T Truth to accommodate everything he said in Step 1 and 2.

Outcome of *The Clearing Process*: "In Step 1, I expressed all of my ego thoughts in a clear format such as, **'What I want you to know,** men at church, **is that I feel** you are judging me to be inferior and not as smart and as good as you, **which makes me feel** alone and separate, just like when...' After completing the entire Clearing Process, I feel quite empowered and feel my desire to express myself clearly and openly now. I had never before said those things aloud in such a clear way and they had even been hidden to me. In Step 1, when I was focused on my teachers in school, I had a glimmer of the feeling that this fear is just an illusion. I could see how my negative beliefs about my parents carried through to all aspects of my interactions with everyone. I am feeling much more peaceful after the clearing and more joined with others. In talking afterward, it came up that a possible next clearing would be on watching pro football games and why it is *so very* important not to have my team lose."

Case Study #5

The client is in her mid-fifties, married with two adult children, and is currently unemployed due to health issues.

Issue for *The Clearing Process*: The client perceives her mother as controlling yet needy to the point where the client feels she has always had to put her mother's needs first.

Clear intention by the client for *The Clearing Process*: "To feel my own sense of self as individuated from my mother and to hold us both as innocent, whole, and complete as we are."

The client describes her life experience: "My mother is controlling yet needy to the point where I feel that I always had to put my mother's needs first. As a result, I came to believe that I am a victim and incapable of making my own decisions, always feeling like I have to run my life as my mother sees fit and have no opinions of my own. I am constantly afraid of hurting people's feelings, yet I am outspoken. I feel like I need to hide, yet I act out to get attention. I feel that I can never live up to my mother's expectations and needs, and that I have to take my mother's word as law when trying to make decisions in my life."

Experience of *The Clearing Process* by the client: The client cleared quite extensively with her beliefs that she has been trapped all her life by her mother's neediness and belief that she has to come to her mother's rescue. She was able to see that she has put herself in the position of victim and how that has carried through to other relationships in her life. Feeling so out of control in her life, she sees how she tries to control her son "for his own protection" and how she accuses her husband of things that she really judges herself about, and how this has really come from her own fear.

Outcome of *The Clearing Process*: "After my first session, I had a couple of days of true peace (extraordinary for me!). When my ego kicked in a couple of days later, I knew to call and schedule another clearing. After this second clearing, again I put connections together that I had never before seen, and upon leaving, I felt peaceful and happier. My intention for *The Clearing Process* has been met."

Case Study #6

An 80-year-old woman who has always overworked and over-stressed herself about her relationships and her role in life. She has little education and can read but cannot write. She suffers from headaches, tinnitus, exhaustion, and stomach problems. She seems to lurch from one crisis to another and she has more friends than anyone else I know, yet she feels alone and often unloved.

Issue for the clearing: Her hatred of the way her father treated her as a child and young woman. She intended to clear her constant reversion to feelings of abandonment, unworthiness, insecurity, imprisonment in work, and poor self-image.

Clear intention by the client for *The Clearing Process*: "To feel at one with my father."

The client describes her life experience: "My father manipulated me when I was young by keeping me out of school to work on the market stalls of the city and run his broken business. He chastised me constantly for being stupid and not doing things properly. He undermined me in public, using me as a kind of "fall guy" as he flirted with his customers. He constantly told me that I was fat and would never be as good-looking as my mother. He left me with all the responsibility for running the stalls and later the café we jointly owned, while he went off gambling or with his girlfriends. I felt that I had to look after everyone: my mother, brother, and sister, and keep the whole family relationship going."

Experience of *The Clearing Process* by the client: The client seemed to get into the swing of things very easily in Step 1 as she described her father's manipulation of her as a young girl. She literally shouted her anger and distress as she recounted her father's deeds and her feeling of being totally discounted, undermined, unloved, and excluded. She became very tearful when she talked about how his attitude had made her terrified of men and had ruined her sex life because she could not open up to men. She cleared deeply and extensively with her father, her mother, and herself in the 3-step process.

Outcome of *The Clearing Process*: "We talked about what the ego does to our lives and how the self-condemnation keeps on running and bringing us the same lessons over and over. After *The Clearing Process*, I feel very different, with solid and clear thinking."

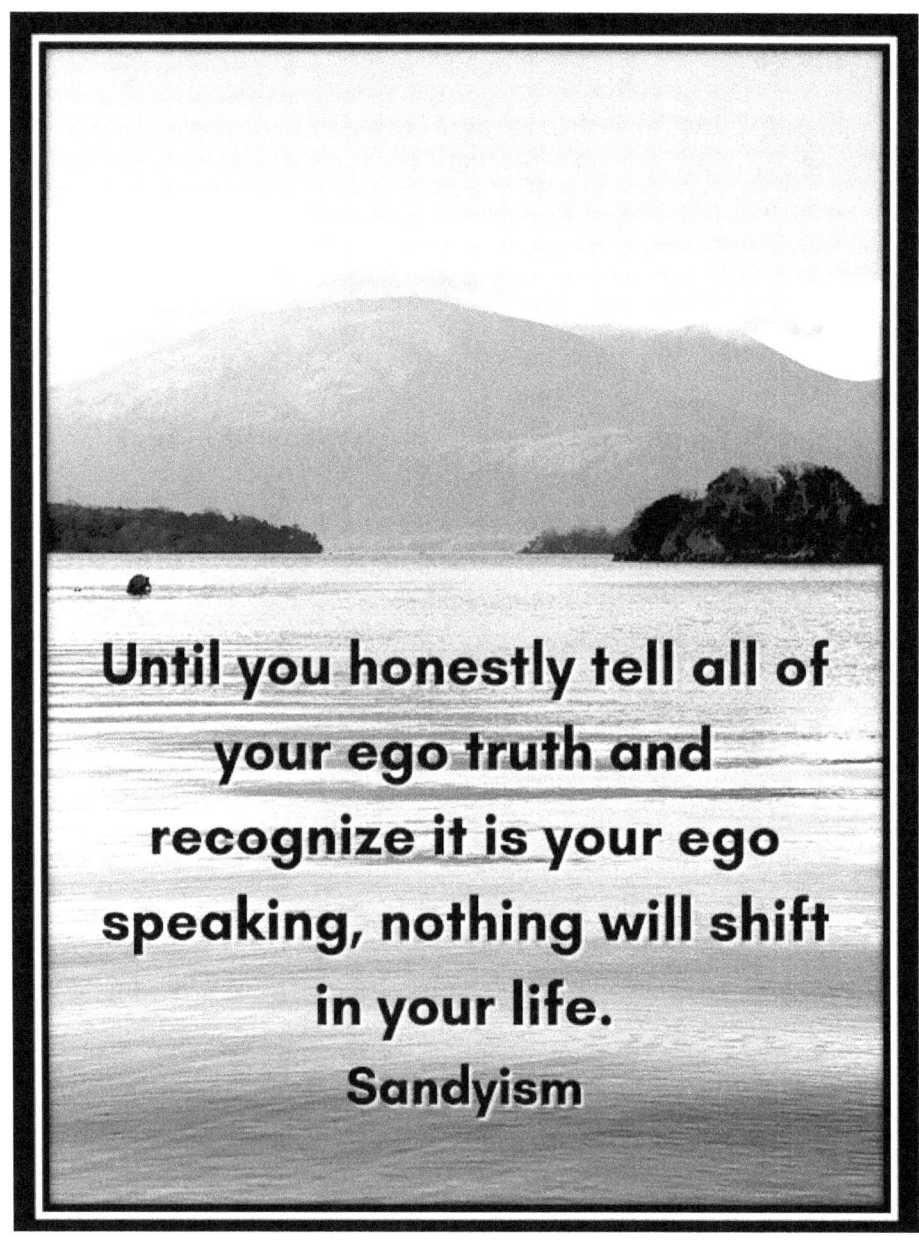

CHAPTER 11

MOVING FORWARD IN PEACE

Postscript by Sandy

Before Angela Hahn and I began to write this book in 2014, we joined in our intention to allow the Holy Spirit to move through us and bring His message to the world with Love and Innocence. We intended that this book be easy and joyous to write and that it would reach everyone who is ready to accept its message and teaching. This teaching did not come from us. It is a teaching that came through us to radiate out into the world. We are the vehicles to make that happen.

Once we had set our intention about joining in purpose to write the book, we asked for guidance and chose two ACIM cards each.

Together our four cards said:

God is praised whenever any mind learns to be wholly helpful.
(ACIM, T.4.VII.8:1)

No one who truly seeks the peace of God can fail to find it.
(ACIM, W-185.11.1)

And be the means whereby your brother finds the peace in which your wishes are fulfilled. (ACIM, T-26.VII.19:1-2)

Having rests on giving, and not on getting. (ACIM, T-6.V.C.6:1)

It was clear that everything we did from that moment on would be aligned with our intention to share this teaching of the way to peace to all our human family and to recognize it as a gift to us and everyone else who is ready to receive it. Since you are reading this, then you are ready to receive this teaching.

> *It is a journey without distance to a goal that has never changed.*
> (ACIM, T-8.VI.9:7)

And we join with you in your intention to live in peace.

Angela Hahn and Sandy Levey-Lunden in 2016

Special clarifying points from Sandy in 2022

I feel that my story echoes with many. The energy of the Creator moves through us in different ways, or at least, in a way that manifests differently. Part of my manifestation of a Higher Power moving through me is this book, *I Just Want Peace*. For me, the writing comes effortlessly in a Voice that is coming through me as if I was teaching one of my trainings that have also been coming through me over the years since the 1980s.

The premise of this work and all I have described in terms of process is quite simple in theory, yet very challenging to live in daily life. We have so many egoic pulls from all sides that appear to be extremely convincing. The Divine Spirit lives in each one of us and can inspire each moment of our existence, living into individual and collective peace for humankind. How Spirit guides us to realize peace in our lives, uniquely and universally, is interesting and often surprising! Yet, ultimately, the motivation to reach full and complete Peace within and in our world is a pure intention for each one of us who is awake and aware in the moment. To live the way you ideally envision, which is in Peace, you change the way you function and the way that you perceive the meaning of life. You will want to ask yourself, "How do I really want to be? Am I at Peace now? What will it take for me to be at peace in my mind, in my heart, and in my life?"

- *Everything is for your own best interests.* (ACIM, W-25.1:5) We never know if something is "good" or "bad." To see the whole picture of the purpose of an event, we would be at a level of higher power to be able to look back and see how this "good" or "bad" incident moved us further in our knowledge along our journey to awakening. Therefore, *The Power of Clearing* process is non-dualistic thinking, which means nothing is "good" or "bad," it just is. "Good" is absolute; you don't need to go through "bad" to experience "good."

- *All things work together for good. There are no exceptions except in the ego's judgment.* (ACIM, T-4.V.1:1-2)

- The ACIM book says, *there is only love* (ACIM, W-127.1-4) and all other ways of seeing it or defining it are how the ego puts love in special boxes. People make up very special ways of what Love should look, feel, and sound like, and anything other than these strict pictures of the way Love is, is seen as irrelevant or not noticed.

- *Seek but do not find.* (ACIM, T-16.V.6:5) This story is the ego's favorite motto. "I will keep trying but I will never quite get there." It's about seeking things outside yourself. The complete section is: *Such is the ego's plan for your salvation. Surely you can see how it is in strict accord with the ego's basic doctrine, 'Seek but do not find.' For what could more surely guarantee that you will not find salvation than to channelize all your efforts in searching for it where it is not?* (ACIM, W-I.71.4:1-3)

- Everything we're not communicating clearly will be left to chance. Sometimes we are very afraid to communicate precisely what we want because then we will be criticized if someone doesn't agree with us. If I'm ambiguous then I can always change what I meant, depending on feedback and thereby believe myself not to be guilty.

- I must ask myself in every situation, *What do I want to come of this? What is it for?* (ACIM, T-17.VI.2:1-2) In lesson five of ACIM, it says, *I am never upset for the reason I think.* (ACIM, W-5) There is always a reason for why we are getting upset and that is what *The Clearing Process* can locate—the actual origin of the feeling, trauma, or experience that is causing the upset. Therefore, we are still feeling upset, betrayed, or separate because of the trauma that we have never brought into the Light before seeing the Light in *The Clearing Process*. This first step of the 3-step *Clearing Process* may reveal the incident when the subconscious is ready to release the trauma. Note that it is not necessary to find the source of the trauma to clear the feelings of trauma.

- When we enter *The Clearing Process,* it is like being a wilderness guide. We don't know where we are going with the clearing, or what we're looking for. We are moving gently along. We are looking under every stone, down every rabbit hole, and lifting every dark cloth to gradually piece together the main themes that are driving the ego's pain. The pain comes consciously or unconsciously in thoughts of the past that we project onto ourselves and others. When we are investigating old connections, it's like searching with a spotlight in the basement looking for everything that we can possibly uncover.

- "It is the Holy Spirit that does all the heavy lifting" if we allow it to. Some of us don't want the Holy Spirit to take away our burdens when we believe that we should have the strength, courage, and power to do it ourselves! When we believe we can't do it ourselves, the feeling of powerlessness can dominate our lives and create a feeling of lack of control and lack of faith that the Holy Spirit is directing our lives. That is because we cannot see, from our egoic perspective, that anything else is possible.

- In *The Clearing Process,* we don't heal anything; we surrender it. In other words, we likely are going through the same scenario in our lives with only the details appearing to be different. We may be tired and bored of the repeating pattern and not sure how to change it. Then, the coach's pivotal questions in *The Clearing Process* illuminate the root cause of the pattern or story. By clearing away the surface ego thoughts, *The Clearing Process* guides us to locate, explore, accept, and surrender the root cause of all the pain. When we no longer have a benefit or payoff to hold onto the negative ego thought, negative feeling, or negative belief, we gently surrender this pattern of pain to the Holy Spirit who takes it from us and brings us to peace. The Holy Spirit cannot take anything from us that we are not willing to give. So, we must be in a "ready" state to completely let go. It will go easily then, like ripe fruit easily comes off the tree. It can take a person years to get to that state of ripeness where they are ready and willing to let go of what they have been holding for a long time.

This legacy book documents my years since the 1980s as a professional counselor, life coach, and creator of original pieces of training. My favorite courses that I teach with my company *On Purpose*, are *The Art of Surrender, Choosing Freedom: The Way Out of All Pain and Suffering*, the *Power of Clearing Coaching Certification Program* (**POCCCP**), *True Woman's Power, The Holy Relationship, The Art of Giving and Receiving Love, The Art of Joining a Family, Youth on Purpose (A Youth and Family Project Program)*, and *The Art of Transforming a Business*. I can bring any of these courses to your friends, family, or workplace, to anyone anywhere in the world with my team of coaches. Please feel free to connect with me and we can talk about how we can work together.

You can find me on LinkedIn:
linkedin.com/in/sandy-levey-lunden/
and on Facebook: facebook.com/sandy.leveylunden/

You can call me at my home office in Bellingham, Washington in the United States, in Pacific Time at 360-527-2796 or my cell phone at 360-739-4602 for your free 20-30-minute consultation on any aspect of your life. I teach individualized courses based on your needs, your family, or your business. My website is Sandylevey.com and onpurpose@sandylevey.com is my email.

Reflections on the Path of the Past

The first training I wrote in 1984, *The Art of Personal Marketing*, about your life's purpose, mission, and vision, took me from making a speech for 100 people in Hawaii to Sweden. There are no accidents in who is where at what time.

I fell in love with personal marketing, as did almost everyone I introduced to this remarkable, heartfelt marketing method. Everyone went into their deeply-held belief systems about their fear of being remunerated for their gifts and talents. Most felt they were not good enough at their special abilities for someone to pay them for what they love doing and that it would be too easy to do what they love. I had many artists in the training who had yet to make money from their paintings or creative abilities. One such artist (now well-known) paid for the training with two paintings and told me that he would take his life if he did not start to make money from his art. Those two paintings are of significant monetary value today. At the time, *The Art of Personal Marketing* was 72 hours on two weekends. After that particular artist went through my processes on his first weekend, I told him his art was magnificent. On the second weekend, I sold 10 k in value of his art. He was ecstatic. After I gave him the money, he said to me, "I can't believe it. I can buy a simple car, have food, pay the rent, and buy some clothes that fit and look good. I can be a normal person with my normal needs and desires met. It's been years that I've been starving and only buying paints for my paintings. You have saved my life." He is still alive today and has a huge following, an agent, a promoter, and a publicist.

Everyone who took *The Art of Personal Marketing* training found a vision for their purpose, special talents, and abilities, and a way to market from their heart with true integrity from their soul's purpose. Each had a video of themselves talking about their purpose, talents, and vision before and during the training. People tell me they still have their videotape to this day because they could see the transformation as I did. I could see the difference in every person in these trainings, from the beginning to the end.

In the 1980s, Prentice Hall offered me an advance to write a book about living your life from purpose, vision, mission, and the art of personal marketing. I wrote the book, but I stopped myself from sending it in because my ego's voice was stronger than my true voice, telling me that it was not good enough to be published. It would have been one of the first books written on these subjects. If I had followed through and sent it to the publisher, I could have let them decide if it was an important book to be published. Now, in 2022, I am grateful that I allowed myself to move forward with completing this legacy book. Eight years ago, my first scribes were in England, where I would go three or four times a year to do trainings. I would devote several days to working with the material for the book. Since then, with numerous scribes, assistants, editors, and a gifted publisher, we now have this book as a guide.

Now there are 24 *On Purpose* trainings, and while there is no replacement for the experience of being in the workshop with others who show up as mirrors, this book portrays the essence of the materials, philosophy, and possibilities for clearing your way to Peace.

Comments on Relationship as a Path to Enlightenment

In my CD, *Relationship as a Path to Enlightenment*, I explain why our perception of relationships can be so difficult and painful. For one thing, we *unconsciously* place expectations on our partners and when they don't meet those expectations, we believe they have failed us or don't truly love us. Then we make a case against them, and pull away. Instead of loving them unconditionally, we blame them for things we perceive that they have done or not done, and we let the blame destroy the relationship. Or we turn the blame onto ourselves and believe we have failed.

There is no failure in any relationship; it is our individualized learning process for us to see and awaken to what our lessons have been. Often, the lessons are repeated until we get them. Failure is a learning process. So, we need to be gentle with ourselves and hold ourselves in love until we can let go of judgment and see ourselves truly as the magnificent beings that we are.

We have no new relationship issues; what we have are unresolved issues of the past with our parents and family that we bring to our current relationships and project onto them, including our present partnership. When we come into partnership (marriage, love affair, working), a co-worker or lover is actually in relationship with everyone from our past with whom we have yet to clear about and come to peace. At any moment, when the situation resembles a past feeling or incident for us, we welcome the familiar response of anger or negativity similar to what we experienced in the past toward someone else. To be at peace in the present, our only choice is for each individual in the relationship to clear and come to peace with those past relationships so they can be fully present in their relationship now. Only then will they enjoy knowing who this person is in the fullness of their true self, clear of any projection. Of course, in order to do this clearing, we first need to become aware that we are feeling bad, which means we need to clear. That's why we value The Watcher. (Please see the Resources section.)

My teachings are based on the Truth that there is no lack of love. We are the love we seek. Therefore, we will never fulfill the illusion or story that we are lacking love and that we need to find the right person, a "soul mate," to fill this lack that we perceive is in us. We can try and we will never succeed. That realization is the dawn of a new world in our life.

Many relationships are rooted in the fear that "If my partner knew the truth about me, they wouldn't love me" and "I am ultimately a fraud and unlovable." The ego is always trying to convince us that we are frauds and that if anyone really knew us, they would see us, reject us, and run away in horror. To protect themselves from this feared rejection, people hide in a subtle web of lies, avoidance, and drama. And they do this unconsciously. As a result, they never allow the real truth of who they are to emerge. The fear of truly being known by themselves and by their partner can be terrifying.

That is why, for many couples in my trainings, they would be scared to have their partner in the training room, because then they would witness the expression of their true feelings. The personal clearing of someone's issues is done in private, one-to-one with a *Power of Clearing* coach. The coach knows how to hold the space for the person for them to fully say anything and feel safe in love and compassion. So, when the couples are doing the clearings, they are usually not clearing with each other about each other. The reason being that when they are just learning how to clear there could be many triggering points, especially in Step 1 of the clearing, that would take them out of being present.

In my couples sessions and the trainings, I saw many relationships change and transform from ego purposes into a higher purpose. This unique journey of owning your evolution out of the circles and patterns of your original family—especially in the area of love, communication, family, and relationship to God—is one that each person chooses to undertake. Whatever way the other person triggers them now becomes an opportunity to see how they can use that upset to heal something within themselves. Ultimately, they are letting go of blame for the other person and taking responsibility for their own process. They now commit to healing any obstacle to mutual peace and love. When they are scared and overwhelmed by something they fear is impossible to get through, they can hold the other person's hand lightly and firmly for support. Either of them can ask the Holy Spirit to gently remove the specific obstacle from them and return them to complete peace and love.

I love seeing all parties fully communicate only to discover there was nothing to be upset about in the first place. It was all one big misperception between two egos. As a psycho-spiritual counselor, I am here to remind us to and completely let go of our belief in "lack of love" so that we can truly experience Love and connection. If a person has yet to honor and appreciate their partner unconditionally now, they are still learning the lessons that they came to learn. The true purpose for relationship is for healing. Many never get to that realization. They will recreate these lessons with other people until they learn them. No one can escape their lessons. They follow us everywhere.

In each the other saw a perfect shelter where his Self could be reborn in safety and in peace. (ACIM, T-22.I.9:8)

In looking back, one of the highlights of my life was the original training that I did in the *Youth on Purpose* project named *Fri Sikt* from 1996-98 in Sweden. It is still relevant today and would be beneficial to create more of these projects to include youth, family, and their communities. Empowering and training more youths in *The Power of Clearing* process will create more Peace teachers and leaders in the world.

I welcome benefactors to establish new locations for the *Youth on Purpose* project and program. Maybe you are a youth who would like to be in this training, or you are a potential benefactor to support our shared vision. This training will be international because the obstacles to peace are presently in many minds around the planet.

Yet the peace that already lies deeply within must first expand, and flow across the obstacles you placed before it. (ACIM, T-19.IV.2:2)

By sharing my philosophy and experiences with you, I trust you will understand the benefit of *The Power of Clearing* process in freeing you from all limited thoughts, feelings, and beliefs that appear to be holding you back from standing in the Truth of who you are. My purpose in writing this book is to share my legacy journey of Peace with you.

The truth in you remains as radiant as a star,
as pure as light, as innocent as love itself.
(ACIM, T-31.VI.7:4-5)

PART V

ADDITIONAL MATERIAL

APPENDICES

APPENDIX A

DEFINING MOMENTS IN PEOPLE'S LIVES AND WHAT THEY LEARNED

1) Oriana, Gerrards Cross, UK

What are the benefits of *The Power of Clearing* process with Sandy Levey-Lunden?

"You will discover an abundance of benefits with *The Power of Clearing* process. You will feel lighter, freer, and more peaceful from uncovering and releasing unproductive patterns of thought that have kept you stuck. You will remember that you are perfect exactly as you are right now—whole, complete, and lacking nothing. You will find you laugh more with increased ease and flow in your life. You will be able to use this practical and straightforward process on your own, and you will discover that you have within you all the resources and inherent gifts you need to lead an abundant, rewarding, and joyful life. You will sleep better because your mind won't constantly be replaying hurtful incidents from the past or fretting about something that's coming up in the future. You will come to truly understand that you are so much more than your thoughts and behaviors. After bringing to light and releasing pain and emotional suffering, you will stop recreating the same issues and patterns that cause it. You will feel more loving and compassionate with yourself and others because you will understand that you have done nothing wrong and that you are not at fault despite what you think. You will fall in love with yourself all over again!

"Whenever I have a particular issue that is causing me emotional discomfort or pain, I do a clearing and then I feel so much lighter and more peaceful. *The Clearing Process* lifts the weight and burden of that worry from my shoulders.

"Sandy is an amazing facilitator, and I adore her. For years, I have been constantly enthralled by her ability to hone in on exactly the issue to uncover for breakthroughs. She is compassionate and kind yet never holds back and says what needs to be said, even though that can sometimes be uncomfortable. She teaches about full communication and models this ability superbly. I trust her implicitly and wholeheartedly recommend her."

2) Tami Visser
Ego & Spirit: A Story

Ego and Suppressed Spirit lived together in a little house in a dark, dark land. Ego was the boss; very loud and clear. He ran the show and took great delight in telling Suppressed Spirit how to feel and that the world outside was big and scary. He would say to Spirit, "I am all-powerful, I am strong. I will protect you. Do not wander far because The Watcher may follow you back, and then we surely both shall die."

So, for a long time, Suppressed Spirit played happily under Ego's watchful eye. Sometimes, while playing all by herself, she would see a light in the distance. It gave her comfort to see the light. Sometimes the light came closer, and it made her feel curious. So, she began to ask others about the light. Some people seemed very familiar with it, and others very fearful. In books, she read that some people lived in a land enveloped in the light all the time, and she wondered to herself how that must feel.

Ego got very angry when she asked questions about the light. "Why do you want to know about the light? Don't you think I am doing a good job taking care of you? Shame on you!" But even with the Ego's presence, Spirit still felt alone.

So, she began a journey to go to the land of light. She read books and looked for guides along the way. She found out that many helpful people could show her the way to the land of the light. Eventually, she met a group of loving people who knew about the land of the light. They had the light shining in their eyes and were not afraid to venture into the land of darkness; they didn't even seem to see the darkness. So, she asked them to teach her how to see the light all the time. They did, and then, she found she saw Ego in a very different way, too.

The Watcher, who the Ego had warned Spirit about, became her new friend; they were always together. The Watcher helped her be aware of Ego and how it tried to get her to return to the little house in the land of darkness. With The Watcher, she could see the light everywhere, and it made her feel so full and connected to everything that she wanted to share what she learned with everyone.

With the light guiding her way and The Watcher by her side, the no longer Suppressed and now Free Spirit then helped others in the darkness see the light that is always shining on them and in them.

3) By Joan Trinh Pham
Power of Clearing Coaching Certification Program Testimonial

What exactly did you get out of this course?

- I learned about a simple, potent, and effective method to become aware of negative subconscious patterning, which creates outcomes in my life that I do not like and for which I do not want to take responsibility

- I became aware of the amazingly creative responsibility I have for all the pain, suffering, peace, and joy in my life. I feel wonderfully empowered because *The Clearing Process* gives me a tool to clear illusions that I want to let go of to cultivate Truth

- Through experiencing and using this tool, I cleared a tremendous amount of guilt, fear, and feelings of worthlessness which I had internalized through emotional traumas from a very young age

- I regained feelings of safety in a profoundly visceral way and the knowledge that I am innocent, perfect, whole, and complete just as I am

- I confronted my pattern of making just enough money to survive and released the guilt and fear that I had come to associate with personal abundance

- I have become much more precise, committed, and present in my language and communication

- I have become aware of my deeply internalized voice of criticism and judgment (ego) and now can employ the loving, neutral voice of my Watcher to acknowledge and appreciate the ego voice

- With the voice of my Watcher, I am much more able to make conscious choices of how to direct my attention and energy in thought, word, and deed. This positive approach allows me to respond consciously to life rather than to react impulsively

- In recognizing how I create my suffering by projecting my beliefs onto others, I am now able to feel much more connected to people in my life, honoring them for their valued role in helping me to learn about myself and clear up negative beliefs

- I gained a deep appreciation for the healing power of presence, eye contact, and listening deeply. I feel confident in offering it to others both in everyday interactions and in holding space as a Clearing Coach

- I deepened my appreciation for the body. Though it is also from the world of illusion, the body is an impressive conduit of feelings that help me to discern in each moment Big T from little t (feelings of lightness and expansion from feelings of darkness and contraction)

- I learned that I am limitless and abundant. Specifically, I can make a joyful living doing something creative and healing (being an artist/hand analyst/coach). I released the belief that the only way to earn my parents' love, acceptance, and respect is to do work I do not care for and struggle to make money

- I have learned to be much more loving, kind, and gentle with myself, knowing that the work of life is to love imperfection by living little t and Big T in the most transparent awareness (to myself and others) as possible

- I now have concise, clear language to articulate and navigate my reality. For example, The Truth is that I am an expression of love, the same as every person in my life. Any upsets I encounter are rich learning opportunities to clear false beliefs that keep me separate and suffering instead of my natural state, which is to be in communion and at peace

How will you use what you learned from the course to change your life?

- I have learned that the Universe and all of life conspires to help us humans return to our natural, beautiful, unique, and perfect way of being. This knowledge helps ground me when I notice that I am acting out of fear rather than love—always, I choose to be motivated by love

- I have learned the value of clarity and will use the clearest, specific language I have in speaking about what I want and truly desire in my heart and envisioning it

- I have learned that the essence of communication is the intention, so I change my life through mindful intention to be heard and seen in the full expression of who I am

- I have started a personal practice of reading the ACIM lessons every morning to gently train my mind to return to Big T

- I am now aware that hurts and upsets in life are opportunities to clear false beliefs, so rather than getting lost in the suffering of my upsets, I acknowledge them and clear them as they come up

- I have learned that I am safe to be courageous and take risks in my life in expressing what is true for me in each moment and then taking action that feels most authentic. In this way, I allow myself to be friends with fear, and beyond fear, I choose to be epic and grand, a creative, unique facet of Love itself

- I will use the clearing tool to free myself from pain and suffering created by perpetuating illusions of separation and guilt

- I will practice every day to know, trust, embrace, and live my wants, knowing they also come from Big T

- I have learned to offer up all my intentions and wants to the Holy Spirit. May the Holy Spirit guide me to listen and act from Big T

- My life is changed by knowing I can release the illusions of guilt, scarcity, and suffering. Instead, I live in innocence, abundance, peace, and joy, my birthright and natural state. I intend to reflect this Big T Truth in how I live in the world

What concrete five steps will you take in the next month to change your life that will demonstrate and put the course in action in your life?

- I will call five friends I have identified with specific reasons for how they may benefit from this work by January 19, 2014. I will enroll them to experience this work. I intend to count these sessions toward my *Power of Clearing* Coaching Certification

- Every morning until March 30, 2014, I will spend at least 10 minutes in quiet, asking the question, "What do I truly desire at this moment?"
- I will commit to one of my POCCCP or *Choosing Freedom* classmates to do a clearing check-in monthly
- I will write a blog post about my experience at the POCCCP and express my truth about the transformative experience by January 13, 2014
- I will have a conversation with my mom, dad, and uncle about what I learned, to share with them my learning and joy by January 31, 2014

Would you recommend anyone to the course? Why?

- Absolutely yes. The POCCCP provides participants with a powerful, practical tool that aims to heal and strengthen one's mind through experiencing it directly. In addition, the transformative, shared journey to learn *The Clearing Process* and share it with others is an invaluable investment

4) Angela Hahn

My Clearing on Bobby the Bunny

The Power of Clearing process always amazed me during the POCCCP. Perhaps the most amazing ego story that linked in with my core beliefs, though, was the one I had held onto for over 30 years about my rabbit, Bobby.

A family, who were friends, gave Bobby to me. They bred rabbits and also ate them. I was delighted to have Bobby—I must have been about nine years old, and Bobby was a birthday present. Although Bobby lived in a hutch in our back garden, he often managed to escape and was found in the field next door or on the building site at the back of our garden. My dad put a collar on him with a long chain to stop him from escaping.

I went away on a short holiday (I think it was with the Guides—Girl Scouts), and when I returned home, Bobby was gone. I asked my parents where he was, and they told me they had given him back to the family who bred him. They laughed about it. I believed that the family would kill him and eat him, so I was extremely upset. This experience reinforced several already well-established beliefs about myself: that I was not of importance (in my family) and that my needs and wants would not be met (by others). The experience also echoed my belief that I was powerless and worthless, that I was not going to be cared for by anyone, and was unable to care for others properly. I also believed that I was unable to protect or save others. Underlying these beliefs was a strong feeling that I was not lovable or worthy of love.

The Clearing Process allowed me to fully release the pain and sadness of this experience and let go of my feelings of blame toward my parents and myself.

Now I feel a complete sense of peace with this episode of my life, both intellectually and with a deep inner understanding. I know this is true because I can speak of it with no emotional charge or "mind chatter." I can even smile about the extraordinarily creative part of me that shows me what I believe my world to be!!

APPENDIX B

ARTICLES ON RELEASING SEXUAL GUILT AND THE PHYSICAL BODY

1) Marietta – 52-year-old saleswoman and trained therapist
Blown away by my first clearing!

My experience with Sandy Levey-Lunden and *The Power of Clearing* process has been completely transformational. As someone who has worked several years in the mental health/therapy arena, I am very picky about who I work with for my personal development.

What I achieved in a handful of sessions alone with Sandy is equivalent to a year's worth of therapy.

I have always been a reasonably successful person, but I have lost a couple of jobs and struggled with relationships with men and my self-worth.

Sandy helped me understand that my belief system (that I was completely unaware of) and my childhood experiences attracted unhealthy people into my life. As a result, I had reached the point where I felt rather hopeless and in despair. Even though I did everything I knew to do, nothing seemed to help, and I could not push through.

Sandy helped me find the source of why I was accepting poor jobs, attracting egocentric people, and struggling with sexual issues.

Sandy taught me that the judgment I placed on my father and mother was a judgment of me.

She showed me that I was drawing the type of men with similar sexual guilt to me due to a childhood experience. It was mind-blowing that the sexual trauma that I experienced as a child was an exact match for the sexual experience that one person, in particular, wanted to do with me. That's why we were so connected in our sexual attraction for each other, reconfirming our mutual sexual guilt by acting out this attraction and fantasy in our real life. When Sandy helped me to realize that truth, it blew my mind.

She taught me that these men attract me to my sexual guilt.

Through the process of clearing, I have had so many revelations, and lightbulbs go off; it's astounding. To see the underlying truths of why I could not see myself as lovable, worthy, or valuable is so freeing.

At first, I thought this was too easy of a process, and I was unsure if it would work. However, I was blown away even after my first clearing.

I continue to do the 3-step clearing in the mirror whenever I see the old ego thoughts coming up. I am doing my part and the coach's part to reemphasize Big T Truth and help me awaken from my fantasy of fear and guilt. I understand that the clearing is a lifelong process of releasing what isn't my true nature and being awake all the time using my Watcher to see when I am falling into my ego. Three of my very good friends worked with Sandy and then recommended her. I am grateful for finding this process and Sandy.

2) **Robert Hand**

My Journey to a Holy Relationship
Owner of Wise Awakening Bookstore and Metaphysical Center, and Haulin' Ash Chimney Sweep
February 2022

Sandy Levey-Lunden was a friend of my wife, Diana; however, I only met Sandy recently after my wife passed away in May 2020. In November 2021, I met Sandy at a dinner party for people who own the Healy healing device; we both own one and love it. We started discussing a concept called the holy relationship and *The Power of Clearing* process. At that point, I was genuinely wondering if there was a better and different way to have a relationship than what most people experience, including myself. I was in a new relationship of eight months, and this woman was with me at the dinner party. A few days later, an incident happened where my new relationship ended abruptly. I was in a state of surprise, shock, and wonder. I wanted to know how, why, and what I could have done differently to have it work out at deep levels and possibly be indeed a life relationship.

My experience of past relationships and marriages is of emotional pain, sexual dysfunction, divorce, and heartbreak. Therefore, I desire and welcome a breakthrough to have a more in-depth and healing relationship where my partner and I commit to clearing any barriers or impediments that come up between us. My most recent marriage with Diana was by far the best, most loving relationship I've ever had. We did everything we could do to heal ourselves, but there were areas in our relationship beyond what we could do.

Sandy did five major clearing sessions with me in which I healed most of my negative ego thoughts, feelings, and beliefs, and I cleared in the areas of self-worth blockages and barriers in my past relationships. The $2,000 I spent on my sessions with Sandy was more effective and brought me further than the over $50,000 I had paid previously with other methods and people working on the same issues. I consider my investment with Sandy as the most significant value that I have ever spent in my life on anything. I felt different about myself, relieved and confident in my new state of awareness and awakening, and very grounded. My sexual feelings came back. I am now more available and present than I've ever been, much more. The voices of fear, emotional pain, and guilt are mostly gone. I'm much more aware of what is happening inside of me, and as my ego voices of fear and doubt come up, I am releasing them immediately to my true nature. I am single now, and I have decided that my next relationship will be a holy relationship, and I will live and practice the philosophy, tools, and concepts. I am eager and ready to meet my next destined life partner. Together, I hope we will go on a profound, deep, healing, connected journey. I am excited about the new stage of my life as a timeless being ready to go to new heights of peace, joy, and love

3) Krista V., Ontario, Canada, *Power of Clearing* coach, and entrepreneur
A Miracle of Conception

From Sandy: Krista has taken my classes and shares an example of how unconscious beliefs can affect current relationships and how forgiving those beliefs is the most significant step toward peace.

Krista's story

"I started menstruating very young when I was only eight years old, and I was devastated when my mother failed to tell me what was happening to my body. Later, when I was 14, she found out that a teenager at my school was pregnant. My mother went into a rage, telling me that if I got pregnant, 'over my dead body,' would she let me keep it. She was seething angry when she told me, 'I will make you have an abortion.' I was not even sexually active yet. Her words cut deep because I love children and always knew I wanted to have a family one day.

"Later in life, I realized that these experiences emotionally and physically scarred me. I felt it wasn't safe to bring a baby into the world. I knew this was not true in my logical mind, but remembering how my mother said multiple times that it was never her intention to have children further complicated this feeling that I couldn't shake. She seemed resentful and had regrets. Any love she had for me could not get through. I felt unworthy of what I wanted most, creating a family.

"My first husband was verbally abusive and could be cruel. When I did not get pregnant right away, he once told me, 'When I married you, I had no idea you were DAMAGED GOODS.' Soon after, I told my doctor I was afraid I might be infertile. After the divorce, though, I suspected I had shut down my fertility psychologically because I didn't feel safe (again). When I was younger, I could 'concentrate' on shutting down my period with my thoughts until I got home, where my supplies were, for a few hours. I could also 'force' a fever to skip school on occasion. I believe my body knew it was unsafe to bring children into the world with my 'abusive' first husband.

"When I did not conceive with my second husband in our first year together, the whole story around me as 'damaged' blew up in my mind. Years after our children were born, I learned that my first husband discovered he was the one who was unable to have children. So, even though I was not infertile in that relationship, we both blamed me. I never questioned whether the men in my life had fertility problems. Believing I was the one with the problem created considerable stress. I'd also used herbs that can trigger or aggravate endometriosis, causing it to rupture and grow. Through seeking the wrong solution, I inadvertently created a bigger problem.

"When I was 30, I was diagnosed with endometriosis, which causes cells to grow outside the uterus. It causes internal bleeding, pain, and infertility. It was extensive throughout my pelvis. Doctors told me that I might never be able to get pregnant. I scheduled a radical surgery with a surgeon in Oregon but changed my mind as I realized I needed to heal my beliefs and childhood experiences first. My husband agreed to adopt if we could not conceive, and then I explored emotionally to see where it would take me. It was a true gift when Sandy convinced me to postpone surgery. There could have been scar tissue from that, and it was a very aggressive and expensive surgery. (Thirteen years later, when I had surgery to remove my uterus and right ovary, the surgeon only found and removed *one* small spot the size of a coin on my bladder.)

"Through a series of clearings in *The Clearing Process* in Sandy's classes, I was able to acknowledge these issues from my past that emotionally impacted me and had become defining moments in my perception of femininity and conceiving a child. As I became more aware of the devastating effect of these fearful beliefs buried deep in my subconscious, I shifted my feelings, perceptions, and focus. I recognized how these ridiculous beliefs had been holding me back (and impacting my body) for over a decade. I made radical diet changes and removed toxins from my home alongside the clearings. I realized how fear had been dominating my perception. I released the burden of blaming my mother for her threatening behavior and scaring me about womanhood when I was so young. Even more profoundly, I forgave myself for believing her. I stepped into love and embraced the truth of who I am, a loving person who deserves to be loved.

"I freed myself from learned helplessness and embraced the truth that I am worthy and lovable, and it is safe for me to have a baby. As a result, I was able to move forward courageously. Within three months, my husband and I conceived our miracle baby, Xavier, born in 2004.

"My work with Sandy also led to me meeting Tina Feigal, parent coach, who was at the course. I have consulted with her over the years and did her parent certification course. Combining these experiences has helped me be the best mom I can be. Even though I am still hard on myself for not being perfect, there is no FEAR, which can significantly exacerbate physical pain.

"A few months ago, our 17-year-old son told us, 'You really are the perfect parents.' We told him no, not perfect, lots of mistakes. He disagreed, so I take it as 'perfectly imperfect.' Nevertheless, we would not be where we are today had we not participated in the clearings. We both often think of Sandy and Len.

Len's teaching around 'The Watcher' (observing your thoughts in a detached way) is part of what helped us to carry the teachings well into the future. I also still use Sandy's ACIM cards. I continue to tell people about my work with Sandy and Len. ACIM and the *Clearing* opened up my mind and freed me from all these burdens I had taken on with a false narrative and intense fear around not realizing my dream to have a child.

"Through the teaching of *The Clearing Process,* I have had the joy and honor of seeing sicknesses healed, marriages saved, and families reunited. Forgiveness lifts the fog from the mirror, and we see our true selves looking back at us, with the Holy Spirit at our side—and, thus, we see the world clearer than before. *The Clearing Process* is true forgiveness. Forgiveness takes diligence, awareness, and the will to be happy rather than right about what you negatively believe about the world and yourself. Forgiveness ends separation. It is our most important function in life—and we get 'paid' in rewards of freedom, peace, joy, and love."

Krista has two healthy children and could easily conceive after taking three of Sandy's 30-hour *On Purpose* courses, *The Art of Surrender, The Holy Relationship,* and *Choosing Freedom: The Way Out.* Krista went on to take the ten-day *Power of Clearing Coaching Certification Program* and became a certified *Power of Clearing* coach.

4) Mark
Releasing Sexual Guilt

From Sandy: Mark's parents divorced when he was very young and his father was not a part of his life. Due to the nature of his upbringing, he developed a very complex relationship with his mother. At 13 years of age, he thought he could replace his father by becoming his mother's partner. However, he was soon frustrated and felt rejected by his mother when she began a domestic partnership with a man. After that, because he wanted to have sex with his mother and now couldn't, he had sex with his sleeping 15-year-old sister on many occasions. She was a very deep sleeper, and he knew that. When the daughter told their mother that she believed that someone had been having sex with her, the mother assumed it was her new partner. When his mother asked Mark if he thought his stepfather had been having sex with his sister, Mark said no, although he never volunteered the key piece of information that he was the one who had been doing it. His mother eventually split up with Mark's stepfather because she thought he was indeed the perpetrator.

Out of guilt for both having sex with his sister and then hiding the truth that he was the one involved, subconsciously he punished himself by "accidentally" riding his bicycle off of a ledge, knocking himself unconscious, thus becoming paralyzed and unable to move at all. For six weeks, the doctors kept Mark on morphine and even though he was conscious, he was having hallucinations at times. When they told him he was permanently paralyzed and would never walk again, Mark was profoundly grief-stricken. He could still move his arms. Since then, Mark has spent his life in a wheelchair, requiring caregivers on an ongoing basis. Even though he was still physically able to, Mark never had a sexual or romantic relationship until after he participated in *The Power of Clearing* process and cleared much of his guilt. After Mark took the ten-day POCCCP *(Power of Clearing Coaching Certification Program),* he could walk downstairs with crutches, which he had never been able to do before, though he still needed the wheelchair in general.

Mark's story

"In my first clearing, the most notable recurring themes were my relationships with my sister Naomi, my caretakers, and stepfather. It was tough and scary to be completely open and express intimate and private things to a stranger (my Power of Clearing coach). However, I began to retrace feelings back to my past when my coach started to talk about my caregivers and how they take care of me. I recognized that in addition to needing their help, I was getting love, support, and acknowledgment from the attention I was getting from them because I was in a wheelchair.

"One of the first things that came to my mind was all about my female caregivers, Meggie and Tracy. *The Power of Clearing* coach guided me through *The Clearing Process* by suggesting scenarios of what might have happened with them. I thought about how these two caregivers were related to my story and started to bring up painful issues with my relationship with each one of them.

"Then, I went deeper into my mind and thought of my accident and when I was in the hospital. I remember being so attracted to all the female nurses that would take care of me there. The feeling I would get when one of them would get close to my body would make me sexually aroused.

"As I was sharing this feeling with my Power of Clearing coach Deana during the clearing, I felt a strong sense of wanting a nurse next to me and being romantically intimate with her. I felt the deep anger toward Meggie, one of my caregivers, because she did not have romantic feelings toward me even though I did for her. When I went even deeper, I felt pain, suffering, and rage toward my stepfather. While I was at college in Sacramento, my stepfather visited me and stayed a few days. He and Tracy fell in love and got married. She was 25 years younger than him. And so, she went away with him, leaving me feeling abandoned and rejected. I felt he stole her from me. I felt it was kind of like repayment for him losing my mother who split up with him because she thought he was having sex with my sister when it was actually me. Going deeper in the clearing with my coach, I traced it back to feelings I had for my sister. I paused for a moment, and a voice within said, 'NO! Do not share this!'

"At that moment, I felt overwhelming guilt with a massive weight on my shoulders—a weight and burden that I had kept locked inside for almost 25 years. I had never shared what happened to me with Naomi with anyone, and here I was resisting with all my might not to share it! Then all of a sudden, the words came out of me. 'I had sex with my sister Naomi!' For one split second, I said to myself, 'This is it—this is the end; now I'm going to be in big trouble!' However, after that split second, a beautiful white Light filled my sight. I saw my coach in front of me in this white Light that completely immersed her, and I felt such a sense of calm, peace, and joy.

"I couldn't believe what was happening, but all I knew was I was *not* guilty and felt truly Happy. For the first time, I had the knowledge that I was always innocent. The guilt I was holding onto for such a long time was gone, and I felt so much freedom! With that first clearing I did with my Power of Clearing coach, especially the past and present connections that I made *and* the tremendous burden that I released, I had some significant momentum for going deeper into my healing process. I continued my work with Sandy a few months after that first clearing. As we went further into my relationship with Naomi, I started to connect the issue with her to issues that I did not know I had with my mom. I was starting to see faces superimposed on Sandy's face that I recognized from my past. I saw my mom, grandma, and other familiar faces whose names I did not even know!

"It was scary at times because I felt like I was almost hallucinating. I shared this with Sandy, and she said it was common to have that experience of seeing faces superimposed on the Clearing Coach's face. I told Sandy that I also felt more frustration and fear with her than with my previous Power of Clearing coach, Deana. She asked me why, and I told her that she reminded me of my biological brother and mom. We went into that association further and started to clear on it. Issues about safety and security came up for me. My mom and biological brother are both, in a sense, my security to me. My mom provides me with motherly love, and both of them represent financial security.

"There was a prominent awareness in my mind that they were my God and Source providing everything for me. However, looking more deeply, I felt at some level that my mom was at the heart of all of these ego feelings. While I couldn't put my finger on it or understand it, I felt uneasiness inside.

"My next set of clearings happened in the *Power of Clearing Coaching Certification Program* in Santa Cruz, California. This ten-day workshop retreat was an intensive process of completely exposing my most inner feelings and secrets to others in a safe environment while trusting my Inner Teacher. Issue after issue came up for healing. I had never been through an intensive program like this before. In addition, with everyone in the program living together in the same house, it was intriguing and challenging at the same time. I was constantly watching my mind and paying attention to my feelings. It was a 24-hour job in my mind; however, it was gratifying to have significant insights and aha moments.

"Someone in the program reminded me of my sister, so I projected those feelings on her. I felt abandonment, unworthiness, insecurity, fear, and uneasiness. I had to work through these feelings the whole time I was there at the retreat. I even had to do a clearing with her, and it felt very uncomfortable, like I wasn't worthy of doing it. I felt like if I did something wrong, she would leave me just like Naomi and my mom left me. Also, there was a massive amount of guilt when I had to look at her face-to-face eyes-to-eyes and clear with her, not knowing at the time that I was clearing the stories I made up about my sister, my mom, and everyone else from my past. There was one moment when she took off her sweatpants because she was hot in the sun. I was extremely uncomfortable and felt guilty about what I had done to Naomi in the past. I was reminded of when I took Naomi's pants off her to have sex with her. Even though this young woman I was clearing with had a bikini swimsuit underneath her sweatpants, I still felt uncomfortable.

"I even shared these feelings of shame, guilt, abandonment, and fear with my coach Deana and we dove into those feelings to find out what was underneath them. I felt and heard, 'You don't have permission.' The woman I was clearing with triggered me and brought up past emotions with Naomi, specifically not getting permission from her to have sex with her. Then I could feel denial and rejection from my mom, and I realized it wasn't about the woman I was clearing with, my caregivers, or my sister; it was really about my relationship with my mom! I connected the pieces between my caregivers, Naomi, and my mom. After that clearing session, I experienced a great feeling and had some excellent insights into my past.

"In this ten-day workshop, I also had the opportunity to role-play how my biological family would react to me when I told them that I had sex with Naomi, my sister. Everyone participating in the retreat got to play someone in my family. The woman I cleared with earlier who reminded me of Naomi played her in the role play. It was the first time I told a group of people that I had sex with Naomi and saw their reactions. What was even scarier was that these people were playing my biological family; to see their responses brought up the most fearful emotions going through my mind at the time. I felt that I would be in big trouble for something I was not supposed to do. I felt tension and uneasiness in the role-play; however, eventually, I saw the absurdity. While I still felt guilt and some shame, the experience lifted a weight off my shoulders. I felt more deeply that maybe it wasn't my fault and perhaps I wasn't guilty.

"I continue to do clearings with Naomi and my mom, and recently I have had new insights and awareness about the situation with my sister, caregivers, and mom. I am retracing back the emotional trauma of the recurring stories with them.

"It also became clear that my next step in healing these issues was to talk with my sister. Before I made the call, it was essential to clear on it with one of my Power of Clearing coaches and then meditate and give it over to the Holy Spirit. I told Holy Spirit, 'Speak through me. Use the words that are most helpful and healing for Naomi and me. I surrender my agenda. Be You in charge.'

"I felt ready and more empowered to speak with Naomi. Our phone conversation centered around what happened over 20 years earlier. I started by asking her if she remembered our sexual interactions when we were children. Right away, she responded with, 'What are you talking about?' I asked her again in a different way to see if she could remember, and again, she said, 'I don't know what you're talking about.' Then she asked me why I was asking her this question. I told her it was important to know if she remembered anything. My intention was not to push her for an answer but to see if she could recollect a memory. I must admit that I was hoping she would say, 'I do remember that time...' Unfortunately, this did not happen, and she said, "Our stepfather molested me, and I don't want to talk about it anymore.' After that, she told me not to talk to him about it because she didn't want to 'stir the pot' and cause drama. She said this was all crazy, and she didn't have the same memory recollection that I did. She told me she had repressed all of this, and it made her sick that I brought it up. As the phone call was coming to an end, I said, 'I am here for you, Naomi, and I am your brother and always love you.' Her reaction wasn't warm, and she said, 'I am dumbfounded as to why you brought all of this up.' It ended with me saying, 'I'll be here, and we'll talk again sometime soon.'

"Once I got off the phone, I felt a sense of peace and freedom. I spoke with Naomi for about 45 minutes, and the beginning of the conversation was tough for me. However, as the conversation continued, I felt confidence and strength from something somewhere deep within myself. I wasn't afraid to face my fear anymore. I knew I wasn't alone and that Holy Spirit was with me. I had to trust in Him. A couple of days after speaking to Naomi, I did some contemplation and sat with the feelings. I realized I had an agenda and wanted in some way to get an answer or for her to remember we had those sexual interactions. I felt I was judging myself for having an agenda. I did feel guilty, so I cleared on it and felt much better, seeing that every situation is for my healing, including this situation. At first, I found it challenging, and then I came to a greater understanding of why it happened and how blessed I am to have this forgiveness opportunity.

"To help in my healing process, I will be using homeopathy under homeopathic health and wellness practitioner Sharon Richlark and continuing Sandy Levey-Lunden's Power of Clearing process to free myself from emotional trauma. That trauma includes breaking my neck, expecting love and security in my caregivers, pursuing unhealthy romantic relationships, feeling guilty about having sex with Naomi, and feeling abandoned by not getting love from my mom.

"Thank you for reading."

APPENDIX C

UNDERSTANDING AND LIVING IN A HOLY RELATIONSHIP

1) David Spooner – Scotland and England tour guide, geologist, and *Power of Clearing* Coach

Living in a Holy Relationship

As the end of my 30-year romance focused into reality, I felt a failure as a husband and father, certain only of my grief, depression, and now a feeling of doom and separation.

Convinced that I was unlovable and unworthy of prospects, I had no idea how profoundly the *Clearing* and *Holy Relationship* work that I had experienced with Sandy and her team of coaches would pave the way to happiness for me and the benefit of those dearest to me.

In the last five years of our marriage, we were determined to ease our children through our separation. Through Sandy's guidance, the POCCCP, and *The Clearing Process* so graciously applied by gifted coaches in the trainings, including in my home, I was able to call for corrections to errors in my thinking. My judgment and condemnation included being unworthy, not good enough, unimportant, unlovable, and nobody would ever want me. The key for me was understanding that the ego is always trying to do its best to protect me and that fighting imaginary battles with my ego never helps.

My ego continued creating damaging scenarios and fearful thoughts of being forever alone. For the past 30 years, I had been a husband with family, and the thought of being completely alone was terrifying. I was learning to bypass my ego and making lighter work of emotional adjustments that had appeared too painful to consider for a long time. I chose to clear myself of all guilt, fears, and feelings of unworthiness with *The Power of Clearing* process. I had many private sessions with Gillian, Sandy, and Len and completed the trainings. There were moments I felt I could die from the pain of such strong emotions. I cleared deeper and deeper until I tapped the truth of my true nature, that I was good enough to be wanted and chosen and worthy of love and compassion. From this point forward, I was able to begin my new life.

Twice in two years, my wife and I attended a spiritual retreat in Väddö on the Swedish Baltic coast, called the Warm Water Rebirthing training for seven days with Lena Kristina Tuulse. Sandy was also present, teaching a part of the course. At first, my wife and I were unaware that we had met our future partners at this course, each trained in or familiar with *The Power of Clearing*. Since then, we have, at different times, lived as two couples in the same dwelling, shared family celebrations, and been able to show our children that loving relationships are forever and that changing the relationship form does not change the love between us.

We have experienced this profound teaching that Love is unchanging, that we are all one, and that we intend to be a joined family forever. We have learned how to love and accept each other for who we really are, beyond our egos. We join now as one family, with full transparency, acceptance, and understanding because we have learned forgiveness of our ego thoughts. It has been a miraculous healing, each of us clearing what was in the way and, joining fully in the whole family dynamic, accepting each other.

I know now that I am profoundly wanted, understood, loved, and cared for in my new marriage and can truly reciprocate fully. It has indeed been a very deep process and journey.

2) **Jean Battersby Spooner**
Living in a Holy Relationship

Power of Clearing Coach, Belief Systems Coach, Master NLP Practitioner

At the end of my husband's marriage, we first met. Invited by my mentor, Sandy Levey-Lunden, I agreed to attend a Warm Water Birthing experience in

Väddö, Sweden. I had never been to Sweden, nor had I ever considered it. And I certainly did not know about rebirthing! But intuitively, I found myself saying yes. I didn't know that across the world, my future husband had also said yes to Sandy to attend the same retreat.

However, his reasons for going were different from mine. While their marriage was ending, Sandy and her coach team supported them through powerful clearings. When I met him in Väddö, he was in such a state of grief that he didn't really "see" me then. What I could see in him was his loving nature, and I wanted to be near him even if I couldn't be with him.

I completed Sandy's POCCCP to further my development as a life coach and thought that I'd surely gain more tools to add to my "toolkit" to help my clients. However, the year-long course I had just finished lacked a process to help me go deeper, so I was hopeful that the Warm Water Rebirthing with Lena Kristina Tuulse and more Power of Clearing would give me what I lacked. Little did I know that this experience would forever change my entire life.

At my first attendance in 2015, I was still doubting my abilities as a coach. Coming from a childhood fraught with a critical mother, I found that I constantly second-guessed myself. I harshly judged myself, felt unlovable, and, at times, unworthy of living. I didn't trust my true nature, and I didn't understand my true nature until I experienced numerous clearings with Sandy. By the time I attended the same retreat the following year, I had become clearer about my true nature and abilities—I knew that I represented joy, heart, a haven, radiance, and source for many people.

For us, the holy relationship emerged slowly. First was the untangling of the strings of marriage, then the clearing of the fog that separated us from our true Selves. We learned how the ego keeps us separate from our true nature and recognize when the ego is at play. And more importantly for me, to strengthen the muscle of helping each other move out of little t truth into Big T Truth. In a holy relationship, you help each other heal the pain and suffering. You don't judge it. You don't measure it. You don't compare it.

Only my husband and his former wife can speak to their profound process. And I am the one who can speak to the miracle that we all share a closeness that few have experienced. With new partners, we have created a larger family unit that amasses several continents. We've reached new heights of Joy and Freedom. All of our children from our first marriages have experienced the loving relationships we have formed and witnessed the closeness we share.

I will be forever grateful to Sandy and *The Power of Clearing* process. My children have benefitted from my happiness, my business has a renewed clarity of purpose, and I continue to grow in my new relationship with my husband.

3) Iona Leishman, certified *Power of Clearing* coach and visionary artist My Journey to My Authentic Self

I understand now that one of the primary things I came here to work on in this life has been my fear of loneliness, blame, and attack. I have attracted many warm relationships in my life, but I have also angered and alienated others. I believe I have not understood boundaries, and I believed that I needed to keep many relationships superficial because I did not trust myself on many levels. I believed people would discover that I was unpleasant. I believed that my birth family knew that already and that, in their eyes, I was irretrievable. I was confused.

Through my years of Power of Clearing work with Sandy, I retrieved myself and found the bravery to do something that many people believe is impossible. I faced my deep fear of anger, loneliness, and ostracization. In the process, I was able to bring a long marriage that has born beautiful children to a calm, peaceful, and loving conclusion through the release of the other. There have been no lawyers involved in our divorce, and the tough, emotional fallout eased, enabling us to meet gladly as a loving family that now includes new partners for each of us. Our partners love our children, understand they come first, and are familiar and comfortable with Sandy's work.

My deep longing was to be seen, heard, and fully accepted for who I am. I yearned to know my value and have the courage to be transparent with a loving partner. I wanted to be with a partner with whom I could deeply explore on every level.

Growing up, asking for what I wanted could attract ridicule and criticism for being selfish. A middle child for the first six years of my life, I do not have any memories of being closely held and feeling totally safe and loved. Blame and attack were acute issues for me. I remember as a teenager thinking, "I will never do anything else that angers my parents." I believed I had angered them too much already, and I could not bear their displeasure anymore. It was too risky.

As a child, I could be brave and funny, but I had early trauma, including being hit by my father. My parents put me into four different schools before the age of seven, so I became distressed and unhappy. Despite my mother being seriously ill after my birth, my sister was born just 17 months after me and subsequently bore the brunt of my bullying. Apparently, my parents talked about taking me to a child psychologist because I was acting out so much emotional pain, but it did not happen. And by then, my volatile, funny, lovable, scary, exciting Church of Scotland minister father was undergoing his own analysis, training to be a psychotherapist, and by the age of six years, I had another sister.

I learned to test my father's mood in my home life before deciding upon my own. I became watchful and tense; I still hear my father's voice shouting "help me!" as he grappled with some task or other, and we had to run to him. Mostly, I kept safe by trying to anticipate his moods and movements.

We four children danced to his tune, and it was a watchful house: exciting, affectionate, and then terrible—both parents ambitious, sociable, driven. Mother's psychological state became the central plank of my father's life work, and sometimes I wondered why they had children. They almost melded one into the other.

My mother was clever and frustrated, warm but distant about many things. She could gaze out the window and change the subject if she didn't want to talk about it. But somehow, she never gave up on me, and I loved and understood her. I felt, in many ways, I mothered her. She was stalwart, lovable, funny, smart, and ambitious but hopeless about sex, periods, and boys, and I felt utterly unprepared for the pitfalls and delights of teenage years. I believed I was ugly and fat. I couldn't understand how I could simply have boys as friends.

My father told me that "men just want to screw you." I was half horrified, half impressed that he knew that word. Mum had no encouragement. I did not have a boyfriend until I was 18, and by the time I met my future husband, I was done with bruising, abusive relationships involving drugs and alcohol. This man was calm and kind, safe and reliable. I loved him for his constancy. He was an experienced world traveler, and I was desperate to go and see the world, living in the UK for most of my first 25 years. While methodical and organized, he was keen to travel off the beaten track. Perfect for me who had seen little of the world outside Scotland, albeit that my deep relationship with this country contented me.

In contrast to his quiet, systematic way of being, I believed I could be the relationship's energy, dynamo, and excitement. I did well, supported by his steadiness and encouragement. He was and is a kind man who hid many emotions and did not want to talk about them. In my inflated confidence, I believed that I could change him and bring him out.

In marrying him, I felt immensely grateful, amazed. I felt rescued and seen as I believed I was a mess. I didn't know what I wanted to do with my life, but I wanted adventure. I didn't realize how messed up and scared I really was. I didn't know how creatively talented I was; I just couldn't see it.

The death of our first baby in childbirth quickly tested our marriage. The pain of her death was mighty. While I wept and grieved, essentially, I felt guilty for causing pain to my birth family. I felt punished, believing that I was fundamentally unpleasant, guilty of historic bad behavior that attracted my father's wrath, and the displeasure and judgment of my mother. Additionally, a rift between my youngest sister pains me to this day, with her seeming determination to block me from her life. I felt I had killed our baby with my cord, and I had to make amends. I had a huge feeling of guilt deep inside of me to clear, even though I didn't know it could be cleared. Over many years, my partner and I valiantly worked individually and in marriage guidance counseling.

Over eight years, we had five children, and all births had their attendant trauma. Exhaustion depleted my body. I could not wake up in the morning; I had such anemia, yet it went undiagnosed. My husband and I were doing a brilliant job on many levels, we loved our family passionately, and we had many wonderful, loving adventures together. Still, I knew that I struggled to feel a vital connection with him.

I felt unsupported by my sisters, parents, and brother. I just could not understand why my own family could not be more loving and supportive. Why did they not come and help me? After all, none of my siblings had children, and I believed they could make time for me. Perhaps they thought all was well. I was loyal to the situation I had created; I was proud and did not want them to judge me as I believed I would be.

My husband and I worked so hard together to mend the feeling that we were operating in parallel to each other, but in truth, I was terrified of being the cause of pain. Again. It was an old pattern coming round again in my life. I didn't want to be the cause of pain, so I would manage. And joyfully and bravely, manage, I did. My spirit could be tremendous; I enormously enjoyed parenting my beautiful children and showing them wonderful places. By now, I was painting beautiful landscape paintings and selling well. At the same time, a counselor was supporting me to not dump all my unresolved stuff onto my now teenage children. While I was so desperate to take care of them, nurture, encourage, love—in truth, though, I dared not admit my need for a truly deep, intimate relationship with a man.

Tragically, my therapist died, although she told me this time was a new beginning for me before she went. I felt adrift. Then a loving friend told me about a presentation by someone called Sandy Levey-Lunden from America speaking in Glasgow, and did I want to go?

Meeting Sandy and her colleague Len Satov that cold, wet March evening, I felt as if they had sent me a life raft. Perhaps there was a way out of all pain and suffering? So, I climbed aboard the life raft, resolved to throw all my despair at them and test their practice.

I saw that bringing Sandy into the heart of my family could help us enormously. We were at a critical time in our lives, with our oldest starting university and the others navigating the challenges of early teenage years. My husband was deeply unhappy in his work, and I was committed to producing many paintings for the prestigious Chapel Royal at Stirling Castle. My father was increasingly unwell, and my relationship with my youngest sister was tense as we negotiated our parents' ongoing care.

Over the next few years, my husband and I hosted Sandy and Len in our family home, helping bring many people to work with them and experience *The Power of Clearing* process and programs. Our children became familiar with *The Clearing Process,* and, as much as they wanted, also formed relationships with Sandy and Len, and the other coaches, Gillian Hibbs, and Oriana Howes who were part of the course teams that came to my home. I became a certified *Power of Clearing* coach, joining Gillian and Oriana, forever enriching my spiritual practice with the skills I learned through my own clearing with Sandy and helping others with the course. I gained irreplaceable knowledge by sitting for many hours over many years with Sandy during the trainings as she skillfully got to the root of a person's behavior and skewering tenacious ego. It was masterly.

I grieved my father's demise into dementia, and when I lovingly witnessed his final passing, I felt his release and mine. Accepting Sandy's invitation to "come to Sweden and deepen your process," my husband and I flew there, just after my father's funeral, for warm water rebirthing where there were also many different spiritual healers. We were to both meet our future life partners during that week, although neither of us realized it then. I felt dazed after all that had just happened in my life, bruised by the enormity of it all. I felt greedy for all there was on offer for me to experience.

Then life was accelerating, and I felt free to venture to Southeast Asia with Sandy for OUTLAW, *Outrageous Unstoppable True Leadership Adventure for Women*. I was determined to leave all my shame and guilt there in Bali, telling my husband that I knew something enormous was going to happen, I didn't know what, but I had to go. He accepted and encouraged me. It was an immensely powerful place in which to let go. Mama Bali. I felt that Sandy was my guiding mother in human form. I underwent a deep spiritual transformation in the group of women in the intensely female place of powerful heat, beauty, and volcanic energy. The experience changed me forever. I was so much more confident of my power as a woman. I understood how my essential goodness would enable my Loved Ones and me to be free and loving to one another; it would just look different. Finally, at long last, I felt robust enough to hear and accept the hurt, anxiety, and anger that inevitably would come my way. I explained to my Beloved children that, while on many levels, I still loved my husband, their father, I loved another man too. I wanted to be transparent. I hated secrecy and obfuscation, and I wanted to live honestly. A Sandyism made a big impact on me: "You don't have a secret. A secret has you."

Although it was very hard, I knew I was showing my Loved Ones how to be authentic, bold, loving, and compassionate to self and others. Throughout the process, our children had access to Sandy and her compassionate team and the choice to take up help to understand what life was bringing.

For David and me, the release of each other has flowed into warm acceptance of each other with new ways of communicating because we understand the freedom and a new way to communicate. We both have new partners, people who know and understand Sandy's teachings. Many key players know, welcome, and accept the others in this new scene: our children, ourselves, and our two new life partners. Perhaps unbelievably for some, with our new partners, we have lived together under the same roof, welcoming our children when they felt to join us.

As I undid and rebuilt the shape of my family, I had to trust and trust again by repeatedly calling for help from Source Energy to show and guide me. I trusted to lean in to Source through *The Clearing Process* that I resorted to time and time again. I would call on Oriana Howes and Gillian Hibbs to please hold space for me. Hearing Sandy's unmistakable voice was enough to remind me who I was in my Higher Self. She helped me navigate years of stormy emotional waters with a lot at stake. I remember feelings of utter calm in knowing Divine Strength within me. Love was all, and no matter what was said or done to me, I knew and experienced Divine Power.

I understand more and more about how and why my life has unfolded the way it has. Through deep discussions with my partner, I understood that my soul agreed to all of it before this incarnation. I realize that those I love and those who challenge me also agreed to meet with me, and this knowledge fills me with gratitude. I am gaining more peace and understanding in my reason for being here in this Life.

4) Adam Shapiro, certified *Power of Clearing* coach, ACIM teacher and student, Alexandria VA.

Understanding and Living in a Holy Relationship

From Sandy: Adam Shapiro has been a committed and dedicated student of ACIM for many, many years. This article describes what it is like to practice the philosophy of a holy relationship that he is now living with his partner and new wife, Mia. Only someone who has read *A Course in Miracles* will understand many of the terms he uses here in the way he means them as the conscientious student he has been. Adam is a trained *Power of Clearing* coach and a graduate of the ten-day *Power of Clearing Coaching Certification Program,* as well as many of the other courses he took from me.

Adam and Mia living in a Holy Relationship

To me, the holy relationship means seeing and holding your partner's incorruptible and changeless innocence no matter what seems to be happening. In my experience, the holy relationship is beyond the two people in the relationship. It is more about the Holy Spirit and Jesus guiding and directing the inclusive relationship. Eventually, when the holy relationship becomes increasingly advanced, it is clear that the relationship is healing the two holy relationship partners and the Sonship, or the One Mind. In other words, as the two holy relationship partners heal their minds, they are healing the One Mind. As Jesus states in *A Course in Miracles*, *The holy relationship is a phenomenal teaching accomplishment.* (ACIM, T-17.V.2:3) This statement reflects one's growth and development on the spiritual path. It represents the willingness and desire of my partner and me to pursue the goal of seeing each other as perfect and innocent.

Through my holy relationship with my wife Mia, I am healing past issues and traumas that I have held onto since I have been a child. I am 39 years old, and my Mia is 22 years old. There has been tremendous resistance from the ego projecting through blame and countless relationship conflicts onto each other to keep us from coming together and joining mind to mind. I have been with Mia for three years, and it's only been in the past two years that we both willingly accepted the Holy Spirit's goal of seeing each other in holiness (innocence). There are numerous things I have been learning in the holy relationship with Mia. One thing I am learning is to be grateful for being triggered. Sometimes I don't even know when I am triggered, so it's a blessing to have my holy relationship partner show me, helping me to heal the issues. When Mia triggers me, I realize quicker and quicker that she loves me so much that she will show me my upset over and over again until I learn to forgive myself for using her to attack myself. Once I take accountability and bring it back to my mind, I can see the jewel of the miracle behind this false appearance.

I believe forgiveness (ACIM-based forgiveness) is not complete until I express my gratitude for her. The image I get is being in so much gratitude that I want to kiss her feet for showing me all my unconscious guilt that I wouldn't be able to see if it wasn't for her. And then we, together with the Holy Spirit, can heal it together. By joining with the Christ in Mia, we can access our One Mind and dissolve all seeming problems because there is no more separation.

I see the holy relationship as the holy grail to Awakening from the dream entirely. I feel it is a gift from the Holy Spirit to help us return to our shared incorruptible innocence. The holy relationship demonstrates by helping me see my partner as innocent, sinless, and guiltless NO MATTER WHAT the ego in my partner says. "I hold and see the Love that is and always has been in you, which you see as who you are as well." I'm learning that unless it is shared, it isn't real, and we cannot feel it in our hearts until we can share innocence, love, gratitude, and peace with each other.

All of this learning and experience in living the holy relationship is due to meeting Mia in this lifetime. When I said "yes" two years ago to pursue this relationship with her and the Holy Spirit, shortly after that, Mia joined me in my intention and goal of seeing each other's innocence and guiltlessness regardless of any seeming obstacle. I am truly grateful to Mia for having the desire to wake up with me in this lifetime and not waiting any longer. I understand that this world is not real and is an illusion. However, Jesus states in ACIM, *Delay does not matter in eternity, but it is tragic in time.* (ACIM, T-5.VI.1:3) Therefore, as long as we believe this world is real, it will be painful until we desire to wake up and see that the only way to wake entirely from the dream is through the holy relationship; it is truly miraculous! And the great news is EVERYONE can have a holy relationship with another. It all comes down to your genuine desire for it. Then the Holy Spirit will not fail in assisting you to become a holy relationship partner and providing the perfect holy relationship partner for you.

APPENDIX D

DEEPER MEANINGS OF THE TRAININGS

From Chapter 9 – *True Woman's Power*

Psychodrama re-enactment is taking a current upset and role-playing in order to access a deeply embedded memory in the mind. In this method, we explore the drama around the trauma in physical, psychological, mental, and emotional terms. By opening it up and giving someone full permission to recall, feel, and express long-repressed emotions, they can fully let go and release their negative past. In many of my *On Purpose* trainings, Dr. Jack Shupe, Gestalt Therapist, and certified master teacher of psychodrama was on our coaching team. He was also one of the psychodrama teachers of Howard Staples, who held the space for the naked man exercise in the *True Woman's Power* course.

Further in-depth description of the naked man exercise: In this exercise, as in many real-life situations, one man represents all men. When I first introduce Howard to the group of women, he is fully dressed. I tell them that he is a good friend for many years, a skilled coach, a master re-birther and *Power of Clearing* coach, working on and dedicated to his enlightenment process for countless years. He is an avid ACIM student, and a student of psychodrama.

Howard then leaves the room briefly and when he returns, he is completely naked, and I invite him to stand in front of the whole room of women. One at a time, each woman stands up at a three-foot distance from him, facing him with the spotlight of attention on the two of them. The rules of the process include no touching. They are encouraged to especially focus on the man's genitals in order to get the maximum benefit from the exercise.

Because the penis clearly represents manhood, some verbally attack the penis for every indiscretion, sexual abuse, and power struggle she has felt, experienced, and recalled from her past. The woman is free to express herself in whatever way she feels. She can choose to stand there alone, have up to three women on each side to encourage her, or have the entire training group stand behind her, supporting her by saying such things as, "Louder! More! Be specific! Go deeper!" They encourage her to vocalize with gestures, sounds, and words like, "No!" "Stop!" "How dare you?" "I'm so angry because …" and the most popular words are "You f—ing b—tard" because the women in the training are no longer trying to be nice, which is a result of women's standard upbringing. They have full permission to express every projection, perception, past trauma, passion, belief, grievance, angst, and feeling they can access with every memory and cell in their body about men. It might take several rounds of facing the man, in no sequential order if someone feels like they left something out, until every woman feels spent and complete. Each round goes deeper, uncovering and revealing another layer, often triggered by a sister's share. After completing this exercise, the women have the opportunity to do a whole forgiveness process in a 3-step clearing to clear all their negative feelings, judgments, blame, and projections toward all men in their life.

It's the completion exercise for the day. As with each exercise in the course, it is up to each woman what level of participation they are willing to play. There are always a few who choose to sit this one out for various reasons; they may be shocked and scared by the whole exercise. Women can choose to leave the room at any time, before, during, or after the exercise to work with a coach about what this process brings up for them, mainly their fears about men, power, and control. The ones who stay in the room witness and hold sacred space for their sisters.

By the end of the whole exercise, even though the women are exhausted and spent physically emotionally, they celebrate their courage with a group hug and a cheer.

APPENDIX E

HOW IS HEALING ACCOMPLISHED?

Here is the link to the text from pages 17-18 exactly as it appears in the Manual for Teachers in the abridged edition of *A Course in Miracles* published by the Foundation for Inner Peace.

https://acim.org/acim/manual/the-perceived-purpose-of-sickness/en/s/818

5. How Is Healing Accomplished?

1. Healing involves an understanding of what the illusion of sickness is for. ²Healing is impossible without this. (ACIM, M-5.1:1-2)

I. The Perceived Purpose of Sickness

1. Healing is accomplished the instant the sufferer no longer sees any value in pain. ²Who would choose suffering unless he thought it brought him something, and something of value to him? ³He must think it is a small price to pay for something of greater worth. ⁴For sickness is an election; a decision. ⁵It is the choice of weakness, in the mistaken conviction that it is strength. ⁶When this occurs, real strength is seen as threat and health as danger. ⁷Sickness is a method, conceived in madness, for placing God's Son on his Father's throne. ⁸God is seen as outside, fierce and powerful, eager to keep all power for Himself. ⁹Only by His death can He be conquered by His Son.

2. And what, in this insane conviction, does healing stand for? ²It symbolizes the defeat of God's Son and the triumph of his Father over him. ³It represents the ultimate defiance in a direct form which the Son of God is forced to recognize.

⁴It stands for all that he would hide from himself to protect his "life." ⁵If he is healed, he is responsible for his thoughts. ⁶And if he is responsible for his thoughts, he will be killed to prove to him how weak and pitiful he is. ⁷But if he chooses death himself, his weakness is his strength. ⁸Now has he given himself what God would give to him, and thus entirely usurped the throne of his Creator. (ACIM, M-5.I.1:1–2:8)

II. The Shift in Perception

1. Healing must occur in exact proportion to which the valuelessness of sickness is recognized. ²One need but say, "There is no gain at all to me in this" and he is healed. ³But to say this, one first must recognize certain facts. ⁴First, it is obvious that decisions are of the mind, not of the body. ⁵If sickness is but a faulty problem-solving approach, it is a decision. ⁶And if it is a decision, it is the mind and not the body that makes it. ⁷The resistance to recognizing this is enormous, because the existence of the world as you perceive it depends on the body being the decision maker. ⁸Terms like "instincts," "reflexes" and the like represent attempts to endow the body with non-mental motivators. ⁹Actually, such terms merely state or describe the problem. ¹⁰They do not answer it.

2. The acceptance of sickness as a decision of the mind, for a purpose for which it would use the body, is the basis of healing. ²And this is so for healing in all forms. ³A patient decides that this is so, and he recovers. ⁴If he decides against recovery, he will not be healed. ⁵Who is the physician? ⁶Only the mind of the patient himself. ⁷The outcome is what he decides that it is. ⁸Special agents seem to be ministering to him, yet they but give form to his own choice. ⁹He chooses them in order to bring tangible form to his desires. ¹⁰And it is this they do, and nothing else. ¹¹They are not actually needed at all. ¹²The patient could merely rise up without their aid and say, "I have no use for this." ¹³There is no form of sickness that would not be cured at once.

3. What is the single requisite for this shift in perception? ²It is simply this; the recognition that sickness is of the mind, and has nothing to do with the body. ³What does this recognition "cost"? ⁴It costs the whole world you see, for the world will never again appear to rule the mind. ⁵For with this recognition is responsibility placed where it belongs; not with the world, but on him who looks on the world and sees it as it is not. ⁶He looks on what he chooses to see. ⁷No more and no less. ⁸The world does nothing to him. ⁹He only thought it did. ¹⁰Nor does he do anything to the world, because he was mistaken about what it is.

Herein is the release from guilt and sickness both, for they are one. Yet to accept this release, the insignificance of the body must be an acceptable idea.

4. With this idea is pain forever gone. ²But with this idea goes also all confusion about creation. ³Does not this follow of necessity? ⁴Place cause and effect in their true sequence in one respect, and the learning will generalize and transform the world. ⁵The transfer value of one true idea has no end or limit. ⁶The final outcome of this lesson is the remembrance of God. ⁷What do guilt and sickness, pain, disaster and all suffering mean now? ⁸Having no purpose, they are gone. ⁹And with them also go all the effects they seemed to cause. ¹⁰Cause and effect but replicate creation. ¹¹Seen in their proper perspective, without distortion and without fear, they re-establish Heaven. (ACIM, M-5.II.1:1–4:11)

RESOURCES

1) *On Purpose* Courses, Sandy Levey-Lunden, Leader and Founder

The *On Purpose* courses can be done for one person or for a group online by Zoom with trained *Power of Clearing* coaches and Sandy Levey-Lunden as the main facilitator for anyone anywhere in the world. The courses can also be done with a full *Power of Clearing* coaching team traveling to any location. All courses will be taught personally by Sandy Levey-Lunden. Sandy trains certified *Power of Clearing* coaches with the ten-day *Power of Clearing Coaching Certification Program* (POCCCP), online, in a group, or in a person-to-person experience with Sandy. Then, as certified *Power of Clearing* coaches with knowledge of the method, they can coach people in one-to-one sessions.

Here are the courses that Sandy offers, by category.

Personal Development, Addiction, Depression, Grief, and Fears

- The Power of Clearing
- The Art of Surrender
- Choosing Freedom: The Way Out of All Pain and Suffering
- True Woman's Power
- True Man's Power
- Taking Your Place as a Leader in the World
- The Breakthrough

Focus on Relationships, Marriages, and Families

- The Holy Relationship
- The Art of Merging two ego wills into one true will
- The Art of Partnership
- Opening to the Power of Love
- The Art of Giving and Receiving Love
- The Art of Joining a Family
- Partners on Purpose
- Fathers in Distress
- The Fear of Love

Career Advancement and Personal Marketing

- The Art of Personal Marketing
- The Art of Transforming the Workplace
- The Power of Clearing Coaching Certification Program (POCCCP)
- Outrageous Unstoppable True Leadership Adventure for Women (OUTLAW)

Special Retreats of one week, ten days, or three weeks, with Guest Teachers invited to certain trainings

- Youth on Purpose
- Warm Water Breathwork with Lena Kristina Tuulse

2) List of Coaches and Therapists

The following list of certified *Power of Clearing* coaches are familiar with the material in this book and from their *Power of Clearing* course training. If you would like to learn more about *The Power of Clearing* process and go deeper with your personal breakthroughs with this method, they welcome your call, question, and connection with them. Each of the coaches has agreed to offer a free twenty-minute consultation to answer any questions you may have about *The Clearing Process* and to help you decide whether you want to work together. The paid clearing session can be a single session or one of a series of sessions, depending on your needs and your intention. The therapist or coach may ask you a number of questions to determine your issues. Alternatively, you may wish to focus on a single issue to clear on with the coach. If you book a session, before the session be sure you know the coach's fees and how they prefer to be paid.

Please note: "Certified Power of Clearing Coach" means they have taken the ten-day class to become a Power of Clearing Coach, which has only been in existence for the last several years and additionally, they have done eight supervised clearings with me and eight supervised case studies with clients.

The Power of Clearing coaches have an intake process asking in-depth questions (approximately two hours) about the person's whole life to bring forth what they are looking for and wanting to clear as a hindrance or barrier to their peace. These questions are taught to the coaches during the ten-day *Power of Clearing* Coaching Certification Program, which I presently do online to train coaches. Because of the pandemic, I train coaches individually all over the world on Zoom, Facebook, and phone.

These coaches are available for counseling and life coaching using *The Power of Clearing* method as a tool. I have listed them by area, although now being global, you can call anyone to connect by Zoom, Skype, Facebook messenger, or other channels.

UNITED STATES

Sandy Levey-Lunden – Bellingham, WA
Creator of *The Power of Clearing* Process
Founder of *On Purpose* and 24 trainings
Transformational Life Coach, Personal and Relationship Counselor
Creator of the *Power of Clearing Coaching Certification Program*
sandylevey.com
onpurpose@sandylevey.com
Home: 1-360-527-2796 Cell: 1-360-739-4602

Valerie Shahan – Washington State
Certified Power of Clearing Coach, Rebirther
innerspiritclearing@earthlink.com
1-360-441-4997

Melanie Aceves – Bellingham, WA
Certified Power of Clearing Coach
melliebellyyoga@gmail.com

Jean L. Battersby Spooner – Seattle, WA
Certified Power of Clearing Coach
Master NLP Practitioner, Spiritual Guide
jeanbattersby.com
Skype: 1-206-973-7500 (US or UK)

Rachel Curry – San Francisco Bay area, CA
Certified Power of Clearing Coach
Certified Family Coach
rachelcurry.com, rachel@rachelcurry.com
@RachelCurryCoaching
1-510-214-2347 call or text

Richard Unger – Sausalito, California
Soul Psychology, founder and director of
International Institute of Hand Analysis
handanalysis.net
richard@lifeprints.com

Adam Shapiro – Philadelphia, PA
Certified Power of Clearing Coach
alshapiro28@gmail.com
1-530-304-7989

Petra Stahl – Sandpoint, Idaho
Certified Power of Clearing Coach
petrastahlmusic@gmail.com
1-208-217-0331

Kylene Ross – Nashville, TN
Certified Power of Clearing Coach
kylene.ross@gmail.com
1-253-740-8943

Elisabeth Hopkins Lynch – Nashville, TN
Power of Clearing Coach
Counseling Professionals LLC
Licensed Professional Counselor (LPC)
Mental Health Service Provider (MHSP)
CounselingProfessionals615@gmail.com
1-615-584-4507

Alanna Zackrison – Knoxville, TN
Student of The Power of Clearing Process
Resonance Repatterning
alannazackrison@gmail.com

CANADA

Len Satov – Vancouver, BC
Certified Power of Clearing Coach
Psycho-spiritual Life Coach and Counselor
lensatov.com
len_satov@shaw.ca
1-604-974-0074

Laura Gibson – North Vancouver, BC
Certified Power of Clearing coach
Master Hand Analyst
lifepurposeprints.com
1-604-916-4813

Gizella Nagy – North Vancouver, BC
Certified Power of Clearing Coach
Spiritual Bodywork and Massage Therapy
bodymindcocoon.com

Kristi Birnie – Campbell River, BC
Certified Power of Clearing Coach
Cranial Sacral Therapy, Jikiden Reiki Practitioner
Yoga Nidra Facilitator
sunspotcarrottop@gmail.com
1-778-928-3653

Miriam Evers – Langley, BC
Power of Clearing Coach
WindSong Cohousing Community, Joy Coach
joyousrenegade.com
miriam.evers2020@gmail.com
1-604-888-1442

Howard Staples – Langley, BC
Power of Clearing Coach
WindSong Cohousing Community, Rebirther
howard@windsong.bc.ca
1-604-888-1442

Sarah Huemmert – Harrison Mills, BC
Certified Power of Clearing Coach
huemmert@shaw.ca
780-445-8121

Denise Leppard – Halifax, Nova Scotia
Certified Power of Clearing Coach
1-902-425-1234

Theresa Thomas – Halifax, Nova Scotia
Certified Power of Clearing Coach
Spiritual Connection Mentor
Author, Speaker, Consultant
Readings Rituals & Resolutions
healingfromtheheart.ca
theresa@healingfromtheheart.ca
facebook.com/groups/healingfromtheheart/
linkedin.com/in/theresa-thomas-yhz

UNITED KINGDOM

Iona Leishman – Inverness, Scotland, Findhorn Community
Certified Power of Clearing Coach, Visual Artist
ionaleishman.co.uk
iona@ionaleishman.co.uk
0044-777-434-7780

David Spooner – Scotland
Certified Power of Clearing Coach
Certified Scottish Tour Guide/Driver Guide
email: david@scottourguide.com
facebook.com/scottourguide
linkedin.com/in/scottourguide/
g.page/Scot-Tour_Guide
+44-0131-618-1164

Gillian Hibbs – Berkshire, England
Certified Power of Clearing Coach
hibbsgillian@gmail.com

Susan Culverwell – London, England
Certified Power of Clearing Coach
Healing Trust Registered Spiritual Healer
Past Life Regression Therapist
BACP Registered Psychotherapist and Counselor
Available Worldwide via the web/zoom/telephone
F2F London 07889-199566
susanculverwell@hotmail.com

Oriana Howes – London, England
Certified Power of Clearing Coach
orianahowes.co.uk

Ian Patrick – London, England
Power of Clearing Coach
A Course in Miracles Teacher
Founder of the Miracle Network
miracles.org.uk

Angela Hahn – Suffolk, England
Certified Power of Clearing Coach
0044-0-7719-790681

Sue Reynard – Suffolk, England
Certified Power of Clearing Coach
sue.reynard@hotmail.co.uk

John Reynard – Suffolk, England
Certified Power of Clearing Coach
Spiritual Business Consulting
John.r.reynard@gmail.com
Tel +44-1449-774994
Cell: +44-7900-363918

Roy Gough – Suffolk, England
Certified Power of Clearing Coach and spiritual healer
Havening Therapist, Theta Healing Therapist
Reflective Repatterning Therapist
Tapas Acupressure Technique (TAT)
springtreetherapies.co.uk
springtreetherapies@gmail.com
+44(0)1284-765071

Sally Peace – Essex, England
Energy Alignment Coach
sallypeace.com
relax@sallysretreats.co.uk
Peace Within Facebook:
facebook.com/groups/peacewithinwithsally/?ref=share

SWEDEN

Mats Stjernqvist – Sandared, near Gothenburg
Degree of Bachelor of Science in Social Work
ACIM Teacher – The Holy Relationship
Mats.Stjernqvist@icloud.com

Lottie Stjernqvist – Sandared, near Gothenburg
Certified Therapist
ACIM Teacher – The Holy Relationship
Lottie.Stjernqvist@gmail.com

Carlos Mosqueda – Stockholm
Certified Power of Clearing Coach
Relationship and Couples Counseling
carlos@casamistral.com
0046-70-725-73-57

Inger Holmqvist – Stockholm
Certified Power of Clearing Coach, Nutritionist Coach
Inger@casamistral.com
0046-70-763-13-88

Lena Kristina Tuulse – Väddö (Stockholm Archipelago)
Master Rebirthing Teacher and Rebirther, Psychologist
lena.kristina@tuulse.se

Anna Margareta Sundberg Reed – Linköping
Certified Power of Clearing Coach
annasundberg@msn.com

SPAIN

Carlos Mosqueda – Estepona (Near Malaga)
Certified Power of Clearing Coach
Relationship and Couples Counseling
carlos@casamistral.com
0034-657-158-760

3) Code of Ethics for *Power of Clearing* Coaches

Principle 1: Miscommunication

In communication with a disagreement in perception, possible misinterpretation, or conflict arising, it is essential to speak to the person directly about the situation; e-mails and text messaging can be misleading and hold back those involved from getting to the root of the whole meaning of the situation. If each person clears on this misinterpretation or interaction, they will see things about their thinking or the past that they will not see without clearing. In general, my motto will apply: "What I think is happening is probably not happening for the reasons I think it's happening; I have made the whole story up to suit my ego's core belief, like 'I can't trust that person, or even trust at all.'" Also, what the person thinks or feels about you may actually be what you feel about them in your projection.

Principle 2: Collusion

With close friends, it is essential always to be aware of the collusion factor—friends may agree with your ego thoughts instead of saying, "please talk to the person about that situation and do a clearing on it." If the situation upsets you, there is something to clear. You must thoroughly do all three steps of the advanced *Clearing Process* to get to the bottom of it.

Principle 3: Judgments

During counseling, life coaching, or training, sometimes I have a judgment about a person based on their story that triggers me into the thought, feeling, or belief that this person is hopeless, damaged, or limited in some way. Then I use *The Clearing Process* to see them in their true light or authentic self. If for some reason, I do not clear with the process, I will refer them to another Clearing Coach, so they can move forward and attain the desired result of Clarity, Love, Harmony, and Peace. Robert Perry's book on holy relationships says, "My partner will live up to or down to the image that I hold of them." Therefore, it is vital to see each client in their true light, without their story.

Principle 4: Completions

I will endeavor to complete and clear all communications in my life and bring them to Peace and Harmony, which means I will not avoid anyone or refuse to speak to them. I will endeavor to attend to all incomplete communication, both verbal and written (though not by text, which is ambiguous and subject to misinterpretation). Whether a current incompletion or from the past, it is essential not to have things in my mind bother me (e.g., money, relationship issues, fear, guilt) because they will impede my ability to be present in the Clearing or counseling sessions.

Principle 5: Daily Practice

Daily, I will be using a tool or practice, such as working in the ACIM lessons, meditation, taking a walk out in nature, and other activities to reconfirm my true nature and my authentic self. The 19 principles from the *Choosing Freedom* course will actively guide me in my daily life.

Principle 6: Language

The language we express becomes our reality, including my negative feelings, thoughts, judgments, and spoken language. It is important never to say something we don't want to create. Also, I have removed the word "whatever" from my coaching language because it implies no commitment to what I want. This word is like a back door, taking no responsibility for what I say, think, and do. It indicates that I don't care. I recognized that it is essential in every communication that I move toward what I wish to create and see happen.

Principle 7: Written Materials

When using written materials from another inspirational coach, therapist, or teacher, I will credit that person and acknowledge their writings and teachings.

4) Frequently Asked Questions about *THE CLEARING PROCESS*

A Summary of Why, Where, When, and How to do a Clearing

WHAT IS A CLEARING?

A *clearing* is a simple yet profound process whereby old patterns of negativity are allowed to rise into conscious awareness in order to be healed and released. *The Clearing Process* takes place within a safe and loving space and can also be called a process of forgiveness since we ultimately choose to forgive what no longer serves us before letting it go. It is an opportunity for us to speak our truth and be acknowledged, without judgment, for who we really are.

WHY DO A CLEARING?

Since few of us grew up in families where we learned how to tolerate our complex feelings or those of others, most judge intense feelings as scary or destructive. As a result, we are reluctant to acknowledge, feel, or share them with anyone. We have mastered many ways to deny, repress, and avoid them. It is hardly surprising then that unacknowledged, unresolved baggage from the past obstructs our current relationships. Frequently, the very focus of our intimate relationships becomes the effort to suppress, deny, or manage these intense feelings.

Often, we are afraid of falling apart when the real problem is that we have not learned how to give up control of ourselves, expose our vulnerability, and connect intimately with another person. Clearing helps us achieve the controlled dropping of the ego boundary, thus allowing us to face these uncomfortable feelings and release them. This way, we are freed up to live more rewarding, loving, and peaceful lives.

WHERE DO I DO A CLEARING?

A clearing can be done anywhere and requires only a physical space that is quiet and private enough for the people involved to hear each other from a facing position, preferably seated.

WHEN DO I DO A CLEARING?

Do a *clearing* whenever you feel upset in any way—emotionally, mentally, or physically. You can also do it at any time to clear upsets or issues from your past, which is what the *clearing* does, even when you think you are clearing a recent or current issue.

HOW DOES A CLEARING WORK?

The only way to integrate our feelings is by allowing ourselves to claim them while simultaneously seeing our acceptance in another person's eyes. The psychologist Gregory Bateson says, "It takes two to know one." *The Clearing Process* is working with another person to know ourselves. The Clearing Process "formula" provides the requisite space for cultivating a non-judgmental awareness. In this forgiveness process, stuck energy in the unconscious mind is released and transmuted, thus undoing some of the ego's conditioning.

WHO SHOULD I CLEAR WITH?

It is important to only clear with someone who has learned The Clearing Process; otherwise, your partner could perceive the ego statements in Step 1 as an attack, and react adversely or be triggered by them. (See "Pitfalls" in the final point.)

WHAT DOES "HOLDING THE SPACE" MEAN?

The success of the process is dependent upon the attitude and presence of the person "holding the space" for the other person to clear. It takes courage as well as willingness to clear, so the person clearing must feel safe fully revealing and expressing their deepest emotional self. The receiver of the clearing (the one holding the space) maintains a non-judgmental, open presence, recognizing they are instrumental to the success of the process. It is a great privilege to hold the space for someone in this way. It is a sacred space.

WHY MUST I FOLLOW THE STEPS?

The steps of *The Clearing Process* must be ritualistically adhered to because the ego hates structure. Indeed, it will try to "escape" and distract you whenever possible. Therefore, staying with precise wording is vital to success. In addition, we are forever up against our internal, familial, and cultural conditioning to avoid the intimacy that a genuine clearing affords. As much as we crave being seen, heard, and accepted as we are, we fear that making ourselves vulnerable to another will lead to further disillusionment, pain, and abandonment. For this reason, we deliberately use the "tight container" of the clearing structure to ensure the success of the process.

HOW WILL I KNOW WHEN THE CLEARING IS FINISHED?

Both parties will know intuitively when a clearing has come to an end, as they will find themselves truly in a state of completion and love. However, if there is any sense whatsoever that something is unresolved, then the clearing is not complete.

WHY DIDN'T THE CLEARING WORK?

The success of the clearing is dependent upon being completely unambiguous about the purpose of the process. The intention of *The Clearing Process* is "to get clear." In other words, having a greater insight into things as they are in the present, rather than being temporarily obscured by fear of confronting something painful from the past. Sometimes our ego wants us to use the clearing as a weapon to blame another person, which can never be the highest intention and will therefore never work. We must be sincere in our desire for peace and union throughout.

HOW DO I KNOW WHETHER I AM DOING A BASIC OR ADVANCED CLEARING?

The Basic Clearing is for the family of origin issues. In contrast, The Advanced Clearing often begins with a current issue or relationship and ultimately leads back to the family of origin. As you become more and more familiar with the process, you will begin to work intuitively, without determining beforehand whether you are doing the Basic or The Advanced Clearing. Indeed, it is acceptable to switch between the two, depending on what arises naturally during the session. The label of "Basic" or "Advanced" is not even necessary—it is merely a helpful pointer in the early stages.

WHO DOES THE PERSON SITTING OPPOSITE ME REPRESENT?

Essentially, the person holding the space represents the Big T Truth essence of whoever you are clearing about (mother, ex-husband, yourself). They can also represent the Big T essence of an issue you are currently working with (food, golf, job).

HOW MUCH TIME MUST I ALLOW FOR A CLEARING?

It is challenging to accurately know how long a clearing with last since there are several fundamental factors at work here. At the outset, you do not know what might come up during the session or how many inter-related issues you will need to work with. Furthermore, it depends upon how familiar you are with the process and whether you are in touch with your issues.

If it is a session where the person clearing is learning about the Big T and little t chart for the first time while additionally learning the process itself, the whole session may last up to three or even four hours. However, once the person has integrated the chart and *The Clearing Process,* a clearing may last an hour or two or less. It is also worth understanding that what might begin as a simple current issue may become a significant clearing of a deep-rooted core belief. So, the important thing is to trust and let go of the outcome rather than forcing the process. Ensure both parties have plenty of time, so there is no sense of urgency or deadline. Furthermore, it is beneficial for the person clearing to have some quiet time afterward to integrate all that has occurred in the clearing. It is best not to go straight into busyness and appointments.

WHY IS CLEARING A TOOL, AND NOT A TECHNIQUE?

Clearing is a tool to remove obstacles to inner peace and create a genuine connection with yourself and others. When used as a technique, one party could manipulate *The Clearing Process* by attempting to work toward a predetermined outcome, which will almost always be "right" about something negative or a limiting belief. When the subconscious intention of the clearing is to "attack" the other person, the following is likely to happen:

At least one of the participants will only be willing to do Step 1, or the other steps but they still want to be right about certain aspects of their projections.

The word "you" may creep into segments of the process other than the first part as a way of blaming the other person. Be vigilant.

The clearing experienced as an intellectual discussion leaves one or both parties feeling frustrated and confused, resentful and angry.

There may be a recurrent sense of incompletion.

WHAT ARE THE PITFALLS OF CLEARING WITH A CLOSE FRIEND/PARTNER/ RELATIVE?

It is not recommended for people to clear with each other about each other unless they are both very experienced in *The Clearing Process* and have done significant inner work. Those with whom we have an intimate relationship will likely be triggered in Step 1 when holding space for the person clearing. It is okay to clear with them about anything else, just not each other. It's best to find someone else to hold the space for you if you want to clear about that particular friend, partner, or relative.

5) Books, CDs, and Film

The Dark Side of the Light Chasers by Debbie Ford (a definitive book on projection)

Gratitude by Louise Hay

A Course in Miracles (ACIM) – Foundation for Inner Peace 1996 Edition Audiobooks: https://acim.org/digital-editions/acim-audio-editions/acim-audiobooks/

Wishcraft by Barbara Sher (http://shersuccessteams.com/)

Zero Limits: The Secret Hawaiian System for Wealth, Health, Peace, and More by Joe Vitale and Ihaleakala Hew Len

Rumi: The Beloved Is You: My Favorite Collection of Deeply Passionate, Whimsical, Spiritual and Profound Poems and Quotes by Shahram Shiva

What You Think of me is None of My Business by Reverend Terry Cole-Whittaker

The Disappearance of the Universe by Gary R. Renard

Journey to the Heart: Secrets of Aboriginal Healing by Dr. Gary Holz with Robbie Holz

Rebirthing in the New Age by Leonard Orr with Sondra Ray

Eternal Breath: A Biography of Leonard Orr Founder of Rebirthing Breathwork by Pola Churchill

By Sondra Ray and Markus Ray:
The New Loving Relationships Book
I DESERVE LOVE: How Affirmations Can Guide You to Sexual Fulfillment
Liberation Breathing: The Divine Mother's Gift

Passion for Life by Lena Kristina Tuulse

Flight into Freedom and Beyond: The Autobiography of the Co-Founder of the Findhorn Community by Eileen Caddy

Of Course! How Many Light Bulbs Does It Take to Change? Reflections on A Course in Miracles by Ian Patrick

The Art & Truth of Transformation for Women: The Magic Of Shifting Your Mindset and Opening Your Heart to Consciously Live a Life You Love An anthology of 20 women authors compiled and published by Sue Urda and Kathy Fyler by *Powerful You! Publishing*

By Robert Perry:
Holy Relationships: The End of an Ancient Journey
Relationships as a Spiritual Journey: From Specialness to Holiness
Path of Light: Stepping into Peace with A Course in Miracles
Return to the Heart of God: The Practical Philosophy of A Course in Miracles
Glossary of Terms from ACIM

Glossary Index for ACIM by Kenneth Wapnick

By Jon Mundy Ph.D. and Gildan Media, LLC:
Eternal Life and A Course in Miracles: A Path to Eternity in the Essential Text
Living a Course in Miracles: An Essential Guide to the Classic Text

This Is It: The Radically Simple Message of A Course in Miracles
by Jon Mundy and Better Listen (audiobook)

The Difference: Fri Sikt
https://youtube.com/playlist?list=PL676809A6205E5DC1

The Power of Clearing CD ($15)
This CD is a brilliant synopsis for deepening your understanding of how to do *The Clearing Process*. This psycho-spiritual approach forms the basis of Sandy Levey-Lunden's workshops, guidance, and teachings. By speaking your total truth and being received without judgment through the simple yet profound 3-step process, you can release limiting beliefs, pain, and traumas that have become the filter through which you view the world. As a result, *The Power of Clearing* brings a profound sense of peace and completeness.

Relationship as a Path to Enlightenment CD ($15)
This CD is an interview with Sandy Levey-Lunden and Andrew Barber-Starkey, a Master Certified Coach living in Vancouver, Canada. Learning about the Holy Relationship with Sandy in the 1990s profoundly influenced Andrew's life and subsequent marriage. His experience inspired him to record this CD so everyone could learn how to be in a Holy Relationship and its value.

Digital downloads ($15)
https://www.sandylevey.com/product-page/power-of-clearing-digitial-download
https://www.sandylevey.com/product-page/digital-download-relationship-as-a-path-to-enlightenment

THE WATCHER
-LOVING, NON-JUDGMENTAL AWARENESS-

Foundational to all forms of healing and change is our awareness. While this may seem obvious, it is often not seen and used for that very reason. Without consciously using our awareness we won't notice our attack thoughts and judgments. I call this aspect of our true nature The Watcher.

This part of ourselves, when consciously practiced, expands very quickly becoming our greatest asset and ally in our healing. The Watcher notices what we are feeling, thinking, saying to ourselves and others, and how we interact with others—all lovingly and without judgment. It also acknowledges our progress.

If you are so inclined, it is very helpful to ask your inner guidance to help you monitor your mind for thoughts of attack or judgment.

So, for example, say you've noticed you have a tendency to feel irritable and have the intention to clear the source of it and let it go. Your Watcher will notice (with practice) that you are feeling irritable and you might say to yourself, "I'm feeling irritable for some reason. I'm really glad I can see that." This conscious awareness of feeling irritable brings you fully into the present where you can now choose what, if any, action to take such as doing some form of enquiry, clearing or forgiveness. As you practice using The Watcher you will be increasingly more present and so less likely to react unconsciously, such as saying angry words to someone, withdrawing, or some other form of separation behavior.

After noticing something, The Watcher will always say, "I'm really glad I can see that." You feel genuinely pleased and grateful to be able to notice thoughts and feelings that you were not so aware of before so that you can clear the source of it. And this awareness allows you to increasingly meet with love, acceptance, and forgiveness whatever aspect of conditioning that shows up.

Of course, the ego will not be happy about this and will likely do whatever it can to either make you forget about The Watcher or to take it over. You can tell the difference because the ego will try to make you wrong for what you are noticing. It's definitely not loving and non-judgmental. Using the same example as before, instead of The Watcher saying, "I'm really glad I can see that," the ego might say, "There I go again! I'm never going to be able to let this irritability go!" So, when The Watcher sees that, it will say, "Oh, I see that I just blamed myself when I noticed I felt irritable. I'm really glad I can see that." Whenever you notice your behavior, thoughts, or feelings lovingly and without judgment, that is The Watcher in action.

It does take willingness, sincerity, motivation, and practice for The Watcher to emerge in full power for you and to be able to increasingly spot the ego, but it does not take effort. It is a powerful ally in our healing and a natural part of who we are.

"The Watcher" copyright Len Satov 2001—2022 revised
www.lensatov.com, 604-974-0074 len_satov@shaw.ca

DARING TO RISK

I still have the same inquiring mind as when I was seven and started pestering my mother with questions like, "Why are you here? What are you here for?" Occasionally I would even ask, "Why did God send you?" A single thought constantly repeated in my mind, "What is our real purpose?" I didn't even know what that word meant but knew I needed an answer.

My mother was shocked that such a young person was asking her such deep, thought-provoking questions. She tried her best to find answers that would satisfy me, but they never did. Finally, one day she proudly announced, "I'm here to be your mother!" I had noticed much of the time she appeared to be quite unhappy, so I responded, "If you're here to be my mother, if that is your real purpose, then you would be happy!" Unfortunately, she suffered from painful migraines and nausea that left her helpless and in bed for hours.

The seeds of my becoming a life coach and counselor were there very early in my life. My grandmother, Gussie, had extraordinary abilities to heal people. She was my guide and mentor always. She was selfless and entirely giving. I don't think I ever heard her say "no" to anyone. In turn, I have always tried to find a way to say "yes" as well. I believe that when someone is drawn to ask me something, there must be some purpose in it, something to which I'm supposed to say "yes."

We all have a destiny in the way we move through our lives. Looking backward from the present to the past, we can see what has shaped our lives' flow and meaning. I was always looking for the highest use of myself, where I would be the most helpful and have the most significant effect given my talents, abilities, and natural gifts.

I have always preferred to make practical use of my time. In many ways, I didn't have a childhood because I explored big questions: What is the meaning of life? What are we here for? Who can I assist, and in what way? Many years later, I found this saying in *A Course in Miracles*. This simple quote precisely embodies how I feel, think, and live.

I am here only to be truly helpful. (ACIM, T-2.V.A.18(8):2)

In 1979, I was a career counselor working with migrant workers for the Monterey Office of Education in Salinas, CA. Although it was meaningful work, I felt I could do much more with my life than I had been doing. In 1980, for the first time, I decided to go headfirst into my fear of success. I had read a description for a three-day women's workshop, Women's Success Teams, and it completely resonated with me. Alongside 29 other women, I participated in the first Women's Success Teams (WST) seminar on the west coast. Laura Boxer hosted the course after buying the franchise from Barbara Sher. My experience in the WST was incredibly emotional; I cried more throughout the course than anybody else in the room. I was able to feel my blocks and finally release them.

At the end of the WST course, I felt I had made a tremendous breakthrough. I thoroughly enjoyed the process of the course, the introspective examining, thinking, feeling, and sharing with the other women. I had never before seen the power of such a support network and was so excited at the prospect of what we could accomplish.

After completing the course, I was given my very own team of women supporters. We didn't live near each other, but we could talk on the phone, and we sometimes met in person. This new adventure with these wonderful women fully inspired me.

To my great surprise, Laura Boxer asked me to be the Director of Marketing for the west coast WST. I didn't even know what marketing was and had to look it up in the dictionary. It said marketing is how something is put into the world for people to buy, see, and have. Laura kept calling me and asking me to move to San Francisco and help her find a house for the WST course where we both would live and hold the seminars. I was amazed she kept asking me. I thought Laura should find someone else, but she didn't think so. On some level, Laura knew I was here to be truly helpful. She needed my help and knew others could avail themselves of my support.

I discovered a characteristic inside me over many years of living: I would always rise to the occasion. I would always find a way to get it done, whatever it was, and accomplish the task at hand. Even when I wanted to give up, a part of me would always keep going. So, I gave notice at my job as a career counselor for the migrant workers. When I arrived in San Francisco, Laura informed me that we didn't have the money needed to rent a house. She said we would have to produce a seminar to raise the required funds, and we only had a week to do so.

Anxiety, worry, and fear consumed my thoughts. I usually only slept three hours per night. Miraculously I came up with a way to market the WST course. I knew if I could address a group of women every single evening, I could enroll several and thereby create a seminar every weekend. We would then have enough money to complete the payment for the house and the expenses. I spent my days on the phone talking to women whom I had met the night before. It seemed natural for me to be on the phone talking to these women. I felt a personal connection with everyone I spoke with, and my interest was genuine, always coming from my heart and purposefulness. I was eager to get them signed up and prepared for the weekend course. It was like I was growing everyone I enrolled in WST into powerful, successful women. Many of those women had never been on their own and had recently divorced during the women's movement. Even when someone was afraid, I was right there, supporting her to work through the fear. I said, "Do whatever it is you are afraid to do. That's how you make a fear disappear."

Every night, with a map in my hand, I ventured to a different part of the San Francisco Bay area to connect to someone who had a group of women at their home, office, organization, or library. In the early 1980s, there were very few seminars of this intimate and personal nature where one could get this kind of support and guidance to create a vision for a life they dreamed of. The course encouraged each person to use their natural talents and innate abilities to go for what they dreamed of doing with their lives. Even without formal training, we could directly teach ourselves what we wanted to learn. The WST always filled in with ideas, contacts, methods, referrals, and concrete support. It was a pooled and beautiful effort. Participants would loan each other their clothes, bookbags, homes, and whatever it took to accomplish their dreams.

We generated enthusiasm and passion that I had never seen before. I got more and more excited as we went along. My inspiration was palpable; I could enroll pretty much anyone I spoke to on the phone or in person. I was very successful at marketing this course. I dreamed about it, believed in it, and thought about it constantly. Everything I did, I was doing for the first time, and I had to find the method inside me and follow a map and an inner knowing that was truly unknown to me. I learned to be a public speaker and spoke only from the heart. I even appeared on national television! I thought this would be terrifying, but I loved the experience.

It turned out that one of my most extraordinary abilities was helping women achieve their dreams. I began to have friends and supporters from the WST course each weekend, and these women constantly referred others to the courses I was producing every weekend. There were very few weekends that the WST course didn't take place, and every weekend was a unique adventure. Sometimes the course would go on until 11 pm. At the end of each course, I felt so fulfilled. I was living my life on purpose.

Another miracle occurred when I put out a newspaper ad to sell my rare, vintage convertible. A man named Justin Sterling replied to the ad, and I knew immediately that our meeting would have a profound implication in my life.

He drove my red Mercedes through most of San Francisco with me. We had provocative discussions, mainly about women, sex, and power. Of course, these discussions aligned with what I was working on with Women's Success Teams. Justin seemed to love talking to women, thinking about them, and empowering them. So, I told him I could enroll women in a course called Women, Sex & Power, and he could write the content and teach the course. He loved the idea, and we began working on it shortly after.

There were 75 women in attendance at the first *Women, Sex and Power* course. Justin was extremely daring in his delivery, which increased my fear that the participants would judge me. He wouldn't allow me in the room because he thought I would be worried that the women would disagree with the course content. It was a terrifying time, and there was a lot at stake in my mind. Sometimes I could hardly breathe because of my fear and anxiety. I had done a daring thing in helping Justin create *Women, Sex and Power,* and I wondered how my friends would view me.

In the end, I convinced Justin to cultivate the men's market. We named the men's course *Men, Sex and Power* or *The Guerrilla Training.* Over the next two months, I enrolled 175 men in *Men, Sex and Power.* I was the only woman in the room, which was very scary.

Ultimately, Justin and I had a difference of opinion regarding his philosophy. He believed men got all their power from women and were completely lost on their own. He also felt that women were in charge of every relationship and, if it didn't work out, it was the woman's fault. I didn't agree with these concepts and couldn't support this philosophy. I knew I had to leave and go on a different journey to find out how I could represent this connection between men and women. Leaving Justin and the seminar we had created together was incredibly challenging. I spent many years questioning whether or not I had made the right decision. But, looking back, I know I followed my heart, and that is always the right thing to do.

Counter to Justin's philosophy, I saw men and women as a circle, supporting each other continuously with no end or beginning. This never-ending circle is powerful when there is a unified purpose and passion for this purpose. Today I call this connection a holy relationship. In this relationship, each person sees the other as a Divine, unlimited being. Their function is to support each other and see each other as eternally innocent, no matter what they think of themselves or each other.

In the end, everything boils down to guilt and innocence. In 1990, I received *The Power of Clearing* process, which has allowed me to clear thousands of people from their perceived guilt and help them to live "on purpose" with who they Truly are. This process is a unique and powerful method of releasing mental and emotional blocks. By discovering and releasing these blocks, men and women can live their True purpose and fulfill their destinies.

Everything is about courage; the courage to be your True self and decide that your journey to be at Peace, Love, and Oneness is the ultimate purpose of your life.

By Sandy Levey-Lunden in *The Art & Truth of Transformation for Women: The Magic of Shifting Your Mindset and Opening Your Heart to Consciously Live a Life You Love*. An anthology of 20 women authors compiled by Sue Urda and Kathy Fyler and published by *Powerful You! Publishing* in October 2020, a self-help book and personal growth book. An international bestseller.

HOW HEALING IS ACCOMPLISHED

A part of *A Course in Miracles* that I have felt very drawn to is the section called "How Is Healing Accomplished?" (ACIM, M-5) I have found little written about this section, and I have always been surprised that more ACIM teachers do not focus on it. Some ACIM students might believe that the Course does not support physical healing since the body is not real, but I think an important part of ACIM is to support healing on all levels: mental, emotional, spiritual, and physical.

Since 1990, when I became a student and teacher of ACIM, I have constantly returned to this section whenever I, or anyone else, has a negative feeling in their body that was disturbing their peace of mind. In my course, *Choosing Freedom: The Way Out of all Pain and Suffering and the Way Back to Who You Really Are*, I use this section as part of a process for freeing anyone from the illusion of illness.

When I work with a student, I ask them to go deeply through eight questions about the condition. In 90% of cases, the condition totally disappears, working on the student's mind. Perhaps it disappears because I believe that it will disappear, and the student and I join in the purpose of fully releasing the meaning the condition has for us. I have had people in my counseling or training sessions who were extremely sick with conditions that had existed for years. They are able to clear the condition in the class and are amazed it can happen so quickly and easily by clearing the mind. These conditions include prostate cancer, allergies, colon problems, urinary tract conditions, environmental illness, inability to conceive, and breast cancer. ACIM says: *There is no order of difficulty in miracles. One is not "harder" or "bigger" than another.* (ACIM, T-1.I.1:1-2) I have found this to be so when I practice clearing physical or emotional conditions with the knowledge of "The Perceived Purpose of Sickness" (ACIM, M-5.I) and "The Shift in Perception" sections. (ACIM, M-5.II)

"The Perceived Purpose of Sickness" teaches that we must understand why we created the illusion of sickness? What is the pay-off? Why do we want to hold on to it and keep it in our lives? What does it stand for or prove to us about ourselves (what belief does it reinforce or prove)? What is the benefit of not letting it go or healing it? Who would we blame if we never healed? Does it mean that having this condition makes us the creator of our lives and that we have usurped God's throne? What would it mean to us if we healed ourselves personally and were our own doctor?

In the next section: *One need but say, "There is no gain at all to me in this," and he is healed.* (ACIM, M-5.II.1:2) In other words, I have gone through all the benefits in my mind that this sickness or condition has given me, forgiving myself for making up and believing in these thoughts and forgiving anyone else I think is involved in the illness. It also means that I am reminding myself of spiritual truths and feeding them to myself, that none of these beliefs I made up are true and that I do not need to live in this fantasy or illusion, which is at the core of the physical condition.

This journey without distance is perfectly described in the book by Dr. Gary Holz with Robbie Holz, *Journey to the Heart: Secrets of Aboriginal Healing.* Gary went through multiple sclerosis and healed himself in a process with Aboriginals in Australia, going through every benefit and reason he wanted to be numb and feel nothing in his life, thereby creating MS. When you can feel deeply, taste your reasons for creating the condition, and go through the emotion of the condition, you are on your way to releasing it. Gary Holtz went on to share this process with people worldwide.

When we have hidden a thought, a feeling, or belief in our body, it becomes a sickness. Generally, this is a secret to the person, and when they divulge it to themselves or others, it no longer has a hold over them. Therefore, since I can choose to kill myself with my belief or feeling that I will not release or forgive, I get to be the creator of my own life or death.

The sickness represents the drama we were going through during our emotional challenge, and we felt we could not deal with or go through and release it. Therefore, we stored it in our body as a secret to ourselves, hidden thoughts we would not want to admit about the sickness. Mostly, it is guilt that stops us from accepting these hidden thoughts and thus releasing them.

ACIM says that we cannot be sick unless we think, feel, or believe we are separate from someone. We must forgive the person, persons, or incident we are blaming and thereby release ourselves. As we know, forgiveness is a gift to ourselves. I am only ever forgiving myself for what I think, feel, or believe. I am clearing feelings of worthlessness about myself and forgiving myself for believing in them. In general, I am clearing that I am worthless, not good enough, or that no one loves me, sees me, or wants me. This secret is only released if I am willing to go through all aspects of the purpose of the sickness.

Of course, today, the ego-mind is geared to taking prescription pills instead of being willing to look at the process deeply and clear whatever ego story (or maybe the entire ego life story) the pain or sickness represents. Hence, we never see that it is not the truth of who we are. Of course, it would take time, energy, and effort to do this process and look deeply at the thoughts, feelings, or beliefs that created the meaning and what it says about them, like "no one cares about me because I am not valuable enough to be loved." Therefore, most people's egos convince them that they do not have that time or energy and that the simplest way is to take pills or have surgery.

Sometimes, the pills or the operation are the "special agents" to help release the process and bring it to a conclusion, and this happens after the forgiveness in the person's mind has occurred. Other times, pills are an escape from dealing with a condition of the mind, so the illness re-manifests in another place in the body.

It takes great courage, fortitude, and persistence to heal something in your body through your mind, and your commitment to the process must be one hundred percent. It is easier to do with a holy relationship partner who understands the healing process and fully supports it, knowing that the illusionary sickness is not true and not who you really are. We need another person to remind us of who we truly are when we believe a little t truth (ego) about ourselves or someone else. And the remembrance of who we really are is essential to healing or releasing the condition.

Seeing what the sickness or condition is for, the part it plays in the person's life, and its meaning when they first felt or created the sickness is part of the healing for the person. Therefore, as part of their process of clearing their condition, I ask them the following questions I received as the essence of "How Is Healing Accomplished?" (ACIM, M-5) in the Manual for Teachers, the third section of the ACIM book.

1. When did this sickness begin? What was happening in your life, and what were your feelings in the months or years preceding the condition?

2. What is the value, pay-off, or benefit of your sickness?

3. How does this choice for weakness give you strength? (How does it give you a sense of control or make you feel more powerful? How does it make you think you are better than God?)

4. What (with this insane conviction) does healing stand for?

5. Would you like to be your own physician and heal yourself, with your mind releasing the condition? What would be your purpose for living or healing? Why would you want to die or not heal?

6. Who would you blame, or want to be sorry, if you died or stayed sick?

7. What do you feel guilty about?

8. What do guilt, sickness, pain, disaster, and suffering mean now?

If the sickness has no purpose now, it can leave.

You can practice this process yourself. When someone has answered the questions in my classes and private sessions, they stand up in front of us with their arms straight out like an airplane, fully grounded, sinking their feet into the floor, holding their head up high, and standing erect. Then, in a full declaration in conviction and power, they say several times:

"I declare that I have no need for [name the condition exactly] in any shape or form or effect in my mind, body, and spirit! I declare that I have no need or want for [the condition] and any of its forms anymore! I declare all guilt, resentment, and punishment are released from my mind! I fully release the condition now and establish myself as fully healed on all levels."

This process is very exciting and fulfilling for me when the person gets to the Truth of their condition and the Truth of who they really are.

© Sandy Levey-Lunden, Revised May 2022. SandyLevey.com (360) 527-2796 Pacific. onpurpose@sandylevey.com

GLOSSARY OF TERMS

ACIM terms *(in italics)* are inspired by and taken and adapted from *A Course Glossary* (the last of 16 booklets) by Robert Perry and *Glossary-Index for A Course in Miracles* by Kenneth Wapnick with contributions by Ian Patrick, the author, and editors.

ACIM: *A Course in Miracles* book and spiritual guide. See pages xxxi-xxxii (after Foreword).

Belief (positive or negative): A learned system by which you live and perceive reality.

Clearing: A system of releasing and letting go of limiting beliefs at the emotional, mental, and cellular level, and thereby entering a Big T state of Peace, Love, and Joy.

Condition, Dis-ease: A situation in the body created by living negative, limiting beliefs. When we don't recognize and release these limiting beliefs, they may manifest into a condition in the body that we commonly refer to the symptoms as a dis-ease.

Core: The central essence of who we are as a Being. Example: Each clearing brings us closer to the heart of who we truly are.

Core belief: Core beliefs can come in as early as conception, like "I am not wanted" if there is confusion from the mother or father not completely wanting the baby to be born. A difficult birth with many hours or days of labor can cause a person to believe that "life is difficult." Core beliefs are often held for a lifetime within the mind and, thereby, the body to create the life experience of not being wanted or having a difficult life. In *The Clearing Process*, the coach supports the person to allow their perceptions to be shifted to see, understand, accept, and release old patterns of thoughts, feelings, and beliefs about themselves and their world. Negative core beliefs are the *perceived* meaning that we give incidents about ourselves. They are the root of compounded misperceptions from childhood that are often unconscious and exist in layers. For example: "Life is hard." "I'm not to be seen or heard." "No one cares about me." "I don't matter." I made up my world and what the characters are doing as evidence to prove my negative core (ego) beliefs.

Ego: The self you think you are, the "I." It is the false belief that you are separate from others and your Source (God), that you are a separate mind, living in a separate body, with your own story.

Ego games: Guilt is often related to ego games of money, time, sex, power, and control, and how it impacts our experiences of love in intimate relationships and relationship dynamics in general.

Ego defense: Blaming self (ego identification) and blaming others.

Ego resistance: Blocking flow to the process of Clearing because of the fear that we may come up with something we believe we cannot handle.

God: Infinite, eternal Mind or Spirit, the Source or Creator, pure Love, who creates only like Himself and at one with Him. God has no gender, no form, and no boundary.

Holy Instant: A moment in time of joining in Holy Relationship in which time and the present world disappears. This moment stretches into eternity. All association with the everyday world leaves, and you are present in suspended time.

Holy Relationship: Holiness is recognized in a holy relationship, although it may not be fully manifest. Aspects of specialness (needs, contracts, fear, etc.) may be present but are used as the means for the salvation process, a reversal of the special relationship. The holy relationship is a journey and a process when two people come together and join in a common purpose. They have now entered the Holy Relationship. On their journey toward holiness, they will have ample opportunities to forgive themselves and each other for what they think they each did and what it says about them. No matter their joint purpose, this journey will lead them to holiness in their relationship and innocence in themselves. The

Holy Relationship is one of the most exciting journeys a person can embark on in their lifetime because they will have glimpses, moments, and extended periods of seeing and experiencing their true authentic self, almost like enlightenment. They will also encounter in this journey the **Holy Instant,** timeless moments in which everything stands still, and you enter the world of Oneness. They will accomplish their **special function** together and bring unique healing to the world.

Holy Spirit: Not as a religious term; the Holy Spirit bridges this earthly ego world (little t truth) and our true nature (Big T Truth).

Honesty: One of the ten characteristics of the Teachers of God is "What I think, feel, see, and do, are all congruent." Others are Gentleness and Faithfulness. Each has a particular definition according to how the ACIM would view these terms. The only one used in the book is Honesty.

Holding space: Our *Power of Clearing* coach is there to help remind us of who we are by holding space for us to clear and return to our true nature, Love, Peace, and Joy, no matter what we are going through and no matter what negative story or scenario we are making up by being a vessel in which we can empty our ego and be seen by our coach as purely innocent no matter what we share in the ego statements in step one of the Clearing or in listening to our whole ego story without reacting in judgment.

Illness: Dis-ease, Condition – See "illusion of sickness" in ACIM terms.

little t truth and Big T Truth: The term "little t truth" is what we use for all the thoughts, feelings, and beliefs we can describe that come from the ego-mind that draws conclusions without ever checking to see if it is the Truth or not, or if there is another way to think. The ego structure is a rigid-thinking system, primarily responsive to fear, guilt, and shame. The term "Big T Truth" is the divine, eternal nature, the Truth of who we each are in our authenticity, and the only way we can attain lasting Joy. This true nature can never be changed or altered, no matter what we think, feel, or believe, and whatever negative evidence appears.

Illusion: Includes everything outside of Heaven, in space and time, anything physical, finite, temporary, or imperfect – which is everything here. It also includes our thoughts, beliefs, and perceptions. Truth and illusion have nothing in common; we must choose one or the other. The ego always gives us many choices between illusions, and we think we have to choose between them. These ego choices may always lead to the same place, a lack of total fulfillment and separation. You must always ask yourself, "What is this specific choice for? What will it bring me?" If the answer is a little t truth, it will always lead nowhere. If the answer is a Big T Truth, the choice will be more satisfying, like for Peace, Oneness, and Joy.

Illusion of sickness: Sickness is of the mind, resulting from the belief in separation, resulting in physical symptoms. It is projected onto the body by a "sick" mind (believing it is separate), reinforcing the apparent reality of the ego and the body. Healing comes from the miracle, healing the mind (though physical healing, what the Course calls "magic," may be appropriate).

Inner Teacher: *A Course in Miracles* aims to help us remove the blocks to the awareness of love's presence, which is our natural inheritance, and to start us listening to our inner teacher: the Holy Spirit or "the Voice for God."

Jesus: One of God's Sons, the first to awaken from the dream (illusion), become a pure manifestation of Spirit, and participate in his special function in leading the plan for salvation. Can serve as our model for learning and help when we call upon him in our desire to forgive, truly connecting to him.

Mind – One Mind: thinking with Love, Peace, Joy, with Big T Truth, the mind of God.

Mind – Fragmented Mind: A lot of little t thoughts come together to create confusion.

Mind – Ego Mind: The same as mind, little t truth beliefs, thoughts, and ideas about oneself.

Oneness: The state in Heaven, in which there is no separation, division, distinction between subject and object, no perception, or opposites.

Pacing: The technique of listening and reflecting, like a mirror, saying back what we heard the other say, is called "pacing" in the Neurolinguistic Programming model (NLP). By matching or mirroring the language, experience, beliefs, and words of the other, we gain and maintain a genuine rapport, thus a deeper awareness and understanding of the nature of the relationship between us and the communication that the person is sharing.

Projection: The ego's distorted use of extension throws an idea out of the mind onto a world appearing to be external. The world is, therefore, a projection, appearing to be the cause rather than the effect of the pain we experience.

Relationship: The act of communication, alignment of purpose, and involvement together. Union at the mental level.

Releasing: Total letting go at the conscious and unconscious level.

Responsibility: In the Big T Truth chart. My responsibility is to understand that I am Source, and I create my own world and reality.

Root: *The Clearing Process* uncovers the core issues creating the person's disturbing experience or existence. It's really like peeling an onion: taking away layer after layer to access the root from which those layers have grown. We can allow our perceptions of this "core" to be shifted to see, acknowledge, accept, and release the root cause of behaviors and experiences. We return to our natural state of Peace.

Sin: A mistake that we can never correct. There is no sin except not to know who we truly are and to think we're a body instead of an infinite Spirit.

Source: The beginning of everything. *Creation is your Source and your only real function.* (ACIM, T-3.V.6:8)

Separation: An event in which we appeared to separate from God, giving rise to the entire physical universe of time and space, and which the mind recreates, in every moment, in its mistaken belief in its reality. In our dream, this experience has lasted billions of years; in reality, God's answer ended it immediately. In truth, a part of God, of the whole, of everything cannot have occurred, so the separation never actually happened.

Special function: A term in ACIM about the unique purpose you came to earth to fulfill; the special abilities and gifts that God gave you at the moment your essence was created.

Special relationship: A relationship the ego makes based on pursuing specialness, exclusivity, and special treatment from one special person. It comes from seeing differences and lacks within ourselves and others, which require compensation. It involves needs, jealousy, pain, attack, and abandonment.

Surrender: Total "letting go" to a Higher Power or Knowledge with trust that the highest or most benevolent outcome will occur.

Teacher of God: *(ACIM Manual for Teachers)* There are four definitions for those who become a Teacher of God. 1) anyone who disseminates truth, 2) anyone who's done the 365 lessons in the workbook, 3) anyone who, on their path, has stopped what they are doing to help someone else, and 4) anyone who chooses to be one.

Transformation: A total shift from one condition of ego to another higher consciousness. Known in *The Power of Clearing* process as Big T Truth.

Unhealed healer: One who tries to heal without accepting the Atonement (the recognition of Oneness) and trying to give healing to others before giving it to themselves; this is the ego's version of healing.

MORE ABOUT THE AUTHOR

Sandy Levey-Lunden was born in the Bronx, New York City (NYC), on Norwegian National Day (a Freedom Day), May 17th, 1945. She is a graduate of the City College of NYC with a BA in Psychology and a Master of Science in Education (M.S.Ed.) from the Bank Street College in NYC. Sandy became a teacher of children with emotional disturbances. A teacher's strike in New York allowed Sandy to have children with learning disabilities in the same classroom as the children who were "gifted." She always saw each student as a unique being, filled with talents, abilities, gifts, and individualized learning styles. Sandy's goal was always to find that learning style and teach to that style with each student.

Sandy is an international speaker, counselor, and life coach of over 40 years and has written 24 original training courses. Sandy was one of the first and original life coaches in the 1980s before such a career even existed. Her unique style of coaching has helped thousands of people in North America, Australia, Sweden, and Europe to heal their past negative beliefs, traumas, personal pain, and relationship challenges.

When Sandy was about 28 years old, she initially moved from New York City to Los Angeles, California, to do Arthur Janov's Primal Therapy. He claimed he had a cure for neurosis. Sandy believed from the writing in his book that it would release everyone she knew in New York City from neurotic behavior, known as guilt, in many instances. She later felt that the premise of Arthur Janov's therapy, if your womb experience, birth, or early childhood damaged you, you might never recover, was untrue. She committed the rest of her life to prove otherwise and discovering a way for people to release any emotional pain holding them back from living in peace.

When Sandy moved to California, she lived in West Hollywood, Marina Del Ray, Carmel, and Carmel Valley. She became Beverly Hills Teacher of the Year and received a teaching credential for life. While living in the Monterey area, she became a career counselor working with migrant workers. She successfully found jobs for them and enjoyed going out in a van and speaking in Spanish with them directly in the fields of Salinas and training them in unusual job techniques in the Monterey County office.

In 1979, when the first Women's Success Teams came to the west coast from New York, Sandy became the first marketing director at the request of Laura Boxer (the current owner and director of WST). She felt she knew nothing about marketing. However, Laura repeatedly asked her to become the other staff member. Finally, Sandy felt that since they wanted her to take on this role, that she would do it because she loved WST training and was in the first one held in San Francisco. Several months after working with the WST, Sandy met Justin Sterling from Oakland, California, and felt that he had special gifts and talents unique to him. She then helped him establish the Sterling Institute in 1980 with the training known as *Women, Sex and Power,* and *Men, Sex and Power,* also known as *The Guerrilla Training* to Sandy.

Sandy lived with great excitement for many years in California, mostly in Marin County, Mill Valley, and Tiburon. She became a life coach and counselor in 1980 when she opened her service business called *On Purpose*. Many people referred to her as "the magical lady" or "Magical" because of the "magic" she created in people's lives. Sandy's inspiration for writing each of the two dozen training courses was to answer a challenge presented by someone in their life coaching or counseling sessions with a circumstance or situation ready for a breakthrough from one place in their mind into another expanded space. Her training courses answered these challenges. Ultimately the clearing method demonstrates to people the significance and the way of forgiving themselves.

In 1987, Sandy met the well-known rebirthing teacher and psychologist Lena Kristina Tuulse in Honolulu, Hawaii. In a 7 am speech Sandy delivered at a network meeting called The Winner's Circle, Sandy asked for a volunteer from the audience. Of the many who raised their hands, Lena Kristina was the only one to call out loudly from the back of the room of a hundred people, "Choose me! I don't even need coffee to wake up first thing in the morning!" Lena Kristina, a vibrant, alive, passionate being, invited Sandy to come to Sweden and teach her everything she knew about personal marketing, finding vision and life purpose, and fully communicating. During Sandy's first three-week tour in Sweden in 1987, Sandy met her future husband on her only day off. For the other 21 days, Sandy taught many courses for corporations like the Swedish Telephone Company, Volvo, Scandinavian Airlines (SAS), and Berol Chemie. Sandy moved to Sweden in 1989 and lived there until 2001. A Swedish network was born, and Sandy is still active in thousands of relationships with students and friends from Sweden and other European countries.

The association between Sandy and Lena Kristina continues for over thirty years. In 1996, Sandy put on the first original *Youth on Purpose* training program, *Fri Sikt*, on Lena Kristina's non-profit property known as Life University in Väddö in the Stockholm Archipelago. Life University still exists, and Lena Kristina awaits Sandy's return with her whole coaching team to hold another Youth Project there in 2023-24. They are currently renovating and adding to the buildings on the property that spans many acres and stretches to the Baltic Sea.

Sandy left Sweden only because her daughter wished to attend a performing arts school in Sarasota, Florida. After she changed her mind and decided to go for an academic degree, she told her mother she could go wherever she chose. So, Sandy decided to go to where the *Youth on Purpose* project was happening through a private benefactor in Vancouver, British Columbia in Canada. The closest big city in the United States is Bellingham, so Sandy traveled across the border to Canada a few days each week (45 minutes) to participate in the youth project. She has always loved Vancouver since it reminds her of Stockholm, Sweden.

Since 2000, Sandy has continued to counsel, coach, hold workshops worldwide, and train *Power of Clearing* coaches. She has also been working on this book and planning a feature film project to showcase the fantastic stories people spin with breakthroughs possible!

She has trained approximately 400 *Power of Clearing* coaches. She puts her heart and soul into each client and aspiring coach and stays closely connected, communicating with them regularly about whatever is going on in their lives. These cultivated coaches are like gold to Sandy, functioning like an extended family to her. While not all are operating certified coaches using *The Clearing Process* as the book describes, they are living examples of the embodied Peace they learned in the ten-day course applying the wisdom to themselves and all relationships.

Sandy is devoted to consistently supporting anyone out of stuckness, working diligently with them to find a breakthrough and get to authentic knowledge of their true Self. Once engaged with someone in the process, Sandy holds their situation in her consciousness, constantly seeking solutions to support them in moving forward. Sometimes years after their initial process together, she will see a new angle on their situation and follow up to assist them in clearing their minds and a new way to resolving a specific challenge in their life. She lives what she is teaching all day, every day, guided to engage with those ready to find more forgiveness and Peace within themselves. Her gift of empathetic listening combined with persistent and direct inquiry enables the opening and courage for the client to initiate forward motion. Sandy is acutely aware of the ego being staunchly committed to staying stuck in resistance; therefore, her tenacity is the tough love match needed to enable people's transformation. Sandy holds the faith that there is always a way out of all pain and suffering and chooses to see each person as their higher Self embodied.

Here is an inspiring example of Sandy's tenacious spirit holding space with a dear connection over 13 years of knowing and coaching her. Sandy has recently been able to facilitate a deep *Clearing Process* with this octogenarian to release the blame that she held on herself. The woman finally completely shared her ego (little t) truth and how it has served her for 65 years.

When she was a high-level student in college, involved in a long-term relationship with a man she thought she would marry, that man's friend (of another race) deceived and raped her. While he raped her, he asked her over and over if she would keep the baby, and she said yes. She was a virgin until that moment. She became pregnant and was in great conflict, as it was the late 1950s when there were significant taboos about unwed mothers. Even though she had been raped, she thought her family would disown her if they saw her mixed-race baby and that she would be an outcast amongst her friends and social peers. When she gave birth in the hospital, a set of twin doctors convinced her to give up the baby girl. She held the baby once and then signed a paper surrendering all awareness of what happened to the baby.

She wanted to keep her baby, and her conflict about the whole situation tormented her, torn between social fear of feeling like an outcast and, on the other side, wanting to raise her daughter and be a good mother to her. At the very least, she wanted a contract that would only allow a two-parent couple with Masters degrees to adopt her baby, but they never signed the contract. Looking back at this situation repeatedly, about how these doctors pressured her, she felt it strange that they insisted on her giving them her baby immediately. Her greatest fear was that they would sell the baby into child trafficking. Because of her emotional pain, she doesn't remember the names of the doctors or the date of her baby's birth. When she contacted the hospital years later, no one knew the names of those doctors or how to contact them.

She married a man she met while she was pregnant. He wanted to have children and would have been willing to keep the baby; that didn't happen. She married to save face; however, she didn't love her husband or want to have a child with him. She married him to function as (an ego) punishment to herself for not choosing to keep her baby and not courageously going beyond the social norms of the time. She felt like a traitor, failing both herself and her husband.

She had not forgiven herself after 65 years for not knowing what happened to her baby, her only child, where her baby girl was now, her name, how to contact her, and to find out if she had a good life. In this *Final Clearing* process with Sandy, she forgave herself completely and finally had Peace.

Sandy considers herself a solutionist and a catalyst for Peace by clearing the past with a person so they can open to a new dramatic outcome in the present. She's like a detective with a puzzle. For this client, she conceived a present-day solution for finding her daughter; the woman could write to Dr. Phil about being a guest on his TV show. Even if she didn't go on the show for him to explore her conflict and anguish, Dr. Phil might be willing to help find her daughter through research and investigation so she could meet and reunite with her daughter after 65 years.

After this *Final Clearing* with the octogenarian, Sandy recommitted to the idea of creating a team of *Power of Clearing* coaches all over the world to complete the lives of everyone in care homes who can remember and communicate. So many older people die isolated, separate, and alone and suffer from blaming themselves for something that happened. The coaches could help those willing to let go of something they are blaming themselves for in the past through the *Clearing Process*. Then they can leave the earth free and clear in their hearts, present with love and forgiveness for themselves. One knows if they are blaming themselves if they repeat the same story to themselves or others, trying to relieve their guilt. The *Power of Clearing* coaches could make speeches in the care homes about blame and guilt to see which people would like to clear and ultimately forgive themselves.

As an ACIM-Based Real-World Results Achiever, Matchmaker, Networking Maven, Proud Grandma, and Dog Lover, Sandy Levey-Lunden resides in Bellingham with her extended family and near her daughter and grandchildren.

"I am always looking at who and what can be cleared from the past. I am clearing with everyone I meet wherever I go, if they choose to, and whether or not they pay me. If I died right now, I would feel I have done everything I came here to do for my purpose and have no regrets about anything or anyone. I plan to retire when I expire, resting in Peace. Mission accomplished!"

—Sandy

We welcome hearing from you with your questions, success stories, and Amazon reviews of *I Just Want Peace*.

Connect with Sandy directly.

You can call me in Bellingham, Washington in the USA, in Pacific Time.

Home phone: 1-360-527-2796
Cell or text: 1-360-739-4602

Website: Sandylevey.com
Email: onpurpose@sandylevey.com

LinkedIn: linkedin.com/in/sandy-levey-lunden/
Facebook: facebook.com/sandy.leveylunden/

I offer you a free 20-30-minute consultation on any aspect of your life, and I teach individualized courses based on your needs, your family, or your business by Zoom or in person. You may feel called to commit to your healing and the healing of others by immersing yourself in *The Power of Clearing* material. Your next step would be to enroll in a weekend training with Sandy. For further education, inquire about the ten-day *Power of Clearing Coaching Certification Program*.

www.ingramcontent.com/pod-product-compliance
Lightning Source LLC
Chambersburg PA
CBHW060407010526
44107CB00005B/610